CW01668177

Translation Practices Explained

Translation Practices Explained is a series of coursebooks designed to help self-learners and teachers of translation. Each volume focuses on a specific aspect of professional translation practice, in many cases corresponding to actual courses available in translator-training institutions. Special volumes are devoted to well consolidated professional areas, such as legal translation or European Union texts; to areas where labour-market demands are currently undergoing considerable growth, such as screen translation in its different forms; and to specific aspects of professional practices on which little teaching and learning material is available, the case of editing and revising, or electronic tools. The authors are practising translators or translator trainers in the fields concerned. Although specialists, they explain their professional insights in a manner accessible to the wider learning public.

These books start from the recognition that professional translation practices require something more than elaborate abstraction or fixed methodologies. They are located close to work on authentic texts, and encourage learners to proceed inductively, solving problems as they arise from examples and case studies.

Each volume includes activities and exercises designed to help self-learners consolidate their knowledge; teachers may also find these useful for direct application in class, or alternatively as the basis for the design and preparation of their own material. Updated reading lists and website addresses will also help individual learners gain further insight into the realities of professional practice.

Dorothy Kelly
Series Editor

Audiovisual Translation: Subtitling

Jorge Díaz Cintas & Aline Remael

St. Jerome Publishing
Manchester, UK & Kinderhook (NY), USA

Published by
St. Jerome Publishing
2 Maple Road West, Brooklands
Manchester, M23 9HH, United Kingdom
Telephone +44 (0)161 973 9856
Fax +44 (0)161 905 3498
Ken@stjeromepublishing.com
http://www.stjerome.co.uk

InTrans Publications
P. O. Box 467
Kinderhook, NY 12106, USA
Telephone (518) 758-1755
Fax (518) 758-6702

ISBN 978-1900650-95-3/1-900650-95-9 (pbk)
ISSN 1470-966X (*Translation Practices Explained*)

Printed and bound in Great Britain by
4edge Ltd, Hockley. www.4edge.co.uk

Typeset by
Delta Typesetters, Cairo, Egypt
Email: hilali1945@yahoo.co.uk

British Library Cataloguing in Publication Data
A catalogue record of this book is available from the British Library

Library of Congress Cataloging-in-Publication Data
Díaz-Cintas, Jorge.
Audiovisual translation : subtitling / Jorge Díaz Cintas & Aline Remael.
p. cm. -- (Translation practices explained, ISSN 1470-966X)
Includes bibliographical references and index.
ISBN 1-900650-95-9 (pbk. : alk. paper)
1. Translating and interpreting. 2. Mass media and language. 3. Dubbing of motion pictures. 4. Television programs--Titling. 5. Motion pictures--Titling. 6. Discourse analysis. I. Remael, Aline. II. Title.
P306.2.D53 2006
778.5'2344--dc22

2006028262

SysMedia

SysMedia and WinCAPS

SysMedia specialises in supplying software solutions to the television industry; including subtitling, teletext and interactive TV. The company has over 30 years' experience in the broadcast market, with customers worldwide including the BBC, Sky, and Technicolor.

WinCAPS is SysMedia's professional subtitling preparation software package, used for broadcast television around the world and for many of the latest multi-national DVD releases of many major Hollywood projects.

As with most SysMedia products, WinCAPS is designed with an emphasis on workflow automation and optimum productivity to make the subtitler's work quicker, easier and more productive. Today's software is a result of more than 25 years of experience in the design and development of subtitling systems. It uses the power of a modern multimedia PC to combine text processing with digital video playback to produce a convenient and easy-to-use subtitle creation package.

Its capabilities cover all languages and all forms of television subtitles for both live and recorded programming. It can be used equally well for burnt-in "open subtitling" (often associated with the sort of audiovisual translation covered by this book) as well as viewer-selectable "closed captioning" for the deaf and the hard-of-hearing.

WinCAPS is used not only for recorded television/DVD but also in the particularly demanding field of subtitling for live television programmes, including news and sports - enabling broadcasters to work both quickly and accurately. Automated tools include powerful newsroom data capture to avoid the need for real-time input and speech-text alignment for automatic transmission of short, scripted items. SysMedia also has invaluable expertise in how best to use speech recognition for a cost-efficient live subtitling service without compromising on accuracy.

As you will find from this book, translation for TV/DVD subtitling is a specialised field. WinCAPS helps make the task easier by allowing its user to concentrate on the language work rather than worry about the technicalities and restrictions of the medium. So you can prepare subtitles as quickly as possible and review them with the video just the same as their appearance on the finished DVD or TV broadcast.

The full version of WinCAPS features advanced options that can speed up timing by automatically matching the timing of each caption to the equivalent spoken text in the video.

The accompanying DVD contains a feature-restricted version of WinCAPS (licensed only for educational, non-commercial use). This provides a very good experience of the conventional modern approach to subtitling using software that is truly representative of the full commercial product. When the time comes, you will have already mastered the skills needed for commercial subtitling and you will be ready to make full use of WinCAPS for yourself.

Additional information can be found at www.sysmedia.com.

Contents

Acknowledgements

We would like to express our gratitude to the many people who have assisted and supported us in the writing and editing of this book and DVD, either by generously supplying material for inclusion in the publication, or by providing us with expert help, advice and useful contacts. For this we are indebted to many colleagues in academia and in the subtitling profession worldwide, as well as to filmmakers, production and distribution companies, film festivals, professional associations, graphic designers, students, friends and family.

For giving us permission to use some clips from their films, and for providing us with sundry material like screenplays, illustrations, templates, subtitles, and good subtitling examples: Hanno Baethe & Zaki Omar, (directors of *Boom, Boom, Bang*), Eric Contel & Felip Girbau of Paycom Multimedia (for *Charade*, *Beneath the 12 Mile Reef*, *Father's Little Dividend*, *The Last Time I Saw Paris*, *The Man With the Golden Arm*, *McLintock!*, *Night of the Living Dead*, *The Snows of Kilimanjaro*, and *The Stranger*), Penni Cotton (coordinator of *European Picture Book Collection*), Robbe De Hert (director of *Lijmen*), Jean-Luc Ducasse of Alta Producción (for *Aislados*), ESIST, Valentí Figueres and Helena Sánchez Bel of Los sueños de la hormiga roja (for *Hotel*, *Los accionistas del arte*, and *Movimientos migratorios*), Frédéric Fonteyne (director of *Une Liaison pornographique* and *Max & Bobo*), Fotios Karamitroglou, Firdaus Kharas (director and producer of *The Three Amigos*) José Llurba, Sean Mendez of riceNpeas (for *Bang! Bang! In Da Manor*), Geneviève Mersch (director of *J'ai toujours voulu être une sainte*), Thierry Michel (director of *Mobutu, roi du Zaïre*), Abe Osheroff (director of *Art in the Struggle for Freedom*), Luc Pien (director of *La Sicilia*), Christine Pireaux and Films La Passerelle (for *Mobutu, roi du Zaïre*), Adrian Smith (director of *Blue Star Camp*), Sylvie van Ruymbeke and Artémis Productions (for *J'ai toujours voulu être un sainte*, *Une Liaison pornographiqe*, and *Max & Bobo*).

For the photograph on the front cover thanks to Carlos Neves.

For providing useful advice, practical help and invaluable contacts: Marc Bekaert (Film, Museum voor Hedendaagse Kunst Antwerpen), Patrick Cattrysse (Vlaamse Script Academie), Frederic Chaume (Universitat Jaume I), Doris Cleven (Folioscope), Chas Donaldson, Tonie De Waele (Vlaamse Dienst voor Filmcultuur), Yota Georgokopoulou (European Captioning Institute), Luc Herman (Universiteit Antwerpen), Ilse Logie (Universiteit Gent), Roberto Mayoral (Universidad de Granada), Reine Meylaert (Katholieke Universiteit Leuven), Alberto Mira Nouselles (Oxford Brookes University), Dominique Nasta (Université Libre de Bruxelles), Tom Paulus (Universiteit Antwerpen), Walter Provo (Initiatief Audiovisuele Kunsten), Federico Spoletti (Sub-ti), Adriana Tortoriello (VisionText), Karin Vandenrijdt (Folioscope), Luc Van Dingenen (Broadcast Text Brussels), Susanne Verberk (The Subtitling Company), Luise von Flotow (University of Ottawa).

For their invaluable help with the exercises and the DVD: Miguel Bernal Merino and Isabel Sánchez Gallego. For helping with some of the exercises: Teresa Agost, Clarisa Alonso, Alfonso Belmonte Belda, Nadia Benini, Veroniqué Brian, Marcella De Marco, Ellen Leemans, Chiaki Matsubayashi, Beth Middleton, Itsuko Miyata, Renata Mliczak, Salli Parra, Enrique Planells-Artigot, Eirini Rapti, Pablo Romero Fresco, Zezinha Semedo, Paula Serrano, María José Toboso, Jenny Wich-Knoten and Soldad Zárate.

For their support and constant encouragement: our colleagues from the TransMedia group: Mary Carroll (Titelbild), Anna Matamala (Universitat Autònoma de Barcelona), Josélia Neves (Escola Superior de Tecnologia e Gestão de Leiria), Pilar Orero (Universitat Autònoma de Barcelona), and Diana Sánchez (Imaginables). Warm thanks also to our colleagues at Hoger Instituut voor Vertalers en Tolken, Antwerpen, particularly to Katrien Buyse, Katrien Lievois, Etiënne Mylemans, Paul van Os, Jimmy Ureel, and at Roehampton University, London, particularly to Lucile Desblache, Lourdes Melcion and Jacqueline Page.

Special thanks are due to John Boulton and Andrew Lambourne from SysMedia for allowing us to incorporate a tailor-made version of the Win-CAPS subtitling software, and to Tony Fullman and Simon Collins for there technical know-how; and also to Bram Mylemans, from the Hoger Instituut voor Vertalers en Tolken at Antwerp, for designing the DVD.

We would also like to express our gratitude to Dorothy Kelly, the series editor, for her careful reading of the book, and to Ken and Mona Baker for inviting us to write the present contribution to the Translation Practices Explained series.

Finally, we would like to thank our family and friends for having put up with us writing away on the computer, most of all to Ian Crane and Evy Derycke for their immense patience.

How to Use this Book and DVD

The structure of Audiovisual Translation: Subtitling

This multimedia project is addressed to translation trainers, students, researchers, professionals, and all those interested in the practice and theory of subtitling. It consists of a book and an accompanying DVD, and is fundamentally interactive in its approach.

The publication can be used as a textbook by teachers as well as individuals wishing to master the fundamentals of subtitling on their own, and it offers a wealth of examples and different approaches to recurring subtitling issues that are of interest to professionals in the field. In addition, *Subtitling* raises a number of fundamental research questions and looks at some of the unresolved challenges of this very specific form of translation.

The fact that the book has been written in English shows its authors' intention for it to have a global reach. Writing for an international audience means that a degree of generalization is inevitable, whereas subtitling traditions vary from country to country and even from company to company. However, the degree of variation is relative and practices that were once fundamentally different are often beginning to converge. One could say that not only subtitling, but also audiovisual translation (AVT) generally is in a state of flux. This is due to a number of factors, which are all in one way or another related to the two-sided coin of globalization and glocalization, as well as technological developments. First of all, subtitlers worldwide communicate more than they used to at conferences, through professional organizations, and in journals devoted to translation in all its guises. Secondly, teaching in AVT is expanding, especially at university level. Furthermore, countries that are only beginning to develop some forms of AVT, such as subtitling for the deaf and audio description for the blind, and are still determining which way might be best suited for their needs, are looking to countries with longer traditions for examples and professional support. Finally, new technologies (the development of the DVD, for instance) and the advent of dedicated professional software for AVT also have a homogenizing function. The other side of the coin is that local traditions persist, as do differences related to the medium of dissemination, i.e. cinema, television, or DVD. Besides, relative newcomers on the market do not merely take on existing practices: their choice of AVT and its implementation are determined by their own needs, especially since the market for AVT, including subtitling, is expanding well beyond Europe.

In other words, a textbook that claims universality is certainly ambitious. Having said that, most differences in subtitling practice do not really affect the fundamentals of subtitling. Students who have acquired an insight into these fundamentals and the specific challenges of subtitling practice will be able to apply this knowledge and these skills in any context. Translation, whether for the screen, the Internet or more traditional hard-copy publications will always remain a skill that requires flexibility and creativity. What is more, the different types of subtitling software available on the market may also be on the increase, but the software used in this book, WinCAPS, is well-established worldwide and includes all the functions typical of any professional subtitling software package.

Although written primarily in English, the project resorts to examples and exercises in a limited number of other languages, with back translation, in the book and on the DVD. Most of the exercises and clips included can be used as the basis for the creation of other pedagogical material in other languages, which means that the potential for practice is virtually unlimited. The location of the exercises and other materials on the DVD is always indicated as follows:

4.8.1 Go to DVD > Chapter 4 > Exercises > Exercise 4.8.1

This means that exercise 1, or the material needed for this first exercise, in section 8 of chapter 4 can be found on the DVD under 'Chapter 4', in the section entitled 'Exercises'. See below for more information on the structure and map of the DVD.

The book

The book's seven chapters offer a graded approach with exercises, discussion points and suggestions for research. The chapters in themselves and the book as a whole progress step-by-step, covering all major aspects of subtitling and the subtitling profession. Each chapter starts with a "Preliminary discussion" that aims at stimulating critical thinking, can be used for a warm-up session in class, lends a focus to the chapter, and presents an analytical interactive inroad into the subject matter. All the chapters are subdivided into sections that break down the issues tackled into their major components. They also contain numerous annotated examples taken from existing subtitled films and TV-programmes. All chapters end with discussion points and graded exercises. The discussion points test the users' comprehension of the material covered, help them assimilate the information, offer suggestions for further research and invite students to compare or contrast the issues under discussion to the situation in their own part of the world. The exercises offer real subtitling practice, starting with some of the basic skills involved, without WinCAPS software, and gradually require the users to combine linguistic as well as technical and software-related skills. The various activities clearly state whether or not they involve material included on the DVD and where exactly on the DVD it can be found.

Chapter 1 offers a definition of subtitling, distinguishes subtitling from other forms of translation, and surveys the different types of subtitles and their classification on the basis of different parameters. It ends on a discussion of related translation types such as surtitles, intertitles and fansubs.

Chapter 2 deals with the subtitler's professional environments, taking into account that these may differ globally and are continually changing. Subtopics are: the subtitling process, the different professionals involved in this process, and working conditions, including such matters as clients and rates, the influence of globalization, and the role associations.

Chapter 3 on the semiotics of subtitling, contains the first hands-on exercises, but also provides essential information about the film as text, the complexity of the filmic sign, and how the subtitles interact with it. It includes practical information about the use and structure of screenplays and the specificities of film dialogue.

Chapter 4 focuses on technical issues: subtitling programs and what they can be expected to do, feet and frames, the advantages and disadvantages of dialogue lists, style guides, codes of good subtitling practice, and the spatial and temporal dimensions of subtitling. It also contains concrete instructions regarding the authors' preferred practice for the use of WinCAPS with respect to these matters. The authors' instructions are based on norms and guidelines currently applied today that are gaining increasing support in professional circles.

Chapter 5 is more grammatically oriented, dealing with punctuation and other textual conventions. Since such conventions are language and medium-bound, they can, of course, vary considerably. Due attention is devoted to this variation and to the way subtitling conventions may be evolving. The preferred approach for the exercises is again explained and illustrated with concrete examples. The conventions used in different text types such as dialogue, songs, letters and other written documents, as well as the rendering of numbers, abbreviations, symbols, measures, weights, etc. are also covered extensively.

Chapter 6 is devoted to the linguistics of subtitling in a broader sense and to subtitling as a form of rewriting that requires text reduction through condensation, reformulation and omission at word and/or sentence level. It discusses the syntactical as well as other grammatical and lexical challenges of this specific translation form. It also deals with segmentation and line breaks, offering ample examples of dos and don'ts.

Chapter 7 centres on more specific translation issues, some of which will be familiar to translators of other text types, but involve extra challenges in subtitling: linguistic variation and multilingualism, the translation of culture-bound items, humour and songs. The chapter ends with a discussion of a number of ideological issues.

Chapter 8, the final one, contains further activities aimed at exploiting the subtitling program WinCAPS. Some of the exercises have been devised with particular tasks in mind, **WinCAPS activities**, whereas there is another subsection, **Extra scenes**, with digitized audiovisual excerpts in different languages for people interested in practising with this program in an independent way.

The book is completed with a **glossary** of terms used in the subtitling profession, a list of bibliographical as well as film **references** and an **index**.

The DVD

The contents of the accompanying DVD take up about 3.4 GB of disk space. The DVD will launch automatically and is subdivided into sections. The graphic survey of its structure is as follows:

- WinCAPS
  - Set-up
  - Initiation exercise
- Chapter 2
  - Discussion points
- Chapter 3
  - Examples
  - Exercises
- Chapter 4
  - Preliminary discussion
  - Examples
  - Exercises
- Chapter 5
  - Exercises
- Chapter 6
  - Discussion points
  - Exercises
- Chapter 7
  - Discussion points
  - Exercises
- Chapter 8
  - WinCAPS activities
  - Extra scenes in Dutch
    - Films – Documentaries
  - Extra scenes in English
    - Films – Documentaries – Animation films
  - Extra scenes in French
    - Films – Documentaries
  - Extra scenes in Italian
    - Films

The first main section contains the actual subtitling software WinCAPS as well as instructions on how to install it on your computer and use it. The following sections contain additional exercises linked to the different book chapters, with or without key. Chapter 8 on the DVD includes a section entitled **WinCAPS activities** containing exercises to be exploited with WinCAPS. Besides film clips and dialogue transcripts, you can also find WinCAPS files to work on and a key to these exercises. Instructions on how to work with these exercises can be found in the textbook itself. Subsequent sections contain extra filmic material in several languages (digitized scenes and dialogue transcripts) that can be exploited for exercises or just for practice. This material is not directly linked to any of the chapters and requires combined subtitling skills. The excerpts are from films and from documentary films shot in Dutch, English, French, Italian, and Spanish, giving the user the opportunity to work with other languages besides English.

Finally, the DVD also features a number of practical appendices with information about subtitling companies, software programs and useful websites. It concludes with a list of acknowledgements.

WinCAPS

One of the highlights of this multimedia project is the inclusion of WinCAPS, a professional subtitling software program developed by the company Sys-Media (www.sysmedia.com) and used by many television broadcasters and other subtitling facilities.

Your DVD contains a free release version of WinCAPS [go to: DVD > WinCAPS > Set-up]. In the same section of the DVD, the document entitled 'WinCAPS Installation instructions' states the minimum system requirements your computer must have and explains in a detailed way how to install the program on your PC.

Once you have successfully installed the program on your computer, you can start producing your own subtitles. To facilitate your first approach to WinCAPS, we suggest you start with the 'Initiation exercise' we propose on the DVD [go to: DVD > WinCAPS > Initiation exercise]. The 'Step by step subtitling guide' included in this section of your DVD takes you through the whole process of creating subtitles for a short scene called *Phone*, from the film *Charade*.

A more detailed and comprehensive manual on how to use WinCAPS can also be found on the DVD under the heading 'WinCAPS User Manual' [go to: DVD > WinCAPS > Set-up > WinCAPS User Manual]. Please bear in mind that the version you have with this project also allows the creation of subtitles for the deaf and the hard-of-hearing. You will not need to use some of the functions.

In order to speed up subtitling production, most subtitling software programs offer the option of carrying out certain tasks by means of keyboard shortcuts. A list of the most productive shortcuts to work with WinCAPS can also be found on your DVD [go to: DVD > WinCAPS > Set-up > WinCAPS Keyboard shortcuts].

Restrictions in this version of WinCAPS

Important: The 'Educational' version of WinCAPS supplied has been specially produced for the DVD of this multimedia project and is not licensed for commercial use.

Working with this version of WinCAPS you will be able to carry out all tasks pertaining to subtitling on your computer, but you will be limited to a maximum of 75 subtitlings.

You will be saving your work to files with a .w30 extension, the same way as a word document has a .doc extension at the end. This extension is created automatically, is unique to this educational version of WinCAPS, and means that any .w30 files created with this version of WinCAPS are incompatible with the commertial version of WinCAPS or any other subtitling programs.

When you retrieve any work that you have peviously saved (as a .w30 file) you will notice that the timecode values are only restored to within 10 frames or so of their previous value. Timecode values in files are frame accurate dueing an operating session (however long that may be) and when opening the example files provided on the DVD itself. This restriction can be removed by purchasing a licence. Please contact SysMedia for details and special offers for tutors.

Many of the more advanced features of the normal WinCAPS software have also been disabled (such as files export, shot change detection, visual audio indication, shortforms and text splitting). To upgrade to a commercial software version you should contact SysMedia directly: www.sysmedia.com.

Example WinCAPS files on the DVD

Activities in Chapter 8 ask you to work with clips and read-only .w30 files containing subtitles that have been created for you to correct. The .w30 files and the corresponding clips will be automatically loaded onto your computer hard drive [C:\Example Books] when you istall WinCAPS. In order to work with these files and clips, you will have to open WinCAPS first and retrieve them from your hard drive as indicated in Chapter 8. You will have to create a working copy of the read-only .w30 files. For more details go to DVD > WinCAPS > Set-up > WinCAPS Installation Instructions.

Vedio Playback Difficulties (Codecs)

If you experience any audio or vedio payback difficulties when opening any of the clips on this DVD (e.g. you can only hear the soundtrack of the clip but cannot see the image), then it is possible that the computer you are working with is using an incompatible codec. The solution might be to install more codecs in your computer. You can download some, like:

ACE Mega CoDecS Pack 6.03
Coda Codec Pack
Codec Pack All in 1 6.0.3.0.

These are all a free collection of Codecs (coders/decoders), media player filters, media players and other utilities for vedio watching, audio and video processing, which you will find useful. They are all easily found on internet. Alternatively please consult the WinCAPS support section of the SysMedia website (www.sysmedia.com).

We very much hope that you will enjoy reading the book and using the DVD and software, and that it will reveal all of subtitling's secrets for you.

Good luck!

Jorge Díaz-Cintas & Aline Remael

January 2007

1. Introduction to Subtitling

1.0 Preliminary discussion

1.1 Do you see subtitling as a case of translation or adaptation? What are your reasons for your choice?
1.2 In your opinion, does it matter whether subtitling is perceived one way or another?
1.3 Make a list of situations where subtitles are consumed in your country.

The main aim of this book is to introduce the reader to subtitling, one the most thriving areas within the wider discipline of Translation Studies. For many years ignored by academics and teachers alike, it has since the 1990s gained well-deserved visibility thanks to the proliferation and distribution of audiovisual materials in our society. The value of the image is of crucial importance in our daily lives and we are literally surrounded by screens of all shapes and sizes. Television sets, cinemas, computers, and mobile phones are a common and recurrent feature of our social environment, based on the power of the screen. We come across them at home, in our work place, on public transport, in libraries, bars, restaurants and cinemas. We spend a fair amount of hours watching screens and consuming audiovisual programmes to carry out our work, to develop and enhance our professional and academic careers, to enjoy ourselves and to obtain information. It would not be an exaggeration to talk about the ubiquity of the image in our time and age.

A common companion of the image since the 1930s has been the word, and with the word comes the need for translation. Scholars like Gambier (1994) and Díaz Cintas (1999) differentiate up to 10 different ways of translating audiovisual programmes, although there are three main ones: dubbing (also known as lip-sync), subtitling and voice-over. This chapter sets out to offer a definition of subtitling practice as well as a classification of the many different types of subtitles that we come across in our daily lives.

1.1 Definition

Subtitling may be defined as a translation practice that consists of presenting a written text, generally on the lower part of the screen, that endeavours to recount the original dialogue of the speakers, as well as the discursive elements that appear in the image (letters, inserts, graffiti, inscriptions, placards, and the like), and the information that is contained on the sound track (songs, voices off). In some languages, like Japanese, cinema subtitles are presented vertically and tend to appear on the right-hand side of the screen.

All subtitled programmes are made up of three main components: the spoken word, the image and the subtitles. The interaction of these three components, along with the viewer's ability to read both the images and the written text at a particular speed, and the actual size of the screen, determine the basic characteristics of the audiovisual medium. Subtitles must appear in synchrony with the image and dialogue, provide a semantically adequate account of the SL dialogue, and remain displayed on screen long enough for the viewers to be able to read them.

1.2 Translation or adaptation? Audiovisual Translation (AVT)

For some, this activity falls short of being a case of translation proper because of all the spatial and temporal limitations imposed by the medium itself (§4) which constrain the end result. They prefer to talk about adaptation – an attitude that has stymied the debate about AVT and could be tainted as having been one of the main reasons why the whole area has been traditionally ignored by scholars in translation until very recently.

Audiovisual programmes use two codes, image and sound, and whereas literature and poetry evoke, films represent and actualize a particular reality based on specific images that have been put together by a director. Thus, subtitling – dubbing and voice-over too – is constrained by the respect it owes to synchrony in these new translational parameters of image and sound (subtitles should not contradict what the characters are doing on screen), and time (i.e. the delivery of the translated message should coincide with that of the original speech). In addition, subtitles entail a change of mode from oral to written and resort frequently to the omission of lexical items from the original. As far as space is concerned, the dimensions of the actual screen are finite and the target text will have to accommodate to the width of the screen. Although the figures vary, this means that a subtitle will have some 32 to 41 characters per line in a maximum of two lines. These tend to be the main reasons put forward by those who have looked down on this activity, considering it as a type of adaptation rather than translation. It is indeed this attitude that can be held responsible "for the fact that translation studies of all disciplines have been rather reluctant to include film translation among their subjects of study" (Delabastita 1989:213). For others, this concept of adaptation seems to equate the process to a lesser activity and becomes enough of an excuse to carry out a linguistic transfer that is clearly inadequate but nonetheless justified since it is only a case of adaptation.

Jakobson (1959) is often cited as being one of the first academics to open up the field. He famously established three types of translation: intralingual (or rewording), interlingual (or translation proper) and intersemiotic (or transmutation). Half a century later, this may need some revision to accommodate other dimensions, crucially the audio and visual ones in our case, but the essence is there.

One of the first significant advances in the process of conceding theoretical kudos to translated products such as audiovisuals came from the hand of Reiss (1977 and 1981). Basing herself on the three basic language functions devised by psychologist Karl Bühler, Reiss identifies in a first instance three types of texts (informative, expressive and operative) that encompass the different language functions. In an effort to acknowledge translation forms considered until then marginal, Reiss (1977:111) points out the special attention deserved by written texts co-existing with other sign systems with which they must maintain a constant link. To make room in her taxonomy for this new group of texts of greater semiotic complexity, Reiss creates an additional hyper-text type which she calls 'audio-medial text type'. She defines it as a superstructure that takes into account the special characteristics of the spoken language and oral communication, and sits above the three basic communicative situations and corresponding text types. Despite the fact that the examples provided by Reiss (*ibid.*), "songs, comic strips, advertisements, medieval morality ballads, etc.", seem to overlook audiovisual translation as such, it is evident that it fully fits into her theoretical framework.

Some years later, Delabastita (1989:214), aware of the risks involved in having a limited and normative definition of translation that "is in danger of being applicable to very few, well-selected cases, and of being unsuitable for a description of most actual fact," rejects this minimal kind of definition and opts for a highly flexible notion. He is representative of a trend and an approach that is also shared by Mayoral Asensio (2001b:46), who goes even further by advocating a more dynamic notion:

> The definition of the object of study in translation studies is not the definition of a natural process that assumes an unchanging nature; rather it is the definition of a technological process that continually evolves and changes. Our role is not to close the door on new realities but to favour and encourage them. We need open definitions that can be modified both to envelop new realities (sign language interpretation, multimedia, text production), and to get rid of those that have ceased to be useful and necessary. (Our translation)

We share this opinion. Translation must be understood from a more flexible, heterogeneous and less static perspective, one that encompasses a broad set of empirical realities and acknowledges the ever-changing nature of practice. The traditional notion of formal fidelity, so venerated by the structuralists of the 1960s, has now been revised and made all translations more flexible, but this is especially the case of subtitling and other forms of audiovisual translation. The one-to-one translation approach loses all validity in our field and the concept of formal equivalence must be understood from a much more flexible perspective than in other spheres of translation. If we reject the term 'adaptation', it is because it seems to have taken on a negative connotation, with some academics using it to take away ontological value from this professional practice which they see as inferior to translation. Gambier (1994:278) also considers the use of this all-encompassing epigraph inappropriate, since the mention of adaptation implies, in his words, "to be under the spell of a quantitative, mathematical theory of information (information entropy) which considers cross-linguistic communication in terms of losses or additions and sees translation as a process of mimetically copying a literary word, a duty to repeat". Nearly a decade later, Gambier (2003:178-179) seems to somehow backtrack in his argument when he resorts to the term 'transadaptation'. Although the concept is not clearly defined, it is used in an attempt to justify the hybrid nature characterizing all the different audiovisual translation types, and can be perceived as yet another effort to grant translation status, even if only partially, to our field. The term is probably better suited to give account of another professional practice, in the way Neves (2005:151-154) defines it. She uses the term:

> to refer to a subtitling solution that implies the *translation* of messages from different verbal and non-verbal acoustic codes into verbal and/or non-verbal visual codes; and the *adaptation* of such visual codes to the needs of people with hearing impairment so as to guarantee readability and thus greater accessibility (ibid.:154).

We believe, however, that the battle has now been won with regard to the nature of these practices and translation is perceived by most scholars as a more flexible and inclusive term, capable of accommodating new realities rather than disregarding practices that do not fit into a corseted, outdated notion of a term coined many centuries ago, when the cinema, the television and the computer had not yet been invented.

Once we have accepted the tenet that we are indeed dealing with cases of translation, the following step is to find a generic term that can encompass all the different manifestations we find in the audiovisual realm. Although this may sound an easy task, the fact is that the terminology used is very hesitant and can be confusing. The adjectives 'constrained' and 'subordinate' were regularly used when referring to this type of translation in publications during the 1980s and early 1990s, but began soon to receive criticism for their somewhat negative connotations. It was then that the term 'audiovisual translation', abbreviated to AVT, appeared in academic circles. This coinage has the advantage of including the semiotic dimension, and has taken root to such an extent that today its use is quite frequent. However, despite its popularity, it is not the only term used and some scholars prefer other terms such as 'film translation' or 'cinema translation', but as the field of study spreads to other types of programmes – e.g. sitcoms, documentaries, cartoons, etc. – these concepts also become somewhat restricting. Other umbrella terms, all of them bringing in different nuances, are also in use. One that has caught on in English but not so much in other languages is 'screen translation', which strives to encompass all products distributed on screen, be it a television, movie or computer screen. This term opens the doors to the translation of other products that until now have failed to make it to a more stringent classification, such as computer games, web pages and CD-ROMs. Another designation that is gaining ground is 'multimedia translation', to refer to those products where the message is broadcast through multiple media and channels. This term blurs the boundaries even further and establishes a stronger link with the localization of software and the translation of programmes that are distributed on the Internet, as does the more recent 'multidimensional translation'.

This fluctuation in terms is no more than a reflection of the changing times in which we live. Far from representing a barrier to communication, it could be interpreted as a clear sign of the desire of many academics to maintain an open and flexible approach to our object of study; one that can assimilate and acknowledge the new realities emerging in the translation world.

Fortunately enough, one of the terms, audiovisual translation (AVT), has been gaining ground in recent years and is fast becoming the standard referent. In its inception, AVT was used to encapsulate different translation practices used in the audiovisual media – cinema, television, VHS – in which there is a transfer from a source to a target language, which involves some form of interaction with sound and images. Dubbing and subtitling are the most popular in the profession and the best known by audiences, but there are others such as voice-over, partial-dubbing, narration and interpreting. The translation of live performance was added to this taxonomy at a later stage and that is how surtitling for the opera and the theatre has also come to be included.

New and innovative professional activities such as subtitling for the deaf and the hard-of-hearing (SDH) and audio description for the blind and the partially sighted (AD) are also making a place for themselves within AVT. These new practices have brought in further terminological disarray, especially because of the fact that none of them, at the beginning at least, implied the transfer from a source to a target language, one of the traditionally defining features of any translation activity. Nevertheless, the majority of scholars and practitioners in our field have embraced SDH and AD as an integral part of AVT. The wider concept of accessibility has been put forward to help bridge any possible divides (Díaz Cintas 2005b). In societies that aim at being more just and inclusive, accessibility has a social function and means making an audiovisual programme available to people that otherwise could not have access to it. In this sense, to lip-sync, to subtitle or to voice-over a programme shares as much the idea of accessibility as SDH or AD. Only the intended audiences are different. Whether the hurdle is a language or a sensorial barrier, the aim of the translation process is exactly the same: to facilitate access to an otherwise hermetic source of information and entertainment. In this way, accessibility becomes a common denominator that underpins these practices.

Finally, computer games and interactive software programmes are taking subtitling to the borders between AVT and localization since these games travel not only subtitled, but also adapted to the cultural sensibilities of the target gamers. Likewise, subtitling is re-entering the domain of speech when summarizing techniques and interpreting are combined in teletext subtitling for the deaf and hearing impaired through voice recognition. These trends are representative of a broader move: different forms of audiovisual translation and other translation modes are converging, creating new hybrid forms and sometimes catering for very different and well-defined target audiences. The key word for successful audiovisual translation is insight and understanding of the product and its expected function, combined with desire to learn and willingness to adapt.

1.3 Classification of subtitles

Different typologies of subtitles can be established depending on the criteria that are used at the onset. Subtitling has a very close relationship with technology and one of the main problems encountered when trying to come up with a fixed classification of subtitles is the speed at which technological developments take place. No sooner has one classification been made than new types of subtitles appear on the market.

In an attempt to offer a comprehensive overview of the many different types of subtitles in existence, we have decided to group them according to the following five criteria: linguistic, time available for preparation, technical, methods of projection, and distribution format.

1.3.1 Linguistic parameters

One of the most traditional classifications of subtitles focuses on the linguistic dimension. From this perspective, we can find the following types:

- □ Intralingual subtitles
  - For the deaf and the hard-of-hearing (SDH)
  - For language learning purposes
  - For Karaoke effect
  - For dialects of the same language
  - For notices and announcements
- □ Interlingual subtitles
  - For hearers
  - For the deaf and the hard-of-hearing (SDH)
- □ Bilingual subtitles

Intralingual subtitling involves a shift from oral to written but stays always within the same language, hence the reluctance of some to call it translation. The first type, SDH, is primarily aimed at people who are deaf and people with a hearing impairment, in order to ensure greater democratic access to audiovisual programming. This variety is also known as (closed) captioning in American English. On television, these subtitles are broadcast by means of an independent signal activated only by those interested in accessing pages 888 or 777 of teletext in most European countries. In North America they are transmitted on what is known as line 21. The oral content of the actors' dialogues is converted into written speech, which is presented in subtitles of up to three, or occasionally four, lines. They generally change colour on television depending on the person who is talking or the emphasis given to certain words within the same subtitle. Besides the dialogues, they also incorporate all paralinguistic information that contributes to the development of the plot or to the creation of atmosphere, which a deaf person cannot access from the soundtrack, e.g. the irony of a statement, a telephone ringing, laughter, applause, a knock on the door, the sound of an engine, and the like. Although they are usually presented at the bottom of the screen, they lend themselves more to physical manipulation, as it is possible to move them to the left or right of the screen when it is necessary to identify speakers or to make clear where the sound is coming from.

SDH is undoubtedly one of the forms of audiovisual communication which is developing most at present, thanks to the success achieved by pressure groups campaigning for the interests of this sector of the audience. The fruit of their work is evident from the announcement of new legislation in many countries obliging television channels to broadcast a certain percentage of their programmes with this type of subtitles. The European Year of Disabled People in 2003 helped in great measure to give increased visibility to the issue of accessibility to audiovisual media, particularly in those countries that had been lagging behind (see also Neves 2005). As far as television broadcasting is concerned, the volume of SDH has undergone spectacular growth in recent years. The BBC (British Broadcasting Corporation) is, without a doubt, on a global level, one of the most advanced in this area, having pledged to broadcast 100% of their programming with subtitles for the deaf and hard-of-hearing by 2008. In Canada, the Global Television Network has been subtitling all its programming, twenty-four hours a day, seven days a week, since January 2005. In Spain, the public television station TVE subtitled some 550 hours in 1999, while four years later the number of hours was in the region of 2,500. In 2003, TVE increased its subtitled programming by 73% compared to the previous year (Moreno Latorre 2003). The DVD has also exploited the potential of this type of subtitling and has made it more widely accessible. On a pedagogical note, few educational institutions offer programmes of study that focus on this type of subtitling, and the field is still to be developed.

A second group of intralingual subtitles are those specifically devised as a didactic tool for the teaching and learning of foreign languages. This function of interlingual subtitles has long been recognized. In an article published as early as 1974, Dollerup was already highlighting the didactic value of interlingual subtitles as a language learning tool and stating that in Denmark "many people must [...] be using foreign programmes as a means for keeping up, possibly even improving their command of foreign languages" (ibid.: 197). Watching and listening to films and programmes subtitled from other languages helps us not only to develop and expand our linguistic skills, but also to contextualize the language and culture of other countries. We familiarize ourselves with the foreign language though the soundtrack (vocabulary, intonation, pronunciation), and the images bring us into contact with the mannerisms and behaviours of other cultures (gesticulation, way of dressing, interpersonal relationships, geographical spaces). It is precisely this unique possibility of having direct access to the original and being able to compare it with its translation that has been stressed by many theoreticians as one of the most positive additional bonuses of subtitling (D'Ydewalle and Pavakanum 1992; Koolstra and Beentjes 1999).

But, to return to intralingual subtitling, it can be argued that SDH also offers great educational potential to people with limited knowledge of a country's language, e.g. immigrants and foreign students, but the fact is that it is not openly targeted at these social groups. Many scholars have discussed the issue (Danan 1992 and 2004, Vanderplank 1988 and 1992). Some firms and distribution companies have recognized this educational potential, seen a niche in the market and responded with their own initiatives. Columbia Tristar Home Video, for example, was one of the first companies in the 1990s to launch a collection of English language film videos with English subtitles entitled *SpeakUp*. Viewers were thus able to read on the screen the written dialogue of the actors and recognize or confirm what they had not understood aurally. The conventions applied in this type of subtitling differ substantially from those followed in interlingual subtitling, and it is not uncommon to find subtitles of three lines, full of lexical repetitions and incomplete sentences that are a literal transcription, word for word, of the dialogues, putting some pressure on reading speed. The Spanish newspaper *El País* also jumped on board, in collaboration with Disney, with its collection *Diviértete con el inglés* [Have Fun with English]. Over several months in 2002, many classics from Disney were distributed on video in their original English format with English subtitles so that young people could become familiar with the English language in an enjoyable way.

Although, by and large, the only movies that come onto the market with this type of subtitling are in English, other languages and institutions do seem to be awaking to the attraction exerted by the audiovisual world and the potential it offers for exporting their language and culture. Television has not been immune to these experiments and the international French channel, *France 5*, has for years been broadcasting some of its programmes in French with open subtitles also in French, in order to promote the learning of the language.

The arrival of DVD has also meant the consolidation of didactic subtitles, as a track distinct to and independent from that of SDH. Their use is not confined to helping foreigners learn languages, but can also be an aid to children in consolidating their mother tongues, given that many societies are now so thoroughly immersed in the world of the image and audiovisual communication. Big distributors like Disney and Paramount have for some time been marketing a number of their DVDs with two tracks of subtitles in English: one for the deaf and another which is didactic. Again, to date English is the only language in which this dual subtitling is found on DVD, although the situation might well change in the future.

A third type of intralingual subtitling that is gaining tremendous popularity nowadays is known as karaoke. It is generally used with songs or movie musicals so that the public can sing along at the same time as the characters on screen. The movie *The Sound of Music* has been advertised for many years in a central London cinema as follows: "The classic film musical, now with subtitles so everyone can join in!" It has been a tremendous hit, consistently sold out, and has initiated a tradition with the intralingual subtitling of other movies and programmes such as *The Rocky Horror Picture Show, Abba Live in Concert*, and *Joseph and the Amazing Technicolor Dreamcoat.*

Another example of intralingual subtitling is the use of subtitles in movies and programmes for the dialogues of people whose accents are difficult to understand for audiences who, in principle, share the same language. Languages that are spoken far and wide throughout the world, such as English,

Spanish, or French, are those that are commonly affected. But other lesser spoken languages also transcribe the dialogues. On Flemish television in Belgium intralingual subtitles are often used to 'translate' linguistic variants that the producer of a particular programme feels will not be understood by the entire population. This means that not only are some Dutch programmes from the Netherlands intralingually subtitled on Flemish television, but also some TV series, and parts of reality shows, whenever a character or speaker uses a (regional) Flemish variant that may not be understood by the entire Flemish community, due to phonetic or lexical variation. The language used in these subtitles is standard Dutch, which means that all *couleur locale* is lost. The desirability of such subtitling is the topic of much debate (Vandekerckhove *et al.* 2006).

Although rare, this strategy can be used throughout an entire programme. One such example is the British film *Trainspotting*, where the actors speak English with such a strong Scottish accent that the movie was distributed in the United States with English subtitles. However, the common practice is to resort to these subtitles only in sporadic cases where there is a need to transcribe utterances from people who speak the language either as a foreign language or as their native language, but with a strong, local accent and lexical variation that makes it difficult to understand for the rest of the speakers of that language.

The fifth and last category of intralingual subtitling can be seen on monitors in underground stations and other public areas where subtitles are used for advertising, as well as for broadcasting the latest news. The use of written texts on screen allows the information to be transmitted without sound, so as not to disturb the public.

The other major type of subtitling falls under the category of interlingual, and implies the translation from a source to a target language. Gottlieb (1994) calls it 'diagonal subtitling' since it involves a shift from one language to another along with a change of mode, from oral to written. This subtitling is the main focus of this book and will be analyzed in depth in the chapters to follow.

The traditional, broad distinction between interlingual (for hearers) and intralingual (for the deaf) subtitling has systematically overlooked a professional practice that has existed for several years and that is acquiring greater visibility thanks to DVD: interlingual subtitles for the deaf and the hearing impaired. Historically, in countries with a strong tradition of dubbing, such as Spain, Germany, Austria, France or Italy, the deaf could only watch programmes that had been originally produced in Spanish, German, French or Italian, and later also subtitled intralingually into these languages. Given that the translating custom of these five countries favours the dubbing of the vast majority of programmes imported from other countries, it has been difficult for the deaf and hard of hearing to access the information contained in these programmes and they have had to content themselves with the few foreign ones to be broadcast with subtitles. In other countries with a stronger subtitling tradition like for instance Portugal, Greece or the Scandinavian nations, the deaf have normally been served by the same interlingual subtitles as the hearing viewers, even when these have clearly been inappropriate to their needs since they do not incorporate the paralinguistic information necessary for the deaf to be able to contextualize the action.

However, with the arrival of the DVD the situation has changed and is continuing to change radically. Pressure groups in countries such as Germany, UK and Italy have managed to get many foreign films marketed in their countries with two different tracks of interlingual subtitles: one for the hearing population and a second one that addresses the needs of the deaf. We now have many American films that have two subtitle tracks in Italian and German – one for the hearing and another for the deaf and the hard-of-hearing. This is also the case with films like the Spanish *Women on the Verge of a Nervous Breakdown*, which is sold on DVD with two interlingual subtitle tracks in English and a further two in German. Unfortunately, these are to date the only three languages making full use of interlingual SDH. The rest seem to lag behind in these new developments. Although all languages are supposed to be equal in principle, it would appear that in the film and DVD industries, English, German and Italian are 'more equal' than the other languages in regard to SDH. Strangest of all is that it is generally the same distributor who markets the films in all countries, which makes it hard to understand why some languages can have two subtitle tracks and others just one. Only through pressure groups campaigning for the interests of these sectors of the population can social advances aimed at facilitating access to all media in all languages for everybody be achieved.

Bilingual subtitles are the third type within this category and are produced in geographical areas where two languages are spoken. In Belgium, in an attempt to satisfy the Walloon and Flemish communities, subtitles in the cinema are in French and Flemish. In Finland, where Swedish is an official language on a par with Finnish, bilingualism is also respected in certain regions and television and cinema resort to subtitles in both languages. Outside Europe, in countries such as Jordan and Israel, Hebrew and Arabic co-exist at the bottom of the screen. In these cases, the two lines available for subtitles are in constant use, each one dedicated to a different language. To avoid excessive pollution of the image, they tend to use only two-liners, although subtitles of four lines may also be found. The additional pressure on space renders bilingual subtitling an endeavour that borders on the unattainable.

Another setting where bilingual subtitles are resorted to is in international film festivals. In order to attract a wider audience, many of these festivals screen their foreign films – say Iranian, Spanish or Japanese – with two sets of subtitles. One set is in English, to satisfy the needs of an international audience made up of film directors, producers, distributors, actors, and viewers who come from all corners of the world, and the other set of subtitles is in the language of the country where the film festival takes place, e.g. French in Cannes, German in Berlin, and Italian in Venice.

1.3.2 Time available for preparation

By looking at subtitles from this perspective, the following types can be distinguished:

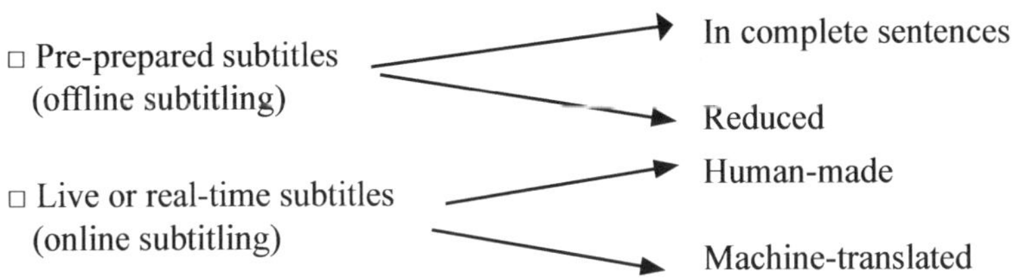

The main difference between these two categories resides in the fact that the pre-prepared subtitles are done after the programme has been shot and some time ahead of its broadcasting or release, giving translators ample time to carry out their work; whereas the online type is performed live, i.e. at the same time as the original programme is taking place or being broadcast.

Pre-prepared subtitles can be subdivided further according to their lexical density. Subtitling in complete sentences, within the limits imposed by the medium, is the most commonly used and the one we normally consume when watching a programme with subtitles. The reduced variety is used when translating television programmes such as the news, interviews or documentaries in which only the gist of what is being said is deemed to be relevant for the audience and translated.

Live or real-time subtitling, also known as simultaneous or online, is a relatively new type, only used when there has not been time to prepare the subtitles in advance, as in the case of live interviews, political statements, sports programmes or news bulletins. This type is much more common in intralingual subtitling for the deaf, but it is also occasionally done interlingually. In the latter case, it is usually done by a team of professionals involving a professional interpreter, who translates the message in a condensed way and in front of a microphone connected to the headphones of a velotypist or stenographer. This is a professional who types in shorthand rather than letters on a special keyboard and can achieve the speed and accuracy required for live subtitling. Irrespective of the linguistic difficulty posed by the source text, this is a very complex activity in which complicated mental processes must take place in seconds. There is also the pressure of coordinating the efforts of several professionals working under stressful conditions, which justifies why this approach is being abandoned in favour of voice recognition. Describing the way it is done in the Netherlands, Den Boer (2001:168) writes: "subtitling involves the very close and concentrated cooperation of two subtitlers-interpreters, one velotypist and, in complicated cases, an editor". Synchrony between source and target texts is the biggest problem here. As subtitles can only be written after the original dialogue has been uttered, this inevitably leads to a delay and lack of synchrony between the dialogues and the subtitles, wich can be confusing for the viewer.

Intralingual real-time subtitling is a daily occurrence in countries with a tradition in SDH and it is carried out following two different approaches. In a similar fashion to the previous type, but without the need for an interpreter, a stenographer or stenotypist – known in North America as stenocaptioner – is in charge of writing the subtitles using the keyboards and writing theories common in court reporting (Robson 2004:119-148). The other approach to live subtitling is to use speech recognition software. It is a simple enough process whereby a person dictates the speech to a microphone, connected to a computer and to a speech recognition program that converts speech into written text. Although the technology has been around since the 1990s, the relatively high number of spelling mistakes that make it to the screen is one of the main drawbacks of this approach. The fact that speech recognition programs only work with a very small number of major languages, simply because more research efforts have been put into them, also makes them impractical in the case of most languages. There are still many other hurdles that need to be overcome before this technology can be put to a successful end (Robson 2004:149-160). However, the industry wants to see it work properly and is investing large sums of money in its development, leading some people like Robson (ibid.:151) to state: "it's only a matter of time before speech-based captioning systems are more broadly deployed".

Technology and subtitling go hand in hand, and machine translation undertaken in interlingual subtitling, without the apparent input of human beings, has for some years been a reality in the USA, in an attempt to attract viewers from certain minority groups. This kind of instantaneous translation into several languages makes use of material that is already available in English. The USA has a long history of subtitling for the deaf and the hard-of-hearing, which is reflected in some pioneering legislation in this field and in high percentages of audiovisual programmes captioned intralingually – i.e. from English to English – for these social groups. Using these subtitles in English and an automatic translation programme, the company Global Translation Inc.'s (www.translatetv.com) has been the first to provide instant machine translation of television content from English into Spanish. Judging by the awards it has received and the enthusiasm it appears to have awakened in certain sectors of the profession, it would not be surprising if, in the not too distant future, this practice were to awaken greater interest in other countries with multicultural and multilingual populations. Despite its potential, however, the problem here resides in the apparent lack of human agents and in the fact that this approach seems to be driven solely by economic forces and interests, as is apparent from the company's own website: "The use of the TTV service provides broadcasters with a cost effective way to reach the Hispanic viewer while also generating additional incremental advertising revenue". Quality seems to be disregarded altogether and the results are still a long way from being satisfactory. If the examples shown on their website are meant to be the flagship of their trade, the situation becomes worrying. Subtitles such as these two from their website:

ESO ES LA PRESENTACION ENTERA. Y ESO ES EXACTAMENTE QUE LO HICIMOS AQUI. [THAT IS THE ENTIRE PRESENTATION. AND THAT IS EXACTLY THAT WE DID IT HERE.]

Ningunas muertes reportaron con esos incidentes, sin embargo. [None deaths reported with those incidents, however.]

are not only lexically and syntactically incorrect in Spanish, but also nonsensical. With their very peculiar grammar, riddled with interferences from English, they are an attack on the Spanish language and do very little to educate their readers.

1.3.3 Technical parameters

From a technical perspective, the following two types of subtitles can be identified:

- □ Open subtitles
- □ Closed subtitles

The basic difference between them is that, in the first case, the subtitles are burned or projected onto the image and cannot be removed or turned off. The programme and the subtitles cannot be disassociated from each other, allowing the viewer no choice as to their presence on screen. In the second case, the translation can be added to the programme at the viewer's will. The subtitles are hidden and can only be seen with an appropriate decoder or when the viewer activates them on DVD.

Until the arrival of DVD, interlingual subtitles were always open on television, in the cinemas, and distributed with the old VHS tape. Intralingual subtitles, on the other hand, were always closed and broadcast via teletext or line 21. With the DVD, a much more versatile format, the situation has changed and we can now also find closed interlingual subtitles, whose appearance on screen is optional and dependent on the viewer. However, contrary to general belief, not all subtitling on DVD is closed and some companies, perhaps rather surprisingly, do distribute their films on DVD with open subtitles.

1.3.4 Methods of projecting subtitles

A classification of subtitles from this perspective represents in effect an excursus through the history of subtitling:

- Mechanical and thermal subtitling
- Photochemical subtitling
- Optical subtitling
- Laser subtitling
- Electronic subtitling

The technical process of transferring the subtitles to the actual film or programme has undergone a considerable evolution, which has led to an improvement in their presentation and stability on screen. We will focus on the last two types, but for those interested Ivarsson and Caroll (1998:12-19) and Díaz Cintas (2001a:101-103) offer a more detailed account of each of them.

The current method of impression most commonly used in cinema subtitling is laser. Introduced in the 1980s, it rapidly proved itself to be much more effective than the previous methods it began to replace. A laser ray of great precision burns the emulsion of the positive copy while printing the subtitle which, thanks to the time code, is exactly synchronized with the actors' speech. From this point the subtitles form an integral part of the film copy, and every time it is projected they will appear on the lower part of the screen. Since they are burned in they are always white, like the screen onto which they are projected. This method permits excellent definition of letters, with enhanced contours that facilitate the legibility of the text. Being actually printed on the copy eliminates any possibility of the subtitles moving or shaking during the projection of the film. To laser subtitle a full-length feature film takes about ten times the film's projection time.

Electronic subtitling is the other method frequently used in the profession as an alternative to laser subtitling, its greatest advantage being that it allows subtitles to be superimposed on the screen instead of being engraved on the image. The subtitles are produced by a character generator and beamed by a projector onto the screen. The technology uses a time code system to ensure that the text is projected in synchrony with the film. Electronic subtitling permits extremely versatile subtitling of a single film print, making it possible to project the subtitles onto (or below) the image, in any language, in any colour (though they tend to be white or yellow), and without damaging the original copy. It is cheaper than laser engraving and is used mainly in film festivals where a single copy of the film can be shown with various sets of subtitles in several countries. The other advantage over laser is that since electronic subtitles are independent of the audiovisual programme, they can easily be revised and modified from projection to projection.

This system seems to provide better access to movies screened in the cinema for people with hearing loss, without imposing on the hearing population as the subtitles may be projected onto a screen adjacent to the movie screen. It is also a solution for cinemas that want to use one and the same film print for alternative screenings with and without SDH. Electronic subtitling is also preferred in television and DVD.

1.3.5 Distribution format

A fifth and last category can be established according to the medium used for the distribution of the programme, which may affect the way subtitles are produced. Thus, subtitles can be made for the following:

- □ Cinema
- □ Television
- □ Video, VHS
- □ DVD
- □ Internet

Although the conventions applied when subtitling a programme will ultimately depend on individual companies, on the instructions given by the client or on the subtitling program being used, there are some differences from medium to medium. We mention here some of the most striking ones, but a more detailed discussion is found in chapters 4 and 5.

To calculate the reading speed and the time a subtitle can stay on screen, some companies have traditionally applied what is known in the profession as 'the six-second rule', which refers to the time it takes the average viewer to read and assimilate the information contained in the two lines of a subtitle, when each line consists of some 35 or 37 characters. The average viewer is, therefore, able to read 70 to 74 characters in 6 seconds and from this main rule we can then calculate the amount of text we can write in shorter subtitles (§4.7.9). However, this calculation seems to be mostly used when subtitling for television and varies when subtitling for other media like cinema, video,

DVD or Internet. The reading speed applied in the other media is normally faster, the reason being that the profile of the television viewer is in general more heterogeneous and the subtitles have to satisfy all viewers.

As far as the line length is concerned, cinemas may use up to a maximum of 40 or 41 characters – 43 at some film festivals – since it is an accepted norm in the profession that the viewer is able to read subtitles more easily and quickly on a cinema than on a television screen. Although this has not been thoroughly investigated, the reasons seem to be the better definition and larger screen dimensions, the cultural profile of the audience, and the greater concentration that movie theatres afford viewers. DVD also tends to go for these long lines, as viewers can simply rewind the movie if they have not had enough time to read a subtitle. The other reason given is that consumers of DVDs – who also have access to the dubbed version and can choose the language combination of their liking for the sound and subtitled tracks – often use subtitles to improve their skills in other languages and prefer a translation that follows the original more closely and abridges as little as possible. Television, on the other hand, varies from as little as 28 characters per line to some 37 as the maximum. With new technological advances, the debate on the maximum number of characters per line is bound to disappear. Not all letters take up the same amount of space. An 'l' or an 'i' clearly takes up less space than an 'm' or an 'o'. However, when working with characters, each has its own space. Many subtitling programs work now with pixels in an attempt to rationalize the space available for the subtitles, since they allow the space to be adjusted according to the size of the letters.

Line breaks and conventions may also vary depending on the media. For instance, cinema subtitling tends to use shorter lines and centre them, despite the fact that the lines can actually be longer than on television. It also tends not to condense the original dialogue as much as television and to show great respect for shot changes and cuts in the spotting. The result is that the same film subtitled for the cinema usually has more subtitles than when subtitled for television. DVD is similar to cinema, but shows less respect for cut changes and prefers to use longer lines that can be easily read on a relatively small screen compared to the cinema one. The result is fewer subtitles than for the cinema, though not more condensation of information.

The typical commercial release of a feature film starts in the cinema, is followed by the copy on video – now defunct and superseded by the DVD – and finishes on television. Three or four subtitled versions of the same movie can be found on the market. Sometimes, even more when the film is broadcast by more than one TV station or sold on various DVDs, in the same or a different region (e.g. in Spanish for zone 1 for Latin America, and for zone 2 for Spain).

The process usually involves a gradual reduction in the number of subtitles; a change in the type of letter; a slight modification of both the structure and the spotting of the subtitles, since the cinema illusion is based on a succession of 24 frames per second, whereas the small screen uses 25 frames per second in Europe and 30 in North America. To adjust the film print from cinema to television, the pace of the movie must be slightly sped up, reducing the length of the movie and the time available for subtitles by 4%. Generally speaking, a movie lasting approximately 90 minutes contains some 900 subtitles in the cinema, 750 on video or DVD, and 650 in the television version. However, to reduce costs the same subtitles are sometimes used regardless of the broadcast medium, which can force a higher reading speed, cause loss of definition, and make subtitles more difficult to read.

1.4 Surtitles

Also known as *supertitles* in the USA and *supratitles* by some scholars (Gambier 1994:276) they are a close relative to subtitles. They were developed by the Canadian Opera Company in Toronto, and the first production in the world to be presented with surtitles was the staging of *Elektra* in January 1983. They are the translation of the words being sung, if the opera is sung in another language, and can be considered the equivalent of subtitles in the cinema. Although they started in the opera, they have been gaining visibility since the 1980s and spreading to other areas like theatre and live performances in general. They have also developed to become more accessible, encompassing intralingual surtitling.

Surtitles tend to follow most of the conventions applied in subtitling and are shown on a LED display, normally placed above the stage. In fact, they are also called subtitles by many in the profession. They either scroll from right to left or are presented stationary in subtitles of two or three lines, which seems to be less distracting for the audience. Of late, many opera houses and theatres have also installed several smaller monitors throughout the theatre that are placed at the back of each seat in the auditorium. They are known as seat-back title screens and allow for subtitles to be provided in more than one language.

Given that we are dealing with live performances, spotting is usually one of the trickiest issues. It is normally done live by a technician so that the subtitles can follow the delivery of the original as closely as possible. Here is a list of events where surtitles can be used:

□ Live performances → Conferences
→ Theatre
→ Opera, Concerts

1.5 Intertitles

Intertitles are at the origin of subtitles and can be considered their oldest relatives, the first experiments with intertitles having taken place in the early 20th century. They are also known as 'title cards' and can be defined as a piece of filmed, printed text that appears between scenes. They were a mainstay of silent films and consisted of short sentences written against a dark background, usually white on black. Their main functions were to convey character dialogue and descriptive narrative material related to the images. Although communicative in essence, some directors also used them as an artistic and expressive device. The arrival of the soundtrack largely eliminated their usefulness, and when they are used in contemporary films they tend to be called inserts.

Very little has been written about their translation (Weinberg 1985), and very little research has been carried out, apart from the work done by Izard (1992) and Díaz Cintas (2001a:53-59). In the old times, the original intertitles used to be edited out and replaced by new title cards in the target language. On other occasions, the original intertitles were left and a sort of master of ceremonies translated and explained them to the rest of the audience. When translated for today's viewers, they tend to be subtitled or voiced-over.

1.6 Fansubs

The extensive technological developments that have taken place in recent decades have had highly significant consequences for the world of AVT, media accessibility in general and subtitling in particular. The Internet has fully come of age. Computer subtitling programs have become much more affordable and accessible, with many of them available free on the net (see Appendix 2). These programs, known by those with an interest in the subject as subbing programs, have facilitated the rise and consolidation of translation practices like fansubs.

The origins of fansubbing go back to the 1980s, when it emerged as an attempt to popularize the Japanese cartoons known as *manga* and *anime*. American and European fans wanted to watch their favourite programmes but were faced with two main problems: on the one hand, the linguistic barrier and on the other, the scant distribution of these series in their respective countries. The alternative option was to subtitle these programmes themselves. Despite the questionable legality of this activity as far as the copyright of programmes is concerned, the philosophy underlying this type of subtitling is the free distribution over the Internet of audiovisual programmes with subtitles done by fans. The translations are done for free by aficionados of these programmes and then posted on the Internet so that anyone who is interested may watch them.

This new form of subtitling 'by fans for fans' lies at the margins of market imperatives and is far less dogmatic and more creative and individualistic than what has traditionally been done. Some of its defining features are the use of colours to identify speakers, the incorporation of explicative glosses and metalinguistic notes in the subtitles themselves or on the top of the screen, and the use of cumulative subtitles (Díaz Cintas, forthcoming). In fact, some aficionados prefer to use the term *subbing*, instead of subtitling, in order to emphasize the peculiar nature of the activity.

In the first instance, this practice dealt solely with the subtitling of Japanese *anime* into English, but nowadays it has spread to other language combinations and other audiovisual programmes such as films. From an academic point of view, little research has been done to date in this field (Ferrer 2005; Díaz Cintas and Muñoz-Sánchez 2006; Bogucki, forthcoming), but it would be very interesting to research and analyze this new activity in detail, and to see whether or not some points of contact and parallelisms can be established between this new form of Internet subtitling and the more traditional types that we have been consuming in formats such as television, cinema or DVD.

1.7 Discussion points

1.7.1 Below is a quotation from Pommier (1988:22). What do you think about it?
It has to be understood that the subtitled text is not a proper translation, but rather a *simple adaptation* that preserves the general meaning of the original (our translation and our emphasis).

1.7.2 In your opinion, how does the fact that some scholars and professionals think of subtitling as a case of adaptation rather than proper translation affect the general perception of subtitling itself? Can you identify any other translating practices that could be considered to be in this intermediate position? Which?

1.7.3 Watch a movie or programme with subtitles in your mother tongue and draw up a list of at least five different features that define the subtitles you have seen on screen.

1.7.4 Watch a movie or programme that has closed captions in the same language for the deaf and the hard-of-hearing audiences and make a list of at least five different features that define the captions you saw on screen.

You can normally access closed captions on the teletext of your television set or on some DVDs.

1.7.5 What are the main differences that you have noticed in the two approaches? What is your personal opinion about the way the two types of subtitles are done?

1.7.6 Are there any techniques, aspects or strategies that interlingual subtitling could adapt from intralingual subtitling or vice versa to improve the presentation or quality of subtitles?

1.7.7 In your opinion, what is the social value of interlingual subtitles? And what would be the benefits of intralingual subtitles or closed captions?

1.7.8 If you want to experience fansubs there are many websites on Internet. You can go to either Animesuki (www.animesuki.com) or Animecubed (www.animecubed.com/anime-videos) for fansubs in English and to Frozen-Layer Network (http://bittorrent.frozen-layer.net) for fansubs in Spanish. In order to download one of the animes from any of these websites you need to have installed in your computer a program called Bittorrent (www.bittorrent.com). Be warned that the whole process of downloading the anime can take some three hours when using broadband.

2. The Professional Environment

2.0 Preliminary discussion

2.1 Here you have a quote from Ivarsson and Carroll (1998:v), in which they make a reference to a previous edition of their book written by Ivarsson in 1992:

It was a book *about subtitling, not translation.* Translation is a different art. I decided to call it *Subtitling for the Media – A Handbook of an Art*, since in my view subtitling, when it is done to high standard, includes so many of the elements essential to art and above all demands so much skill, imagination and creative talent that it *is* indeed an art.

❶ Do you agree with their concept of subtitling as 'art'?
❷ Do you think that this perception is positive or negative for subtitling and its learning? Why?
❸ Is translation, in general, an art form?
❹ Do you think there are translation practices that are an 'art' and other translation practices that are not? Could you give any examples?

2.2 What are your thoughts about this other definition of the subtitling profession and the figure of the subtitler?

A translator has to be multi-talented, but a subtitler also has to be a verbal acrobat - a language virtuoso who can work within the confines of a postage stamp. You only have a limited amount of characters per line to work with, including commas and spaces.

If you have one letter too many, you can't just leave it out. You sometimes have to rewrite the entire sentence. The layout and spotting of subtitles are art forms in themselves, because subtitles have to have the same rhythm as the film.

Reading the subtitles and watching the film are one and the same activity, not two separate ones. If they were separate, watching TV would be exhausting.

Subtitling is the result of a team effort. There are several stages involved in the process from the moment a job is commissioned until we can watch it on one of our screens. Different companies work in different ways and new technological advances and commercial forces tend to have an immediate impact on the subtitling profession. The aim of this chapter is to present the reader with an overview of the several steps followed to subtitle a film. From a professional perspective, feature length films for distribution in the cinema and on DVD tend to go through the most thorough process in subtitling and this is the reason why they are a better type of programme to illustrate the whole process.

2.1 The subtitling process

The client, normally a production or a distribution company, or a television station, contacts the subtitling company with a commission. General details concerning the title of the film, the name of the client, the project manager and translator assigned, etc. are entered.

Somebody in the company watches the film to make sure that the copy is not damaged, to verify that the dialogue list (§4.3) is complete and accurate – if the film comes with one – and to check if there is any other information (songs, inserts, and the like) that needs to be translated too. In the event that the dialogue list is missing, the dialogue exchanges need to be transcribed *ab initio* from the soundtrack.

A working copy is made of the original film, traditionally in VHS although nowadays these copies are digitized. They are telecined to convert from cinema 24-frame rate to video 25-frame rate (PAL and SECAM systems) or 30-frame rate (NTSC system). To avoid illegal dubbing of material, special anti-pirate inserts might be included in the new copy. Some companies may only give translators the scenes that include dialogue, leaving the rest in black. Others add inserts throughout the film reminding the viewer who the legal owner of the copyright is.

Spotting, also known as timing or cueing and more recently originating, is the next task. It consists of determining the precise moments when a subtitle should appear on screen – known as the in-time – and when it should leave the screen – known as the out-time – according to a set of space and time limitations discussed in §4.6 and §4.7. To guarantee optimal quality it is desirable that, if the task is performed by technicians, they have a working knowledge of the language spoken in the film. In an ideal situation, the spotting should be done by experienced translators themselves. In certain cases, the film may come with a very detailed combined continuity and subtitle/spotting list, containing all the dialogue already segmented into master titles for the translator to follow.

A copy of the film and the dialogue list are then forwarded to the translator, although on many occasions only one of the two is actually sent. Unfortunately, it is not uncommon in the profession to have to work from paper without access to the images, or from the soundtrack without a copy of the written dialogue.

The reasons are varied. Sometimes, it is for fear that illegal copies will be made. On other occasions it is sheer lack of time, and whilst the film is still being finished, the distribution company wants the translation to be underway so that the movie can be shown at a film festival, for instance. It may also be that the subtitler works from a different city or simply cannot go to the studio to watch the programme. In all these cases, a thorough revision is in order at the end to make sure that the soundtrack dialogue coincides with the exchanges provided on paper, and that the subtitles do not enter into conflict with the image. Until recently, audiovisual programmes were always sent on a VHS cassette but these days they tend to be digitized and sent to the translators on CD or DVD. Translators can also download the material to be subtitled via Internet (FTP) from the company's server.

Watching the film or programme in its entirety before proceeding to translate is highly advisable, although not always very realistic when having to work to really tight deadlines. If time allows for it, and the translator works from a written dialogue list, it may be a good idea to take notes of the points and issues that could prove problematic at a later stage. Torregrosa (1996) suggests three areas that the translator ought to take into account during the first viewing of the programme, to which we add a further two:

1. Words and phrases that lend themselves to a polysemous reading in the original. The French *encore du rouge* can be translated as 'a bit more of red colour' or 'a bit more red wine' depending on the image. 'Funny' in English can have a myriad of meanings, even opposed ones, depending on the context and the intonation.
2. The gender and number of some nouns, pronouns and adjectives that are not marked in English. 'You are great' can have many different translations into other languages, depending on whether the addressee is male or female, whether we are talking to one or several people, or whether we are being polite or informal.
3. The degree of familiarity shown among the characters, to decide whether a formal or informal form of address is required, and their identity when being referred to by pronoun. The English 'you' can refer to several people in a language like Spanish: *tú* (singular, informal), *Usted* (singular, formal), *Ustedes* (plural, formal), *vosotros* (plural, informal, masculine) and *vosotras* (plural, informal, feminine).
4. Deictic units as 'this/these', 'that/those', 'here/there', etc. may have referents that appear on screen and do not need to be translated. Alternatively, obscure or long terms that are difficult to translate may refer to objects that appear on screen and can be rendered by means of a deictic.
5. Exclamations with no fixed meaning that can only be appreciated in a given context, such as 'oh, my', 'fuck', 'geez', 'Christ', 'blimey', and the like.

After this, the translator can start with the translation from the source to the target language. Due attention has to be paid to the actors' dialogue, but without forgetting other acoustic and visual elements that should also be translated: songs, inserts, newspaper headlines, or voices coming from a radio or a television set, for instance. Besides being aware of the constraints imposed by the medium, translators also have to be familiar with the value added by the images. In the Norwegian film *Elling*, a framed photograph of a woman on a kitchen wall is subtitled to give us her name, since it is a very important iconic referent to understand some of the ironic nuances in the conversation between the two male protagonists. She is Gro Harlem Brundtland, ex-Prime Minister of Norway, from the Labour Party.

A widespread practice in our field is to use English as a pivot language to translate from lesser-known languages. A Japanese, Iranian or Hungarian film may well be translated into Italian, Spanish or Portuguese from an English translation of the film rather than the original soundtrack. Needless to say, any errors or misunderstandings in the English translation will most likely be replicated in the other languages too. But not only errors: ambiguities, nuances and interpretations will also be filtered through English. A practice perceived by many as problematic and worrying, since not only are most of the programmes already produced in English, but even films shot in other languages end up being translated from English.

If the subtitler has been asked to do the spotting of the dialogue too and to come up with the final subtitles, these are saved as file formats unique to subtitling. These files can be either specific to the subtitling software manufacturer or one of the many industry standard files that facilitate the exchange of material (.EBU or .txt). In the case of WinCAPS, the standard program used in the industry creates files with a unique extension (.w32). The version that is included on the DVD accompanying this book creates another type of files, with a different extension (.w30), which can only be used with this DVD WinCAPS version.

Once the translation is finished, the translator sends it to the subtitling company or to the person who commissioned the job, usually by e-mail these days.

Depending on the way the subtitling company works, if the subtitler was not asked to produce the actual subtitles, then the translation may need to go through an adaptation process. Some firms ask their translators to submit a complete translation of the dialogues, without worrying about any medium constraints. A technician or adaptor is then in charge of adjusting the translations to an appropriate subtitling length, according to the time limitations that operate in particular cases and the reading speed applied to the programme. This practice is more prevalent when subtitling for a television station than when working for the DVD industry. It is also commonly followed when surtitling for the opera and the theatre. Some voices in the academic world and in the profession have started to call for this task to be carried out by the translator/subtitler.

Revision and proofreading of the subtitles (in a printed version) is done to detect any possible mistakes and guarantee a final product of high quality. Ideally, a different person should be responsible for this task. Any mistranslations or typos must be corrected. Spelling mistakes seem to be more noticeable on a screen than on a page, and they must be avoided at all costs. Their presence in a subtitle may not only be irritating but may also distance the viewer from the whole process. In the case of languages going through a process of linguistic standardization, like Catalan or Basque in Spain, we also tend to find the figure of the linguistic corrector. This professional works mainly for public television stations and is in charge of guaranteeing that the language used on the screen is appropriate and abides by the rules of the language. As a matter of principle, translators should have a say in the proposed changes and be entitled to a copy of the final, revised subtitles to see the type of amendments and alterations that have been made to their translations. It helps not only to improve one's work but also to become familiar with the likes and dislikes of the clients.

Before inserting the subtitles on the celluloid, a simulation of what the film is going to look like with the subtitles on it is carried out in the presence of the client. If needed, amendments or changes are incorporated at this stage. Some of the big distribution companies have the figure of the supervisor, responsible for this, well enshrined in their working routines. As the two professionals Leboreiro Enríquez and Poza Yagüe (2001:319) state:

> It is important not to forget that both translators and subtitlers do nothing more than come up with a subtitling proposal for the client, who at any moment can change, delete, substitute… whatever s/he wants, in terms of text or spotting (our translation).

The traditional, academic perception of translation as an individual activity clashes here head-on with professional reality.

The simulation of an average film – some 90 minutes and a thousand subtitles – takes about three hours, and the subtitler is sometimes, though not always, invited to be present.

When the simulation is to the taste of the client, the subtitling company can then proceed to the next stage, which consists in laser engraving the subtitles on the celluloid. Laser subtitling is widely used in the cinema and, although relatively more expensive, it has proved to be much more effective and reliable than the previous methods (§1.3.4). But, with the advent of digital cinema, it is very possible that this stage and the next will disappear in the not so distant future, as technology offers new and cheaper solutions.

The laser ray burns the film emulsion in order to engrave the subtitles, producing a black dust that obscures the new written text and makes it necessary for the celluloid to be washed and dried again in a special machine immediately after the impression. The alternative method is electronic subtitling (§1.3.4), cheaper and more convenient for events like film festivals.

Once the subtitles have been laser engraved on the film copy or copies, and before dispatching it to the client, a final viewing takes place to make sure that both the engraving and the washing of the celluloid are satisfactory. The film is then sent to the client who will screen it in the cinema, broadcast it on television or sell it on DVD.

Up until here we have seen the stages that are usually followed when subtitling a feature length movie. However, real practice and theory do not always coincide and some of the stages might be skipped. It cannot be forgotten, either, that some of these operations are being constantly revisited, and what was normal practice a few years back is now obsolete. The digitization of the image and the commercialization of software subtitling programs are some of the milestones that have led to considerable changes in the profession.

2.2 The professionals

Three different professionals can be distinguished in the subtitling process. The spotter – known by some companies as subtitler – is responsible for the technical task of deciding the in and out times of the subtitles, and increasingly for creating templates and master titles with relevant annotations for the translators. These professionals tend to share the language of the original programme, although not always; might not know any other foreign languages; and are expected to be technologically literate, with an excellent working knowledge of subtitling programs. They should be conversant with film language and narrative techniques, and capable of dealing with issues like shot changes.

The translator, on the other hand, is in charge of the language transfer, should have an excellent command of the source and the target languages and cultures, and know the intricacies of moving from speech to written texts. Finally, adaptors are experts in the media limitations that constrain subtitling and are familiar with condensation and reduction strategies in the target language. Their role is to fit the rough translation into the subtitle lines, searching for shorter synonyms and altering syntactical structures without sacrificing the meaning of the original, although in some cases they might have no knowledge of the source language.

This tripartite division is seen by many as unnecessary, its downside being that too many cooks spoil the broth. The fact that traditionally neither spotters nor adaptors have been required to be conversant with the language of the audiovisual programme has always been criticized as a major weakness, particularly since it is at the final stage that the meaning of the original text can be easily distorted and betrayed. Although still rather prominent in dubbing as a professional in charge of lip synchronization, the figure of the adaptor is gradually disappearing from the subtitling profession and is being subsumed by that of the translator. Luyken *et al.* (1991:57) state: "Ideally the translation and subtitling functions should be combined in one person which will reduce the risk of error due to the inaccurate communication of concepts". In fact, many subtitlers carry out both tasks, i.e. translation and adaptation, simultaneously and at the very same time come up with the final subtitle, rather than a text that needs further polishing to fit within the subtitle limitations.

Only a few years back, and given the developments that were taking place in the field of subtitling software, the general tendency in the field seemed to be pointing in the direction of a professional who would embody all three tasks: a subtitler with the technical know-how to do the timing of the original dialogues, and the cultural and linguistic background to carry out the language transfer, condensing the message if and when necessary. In fact, this is slowly becoming the norm in some working environments like cinema and television subtitling. Given that most translators in AVT work freelance and it can be difficult to guarantee a steady source of income, the more versatile the professional is, the more chances of securing different jobs. That is, the more tasks they are able to perform, the greater their employability potential.

However, the advent of the DVD industry has changed the makeup of the profession and the way the process is being done. From the point of view of translation, perhaps the most significant aspect is the possibility of incorporating on one single DVD up to eight versions of the same programme dubbed into different languages, and up to 32 subtitle tracks in other languages. For a client who needs a film or programme to be subtitled into several languages, it is much easier to send the product to a single company that is capable of doing it into all the required languages, than to send it to several smaller companies that will only be able to translate it into one or just a few languages. For a big subtitling company game to deal with multilingual projects of this nature, it is easier and cheaper to create a single document – known in the profession as a template – which contains the master titles to be translated into all the different languages. The original dialogue is then segmented in the same way for all the translators, and the subtitles follow exactly the same timing in all the target languages. In some big companies working for DVD, the distinction between spotters/subtitlers and translators seems to be as relevant as in the past.

In this book, we understand and advocate the figure of the subtitler as a professional in charge of all three tasks: the spotting and the translation/adaptation of the subtitles, both interlingually and intralingually.

2.3 The working conditions

2.3.1 Clients and rates

Subtitlers can work freelance or in-house for any of the following agents:

- Subtitling companies (see Appendix 1).
- Production and distribution companies dealing with films, trailers and other audiovisual material that is shown on cinema screens.
- Film festivals.
- DVD and VHS distribution companies.
- Private and public television stations.
- Publicity companies.
- Production companies dealing with corporate videos.
- Firms working with multimedia products.
- Companies working in the interactive software industry (also called entertainment software industry, or game industry).

Freelancing tends to be the most common form of employment for subtitlers, and only in countries where the volume of subtitling is very high are subtitlers hired in-house. When working freelance, subtitlers can be paid per whole programme, per minute of programme, per number of words, or per number of subtitles. Rates vary from country to country, and company to company, and translators ought to inform themselves about the going rates to avoid unfair competition and destroying the market with unnecessarily low rates.

There are several factors that impinge on the subtitlers' remuneration. When asked to translate from the screen without a dialogue list, they should charge more for their work, since the task will take considerably longer. Some translators' associations recommend a surcharge of some 30 to 50%, although this is not always possible and some bargaining might be called for.

Subtitlers ought to have sufficient time to do proper research on terminology and cultural referents as well as to revise their own work. The less the time allowed for doing the translation, the higher the rates should be. Once again, this desideratum is not fulfilled in practice and it usually depends on the bargaining power of individuals. The medium is another factor affecting rates; subtitling feature films for cinema release normally commands higher rates than subtitling for television, film festivals or the DVD industry.

Some of the biggest changes in AVT come hand in hand with globalization and technological developments. Today it is not necessary to live in the same city, or even country, of the client or subtitling company. Computers and Internet have opened up new avenues unknown until relatively recently, allowing subtitlers to offer their services to companies anywhere in the world, and firms to contract their workforce wherever they prefer. Pros and cons can be attached to this situation. The great advantage for translators is the increase in the number of potential clients that can be contacted without having to leave home. The downside is that competition also grows and, in some cases, companies prefer to recruit their workers in countries where labour costs are lower.

2.3.2 Globalization

The global marketing and expansion of the audiovisual industry also means that the product becomes increasingly diversified. Two obvious products of the joint forces of globalization and technological advances in the domain of audiovisual media are DVDs and computer games. Whereas the diversity of the world 'out there' seems almost limitless, the commercial world of DVD production seems to be pulling subtitling into the opposite direction. As large multinationals dominate the market, more standardization is called for and subtitlers' creativity is curbed. As discussed above and in chapter 4, the use of templates no longer allows the subtitler to decide about spotting or timing. Subtitlers are restricted to translating the English subtitles that are delivered with the film, or with an extensive dialogue list and glossary but without the film. This certainly allows them to work faster and still requires creativity in order to produce idiomatic target language subtitles of a similar length, but opinions on the desirability of this state of affairs vary.

Many of the big international subtitling companies have their main offices in cities like London and Los Angeles, nerve centres of the audiovisual world. The idea that the decisions on the translation into a given language are taken in the country where the language is spoken is becoming fast *démodé*. For clients with audiovisual programmes that need to be subtitled into several languages, a normal occurrence in the DVD industry, the easiest, quickest and cheapest way to go about it is to approach a big subtitling company that can do all the languages, rather than sending the programmes to different countries where the languages are spoken. They leave the programme in the office in London and collect it at the time agreed. It is the duty of the subtitling company to contact and find professionals in the languages requested. In some cases, the work will be conducted by email, and in others, subtitlers and revisers will be called in to guarantee the quality of the final product.

Globalization has also brought along the application of new parameters that are decided outside the country where the programme is finally watched. A greater degree of standardization can be observed in the conventions applied when subtitling the same programme into several languages for DVD distribution. Given that many subtitling tracks are commercialized together on the same DVD and can be accessed by anyone anywhere, the tendency is to use the same conventions in all languages, even though in some cases they might be at odds with domestic practice. This relatively new development raises questions about the balance among languages (and cultures) in the audiovisual world, since not only are programmes and films produced in English, but their translations are also being done and decided in the country of origin. The jargon used in the profession is certainly telling, with concepts such as 'master' and 'genesis' to name the timed English subtitles used for translation; and 'territories' to refer to the countries where the translated programmes are distributed. The problem is even further compounded if we think that some films from lesser-spoken languages are subtitled using English as a pivot language.

In a drive to save money, another practice being implemented by some companies consists in 'converting' languages that are spoken in different parts of the globe, e.g. Castilian Spanish into Latin American Spanish, French into Canadian French, Portuguese into Brazilian Portuguese, Roman Serbian into Cyrillic Serbian and vice versa. The subtitles are initially done from the SL into one of these languages, say Portuguese, and then 'converted' into Brazilian Portuguese. The timing of the subtitles is the same in both languages and the task consists in changing only the words and expressions that are too local and might not be understood by the other language community. Also in expansion is the use of a 'neutral' variety of the language that could satisfy the needs of several countries where the same language is spoken. Many DVDs are now distributed with a subtitling track in Castilian Spanish and another one in Latin American Spanish which is meant to reach all countries in America. Little research has been done into the morphological, syntactical and lexical characteristics of this language variant or into the way it is perceived by viewers.

Ivarsson (1992:11) deplores that "film directors and TV producers seldom show any interest in what happens to their works once they are exported to other countries", an idea also shared by Krogstad (1998). After recognizing that contemporary films are increasingly being produced for the international market, he goes on to state: "Still, it doesn't seem to be an integral part of the planning of a film that its reception abroad depends on the quality of the verbal transmission" (ibid.:63). It is high time this situation changed. In an increasingly globalized market, with the great potential for boosting box office receipts abroad, translation is a fundamental part of the international success of a movie. Many directors still have to wake up to the reality that the translation process is an artistic factor on which more control needs to be exerted and in which it is worthwhile investing the necessary amount of money, generally very little compared with the overall budget. Subtitling, as well as dubbing, has to be understood as an integral part of the process of the artistic creation of a film and not as a mere appendix subject to market forces.

2.3.3 Deadlines

Although projects in subtitling are virtually always urgent, deadlines vary according to the distribution channel. When subtitling films to be screened in the cinema or broadcast on television, translators tend to be allowed more time than when working for the DVD industry, where the rhythm has accelerated considerably in recent years because of the distribution companies' drive to release the DVD very soon after the cinema launch. Film festivals are notoriously frantic and subtitlers can be asked to do a film in a couple of days, or even in just a few hours overnight. If time pressures are great, it is not uncommon to divide a film or programme into several sections and give them to different translators. Needless to say, unless a thorough revision is done at the end, this practice can lead to a lack of cohesion and coherence in the subtitles, e.g. the same terms being translated in different ways by different translators.

It is rather difficult to tell exactly how long it takes, on average, to subtitle a normal length film of some 90 minutes. The time put into it will depend on factors such as the density of the dialogue, the difficulty of the topic, and the date it has to be shown. In a normal situation, the spotting of a film can take some two days, and the translator is given between four and seven days to produce the target language subtitles. Depending on the number of subtitles, their laser engraving onto the film copy and washing takes around ten times the length of the film, so to subtitle a 90-minute production will last between 15 and 20 hours. The final simulation can be done in a morning or an afternoon. All in all, the whole process to subtitle a full-length film can last some 12 to 15 days from the moment it has been placed with the subtitling company.

2.3.4 Subtitlers' visibility and professional associations

According to Ivarsson (1992:106), subtitlers "have the same copyright under the Berne and World Conventions as writers and therefore have the right to see their names on works that are published". Indeed, Point 5.h, Section III of the UNESCO's (1976) *Recommendation on the Legal Protection of Translators and Translations and the Practical Means to improve the Status of Translators* reinforces this right by explicitly stating:

> the name of the author of the translation should appear in a prominent place on all published copies of the translation, on theatre bills, in announcements made in connexion with radio or television broadcasts, in the credit titles of films and in any other promotional material.

Alongside this acknowledgement, it would also be desirable for the translated product to include a mention of the date when the subtitles were done, since they do not always coincide with the production year of the film. Subject to their consent, the names of subtitlers should appear in the credits, normally at the end of the programme, but sometimes also at the beginning. In some cases, subtitlers may decline to have their names acknowledged in a particular production when they disagree with the changes made during the revision process.

However, the general opinion is that the best subtitles are those that the viewer does not notice. From this perspective, the subtitler's task seems to be a contradiction in terms: to provide a translation that is written *a posteriori* on the original programme, flashes in and out at the bottom of the screen, but pretends not to be there. In what can be considered an attempt at invisibility, many subtitled programmes do not offer in their credits the name of the subtitler or the subtitling company, although this practice varies enormously and some countries are more respectful than others. This forced invisibility tends to have a negative impact on the social recognition of subtitlers which is most patent in the lack of copyright for their work. Countries like Spain (Díaz Cintas 2003:103-104) and Greece (Papadakis 1998) do not recognize this activity for copyright, with a rather ironical situation in Spain where dubbing does generate royalties. In some other countries, subtitlers do own the rights to their work, although it is becoming common practice in the profession to sign them away to the commissioning company.

There are many ways of promoting the subtitling profession, and these are only some ideas: including the name of the translator in the credits of the programme, including their details in national film databanks, creating an annual prize for the best subtitled and dubbed programmes as is done in the literary world, publishing works with the names of the programmes and the translators, creating websites with this information, etc. Castellano (2000), for instance, is a sort of encyclopedia of dubbing in Italy, compiling information on translators, dubbing actors, and dubbing directors of films and sitcoms. As for websites, professionals working in dubbing seem to be ahead in this respect, with sites such as www.eldoblaje.com, www.dubbing.de, and www.doublage.qc.ca among many others.

The lethargy that has traditionally pervaded the profession is these days being replaced with some activity aimed at safeguarding audiovisual translators' working conditions. We have in recent years witnessed the creation of several associations such as the Danish FBO-Forum for Billedmedieoversættere, the Norwegian NAViO, and the Valencian Associació Professional de Traductors, Adaptadors i Assessors Lingüístics (APTAA) (see Appendix 3). Perhaps one of the most ambitious is avtranslators.org, an association of union representatives exchanging news in the field of audiovisual translation and information on agreements, contracts, working conditions and prices (www.avtranslators.org). It can be seen as an initiative building on Point 7, Section III of the UNESCO *Recommendation* (1976), which also calls for the creation of these associations, suggesting that:

> Member States should also promote measures to ensure effective representation of translators and to encourage the creation and development of professional organizations of translators and other organizations or associations representing them, to define the rules and duties which should

govern the exercise of the profession, to defend the moral and material interests of translators and to facilitate linguistic, cultural, scientific and technical exchanges among translators and between translators and the authors of works to be translated.

2.3.5 Training

The well-being of the subtitling profession depends, as in many other professional disciplines, on the sound training of experts in the field. If only some thirty years ago the teaching, learning and researching of translation in educational institutions was a rare occurrence, nowadays it is an unquestionable reality. The discipline has advanced and translation has been part of the educational landscape for some time now. From an initial over-emphasis on literary texts, we have slowly moved on to cover many other areas such as localization, economic, scientific, technical, and legal translation.

However, despite the growing importance of AVT in our daily lives, many universities have been rather passive in the preparation of students in this area, and dubbing, subtitling and voice-over have been largely ignored in the curricula. Lack of interest, prohibitive software prices, absence of teacher expertise, vested interests, or mere blindness may be some of the reasons behind this state of affairs. The end result has been that audiovisual translation could only be learnt hands-on, in-house, outside educational institutions, with little academic backbone. Nowadays, the situation seems to be changing and many universities in different countries have taken up the challenge of teaching AVT, mainly subtitling, dubbing and voice-over (Mayoral Asensio 2001a; Díaz Cintas and Orero 2003). This is a very promising development that is now starting to bear fruit. Nonetheless, these subjects tend to be taught marginally – intensive (summer) courses, extra seminars – making it difficult to go beyond the introductory stages. One of the challenges ahead for AVT is to root it firmly in university curricula.

At undergraduate level the courses are offered as options within a degree in translation, and their content tends to favour practice over theory. Given the high costs involved and the speed at which technical changes take place, the use of subtitling and dubbing software equipment has always been one of the thorniest issues. University management has never been willing to invest large sums of money to buy subtitling software that may need regular updates. Hence, some institutions have worked, and continue to work, on paper whilst others have managed large groups of students with just a few open-access subtitling stations from different manufacturers. In order to overcome the financial constraints, some universities have developed their own subtitling software. From the industry perspective, these programs may lack some functionality, but they have two major advantages for the educationalist: they are much cheaper and they are designed with the student in mind, making them much simpler to use; an advantage that cannot be stressed enough if we think of the limited time available at University for training.

Discussion point 2.5 below offers an insight into what some companies believe to be essential qualities of a good subtitler. We share the opinion that a subtitler has to be a professional able to carry out all the tasks involved in subtitling, independently of the fact that some companies might commission only the translation. Students should be trained to time, to translate and to come up with a translation that respects all the media limitations of subtitling. They should also be familiar with subtitling software programs. It is simple: the better the preparation, the better the chances of getting a job.

2.4 Discussion points

Training

2.4.1 Visit the website of at least three institutions offering postgraduate studies on AVT.
[You can find a sample list on: *DVD > Chapter 2 > Discussion points > Discussion point 2.4.1*]

❶ What subjects do they offer?
❷ What are, in your opinion, their strongest points?
❸ And what are their weakest features?
❹ Would you change their structure, adding or deleting some of the modules?
❺ In general, what do you think about these programmes?

Working environment

2.4.2 The following is a statement made by an ex-Managing Director of a French company dealing with subtitling and cited in Pommier (1988:22):

I tend to use women to subtitle love stories, highbrow types to subtitle highbrow films and punchy writers for Westerns (our translation).

❶ What is your opinion of such an approach to translation commissions?
❷ Do you think it still applies or is it rather outdated?

2.4.3 What do you think of the following comment by Ivarsson and Carroll (1998:12)?:

The next process involved writing the subtitles. Using the spotting list prepared by the technician, a translator would write the subtitles, often without ever having seen the film, [...] With rare exceptions, spotting was considered too technical a task for translators. This was better left in the hands of technicians.

2.4.4 Go to this website: www.jostrans.org/llurba.html, where you find an interview with Spanish audiovisual translator José Llurba. Listen to section number 6, entitled "When working in subtitling, do you do spotting work or are your translations passed on?"

What is, in his opinion, the "perfect situation for the translator"? Do you agree with him? Why?

[You also have a copy of this interview on: *DVD* > *Chapter 2* > *Discussion points* > *Discussion point 2.4.4*]

2.4.5 On the same website, www.jostrans.org/llurba.html, listen to section number 4, entitled "What is the situation as regards copyrights in audiovisual translation?"

Try to find out about your own country and compare it with the situation described by José Llurba.

[You also have a copy of this interview on: *DVD* > *Chapter 2* > *Discussion points* > *Discussion point 2.4.5*]

Subtitling profile

2.4.6 Go to the following page on the website of the German subtitling company Titelbild, and read the section 'Future subtitlers require', which lists 11 characteristics that they consider define a good subtitler:

[You also have a copy of this document on: *DVD* > *Chapter 2* > *Discussion points* > *Discussion point 2.4.6*]

www.titelbild.de/english/info.htm#Future

2.4.7 After reading the information contained on the webpage mentioned above:

❶ Do you agree with all of them?
❷ What do you think about the last one? What do you think it refers to?
❸ What is your opinion about the information added to the second bullet point?
❹ Do you agree with the idea that subtitling can only be learned after having a "sound experience in translation"?
❺ In your opinion, are these characteristics different from those expected of any other translator, irrespective of their field of expertise? Why?

❻ Try to prioritize these qualities from most to least important according to your own opinion (give 1 to the most important one).
❼ Can you think of other qualities that might enhance the professional figure of the subtitler?
[You can find some suggestions for this activity on: *DVD > Chapter 2 > Discussion points > Discussion point 2.4.7*]

Subtitlers' visibility

2.4.8 Audiovisual translators in general – and subtitlers in particular – do not seem to be socially recognized.

❶ Do you know the name of a professional subtitler?
❷ Would you know how to find out the names of some of these professionals?
❸ Why do you think they are so little known?
❹ In your opinion, does it matter that they are not well known? Is it positive or negative?
❺ How do you think their visibility could be enhanced?
[You can find some suggestions for this activity on: *DVD > Chapter 2 > Discussion points > Discussion point 2.4.8*]

3. The Semiotics of Subtitling

3.0 Preliminary discussion

Semiotics is "the study of signs and symbols and their use or interpretation" (NOED 1998). The semiotics of film refers to the sign systems a film combines to communicate its message or story.

3.1 What, in your view, might the 'semiotics of subtitling' refer to? That is, which sign systems do you expect to be involved in the way subtitles signify and how?
3.2 In what way might 'the semiotics of subtitling' differ from the 'semiotics of poetry translation', for instance, or the 'semiotics of drama translation'? Do you expect there will be similarities as well?
3.3 Review your initial replies to these questions after reading this chapter.

3.1 The film as text

3.1.1 The complexity of the filmic sign system

Films are texts of great semiotic complexity in which different sign systems co-operate to create a coherent story. The term 'film' and its derivatives are to be understood throughout the book as an umbrella term encompassing all audiovisual material. In film, light and sound create two fundamental systems of space, time, and causal interaction: one on the screen before our eyes, and another within a story world that we conceptualize in our heads (Branigan 1992:34). In other words, viewers make sense of visual and acoustic sign systems that are complemented by an acoustic channel and presented to them on a screen. They see and hear these signs as a story world in which characters evolve and lives take shape. Somehow, subtitles have to become part of this semiotic system. They are an addition to the finished film, and if they are to function effectively, they must interact with and rely on all the film's different channels.

According to some early film theorists, such as Béla Balázs, cinema initially represented a universal photographic language that could be understood by all and would have continued to conquer the world had it not been for the advent of sound, which made translation into different languages necessary. This idea of universal Esperanto, however, is a fallacy that has been demonstrated many times over. As Dwyer (2005:301) states:

> Historical records reveal [...] that the internationalism and supposed universalism of the silent era was in fact underwritten by a vast array of translation practices both linguistic and ideological in nature. During this period translation took many forms encompassing the textual, aural and visual realms. Intertitles were swapped, films were accompanied by live commentators/interpreters, and whole storylines were transformed. Indeed, intertitles were subject to both inter- and intra-lingual translation. For example, US film intertitles were altered for export to England and Australia, as well as foreign-language markets. Indeed, the degree of translation required to preserve the myth of universalism was phenomenal, as is revealed in Ruth Vasey's impressive study *The World According to Hollywood, 1918-1939* (1997).

And yet the myth of the universality of images persists and has also found its way into Translation Studies. Chaume (2004), for instance, points out how it informs the research of scholars working on dubbing such as Izard (1992) and Martín (1994). However, it is safe to state that images are far from universal. Indeed, they are culture-bound references in themselves and always subject to ideological framing. This means that even if the spoken language of an audiovisual programme is the main source material that needs to be subtitled, it is important for subtitlers to be aware of the film text's other semiotic systems, and to be fully aware of how they contribute to the development of the story or the programme as a whole. Visually rendered information must be taken into account because it is part of the message, but also because all cultures have different visual as well as oral and linguistic traditions, especially cultures that are geographically further apart. From a translational viewpoint, the most difficult situation therefore arises when a linguistic sign, a phrase, refers metaphorically to an iconographic sign or image that the source and target culture do not share.

The initial optimism in TS about the universality of visual images may also have its roots in the Eurocentric perspective that has long been one of its dominant traits. Still, to what extent translation, and subtitling more specifically, can or needs to bridge the visual culture gap is another matter. In many cases it can be argued that traditions have grown closer to each other due to the globalization of filmic traditions. Nevertheless, it is an issue that all audiovisual translators must keep at the back of their minds.

What is more, not only do subtitles need to reckon with visually conveyed information when translating speech, the acoustic channel of a film cannot be simply equated with its verbal signs either. In his analysis of the components that constitute the filmic sign, made with AVT in mind, Delabastita (1989:199) distinguishes the following four categories or communication channels:

1. Visual presentation – verbal signs.
2. Visual presentation – non-verbal signs.

3. Acoustic presentation – verbal signs.
4. Acoustic presentation – non-verbal signs.

Visually transmitted verbal signs (1) are, for example, credit titles, street names, letters, newspapers and other written documents that appear on the screen. Visually transmitted non-verbal signs (2) cover the film's photography. Acoustically transmitted verbal signs (3) are basically songs and the dialogue exchanges, and acoustically transmitted non-verbal sounds (4) are instrumental music and background noises. All the above sign systems work together in the creation of a coherent film story, be it fictional or non-fictional. The degree to which subtitles need to relate to each of these systems will vary, and will therefore have to be determined by the subtitler. Some insight into how film works is obviously in order; being an avid moviegoer may not be enough. Indeed, we all watch films, and automatically absorb and interpret the information streams the medium unleashes on us, but we rarely take the time to sit back and analyze how its carefully orchestrated systems really work.

For the sake of analysis, the interaction of the subtitles with the different filmic sign systems is considered separately in §3.2 and §3.3, although in practice all the systems are obviously interrelated. First we consider the verbal elements of the filmic text.

3.1.2 The semiotics of screenwriting and film dialogue

Screenplays are important for subtitlers mainly for two reasons. First, because they are the source of the narrative structure of the film; and second, because they are documents subtitlers can resort to when no dialogue list is supplied. Internet has quite a few good screenplay sites, from where both pre- and post-production screenplays can be downloaded (see Appendix 3). Having said that, some caution is in order: neither pre-production nor post-production screenplays are entirely reliable and they must therefore be double-checked with the film version supplied for translation. Likewise, the spelling of proper names, references to historic events, terms in other languages, etc., cannot be taken for granted.

What concerns us here, however, is the screenplay as a kind of 'virtual' structure. Both documentary films and feature films – most audiovisual programmes for that matter – are highly structured, basically with a view to catching and retaining the attention of the viewers within and for the entire time slot allotted to the production. Originally, screenplays harked back to the well-structured 19th century play, relying on theatrical models to tell their stories for the screen. Classical Hollywood films, therefore, have an exposition, development, climax, and denouement (Bordwell *et al.* 1996). In the exposition, all the details the viewers require about the characters, their background, the setting, the historical period, etc. are supplied. The development follows an initial disturbance in the life of the protagonist, which sets him or her off on a quest. The climax is the moment of no return toward which the entire film evolves; at this point the conflict in which the protagonist is entangled is either resolved or lost. The climax is followed by a short denouement in which all narrative loose ends are tied up. This basic template has produced a lot of variants by now, although screenwriters are sometimes encouraged to learn the basics of story-structure, before embarking on experiments (Dancyger and Rush 1991). An important concept that will return in any mainstream screenwriting manual is that of 'continuity' and 'causality', i.e. avoiding narrative gaps at all costs. In mainstream cinema one action always leads to another and everything is somehow connected: not a single window is opened or referred to, so to speak, if it does not have a narrative significance. Given that reduction and deletion are strategies often implemented in subtitling, this is what subtitlers must always keep in mind, that events and references to events at the beginning of a programme are usually connected to events that occur much later. Early challenges are set up and used or built upon in subsequent scenes, and even documentary films that have little commercial ambition will try to create some form of suspense to keep their audience interested, and improve their ratings (Franco 2000; Remael 1998).

Film dialogue is highly implicated in all this. Dialogue writing is one of the last stages in screenwriting, which starts with a synopsis, followed by a treatment containing a sketch of the different scenes. Only after the outline of the screenplay is thus established, does the writing of dialogue begin. It goes without saying that dialogue will have to support the story thus outlined, which it does in collaboration and interaction with the film's other semiotic systems.

One obvious result of this is that the dialogue exchanges must actually inform the viewers while mimicking the features of everyday conversation, what Chaume (2004:168) calls *oralidad prefabricada* (prefabricated orality). Likewise, interviewees addressing the interviewer of a documentary film are really informing the public of that film, not (only) the journalist. That is to say, there is dialogic interaction between the (fictional or non-fictional) characters on screen, but their words also interact with the film's visual signs, and this interaction determines what the film communicates to the spectator. This triangular relationship is, of course, very familiar to anyone working in film or screenwriting, and it has been discussed in depth by Vanoye (1985:99-118). He distinguishes the 'horizontal' communication between characters from the 'vertical' communication that takes place between the film's apparatus (which includes verbal and non-verbal devices) and the viewer. Indeed, some of the formal features of film dialogue are meant to suggest the interactional build-up of conversation, especially in fictional programmes, whereas much of the content is addressed to the viewers who are witnessing the conversation on screen.

How must the subtitler handle this? Subtitling is an ancillary element added to the finished product. It is extraneous to the diegesis or narrative, and obviously addresses the viewers. It must therefore contain the information that is meant for the public. Usually, this is thought to be the propositional content of utterances, but since form and content cannot be completely separated, some of the dialogue exchanges' formal features, which are part of the diegesis, will have to be rendered too.

Dialogue basically fulfils three functions, which in practice often coincide: a structuring, a narrative-informative, and an interactional one. Consider the dialogue excerpt from the script of *American Beauty* (see example 3.15). The entire dialogue is informative: it confirms that the protagonist's job is endangered; indicates that he and his wife, Carolyn, hold different views on how he should react; tells us that they have new neighbours and that Carolyn is an estate agent; and establishes her nervous-tempestuous character. The first line also has a structuring function in that it links the present scene to the previous one. The subsequent lines have an additional interactional function: the tone in which they are uttered, as well as the verbal and physical interaction between the characters, convey the protagonists' disagreement. In fact, at the end of the scene, as Carolyn heads into the house, followed by Lester, she continues to shout words of protest to which he pays absolutely no attention. Obviously, the interactional features of the dialogue, and their emotional connotations, contribute as much to the narrative and to one of the core themes of the film (estrangement), as do the words uttered by the couple.

Unfortunately, subtitlers will never have enough time to carry out an in-depth script analysis. All the same, they should be aware of the existence of underlying narrative structures, of connotations and interactional features as well as denotations in the dialogue, and the interconnectedness of whatever happens at any time in a movie – feature film or other.

3.2 Subtitling and images

3.2.1 Semiotic cohesion

In what follows, the interaction between words and images is examined. By way of example, we shall analyze how narration relies on both in a scene taken from *The Snows of Kilimanjaro*. A few features stand out. On the one hand, there is camera movement and editing, i.e. extra-diegetic visual manipulation that does not belong to the fictional story as such. On the other hand, there are the gestures and looks of the characters, i.e. diegetic information that does belong to the story proper. Both supply essential information for the understanding of the film. Besides, there is the wealth of details provided by setting, props, casting, costumes, etc.

Example 3.1

Film: *The Snows of Kilimanjaro*	Scene: *Beginning*
Pathway: *DVD > Chapter 3 > Examples > Example 3.1 > Beginning*	
In this scene, camera movement is used to convey information gradually. First, the viewer sees a close-up of the main character Harry, later the camera moves away from him to reveal a vulture flying overhead, and eventually, Helen by his side. Editing, in the form of cuts, varies from a close up of Harry to a shot of a vulture flying overhead, to a travelling shot of the setting, obviously Africa. There is a mountain (Mount Kilimanjaro of the title) in the background, and there are tents in the foreground. Eventually, the camera returns to the people near the tents. This basically takes care of setting the scene for the action. The gestures and also the looks of the characters provide the link between the wound on Harry's leg, the gravity of his condition, and the vultures flying above, or perching on a nearby tree. The dialogues complement and further explain all this iconic information. Looks, gestures, facial expressions and language are inseparable, but also result in a degree of redundancy.	

The redundancy typical of film narration's careful use of its many channels is, in fact, one of the features of filmmaking that subtitlers can use to their own advantage. Indeed, according to Marleau (1982:274), the relation between image and word can take two concrete forms, and these correspond to two functions which the author also attributes to subtitles. In some cases the verbal mode further defines information that is also given visually, which he calls *fonction d'ancrage* or anchoring. In other instances, for which he uses the term *fonction de redondance* or redundancy, words and images communicate more or less the same information. The scene we have just analyzed is a clear example of the first type.

In order to accommodate such filmic features, Chaume (2004:232-237) extends the linguistic concept of textual cohesion to include interaction between the linguistic and the visual channels of a film. According to Baker (1992:218), linguistic textual cohesion is the "network of surface relations which link words and expressions to other words and expressions in a text, and coherence is the network of conceptual relations which underline the surface text". In other words, whereas "coherence is a property of texts that make sense, cohesion refers to those linguistic techniques which are used to facilitate the readers' task of discovering the coherence in your text" (Hannay and Mackenzie 2002:155). Such cohesive devices are: reference (e.g. the use of pronouns and various types of anaphoric or cataphoric reference), lexical choice (e.g. repetition versus variation), tense choice, and the use of connectives.

Expanding the concept of cohesion for film and hence also for AVT, Chaume (2004) introduces the term 'semiotic cohesion'. An ellipsis or gap in the (subtitled) dialogue may be filled with information the viewer obtains from the images on the screen rather than another passage from the (verbal) text. Indeed, in writing, a noun may be replaced by a pronoun, whereas in audiovisual texts pronouns in the dialogue can refer to people or objects on the screen. Consider the following dialogue from the above scene:

Example 3.2

Film: *The Snows of Kilimanjaro*	Scene: *Beginning*
Harry: I wonder is it sight or is it scent that brings **them**? Helen: **They**'ve been about for ever so long **they** don't mean a thing. Harry: The marvellous thing is that **it**'s painless now. Helen: Is **it** really? Harry: Yes. That's how you know when **it** starts.	

Without the narrative context and the visual images to support the dialogue, these exchanges make absolutely no sense. The text has low coherence. Conversely, if you were to watch the film without sound, it would take some guessing to interpret what is happening on the screen. This scene is therefore an obvious example of anchoring, in which one semiotic system supplements the other. What is actually happening here?

- ❑ The personal pronouns 'them' and 'they' refer to the vultures circling above Harry and Helen.
- ❑ The indefinite pronoun 'it' in lines three (Harry) and four (Helen), refer to the festering wound on Harry's leg.
- ❑ The last 'it', in Harry's third turn, refers to the gangrene that has got hold of the wound and that will eventually kill him.

The referents of 'them', 'they' and the first two mentions of 'it' are visible on screen, within the diegetic story world, and constitute an example of semiotic rather than purely linguistic cohesion. The last 'it' is slightly more complicated and left open to the interpretation of the viewers, who can replace it with 'gangrene' basing their judgement on the context or the narration, and their own knowledge of the world.

For this kind of semiotic cohesion to keep working in the subtitles there must obviously be a form of synchrony between the written target text and the image. Subtitles should therefore never anticipate, or be ahead of visual narration on screen. It is equally obvious that synchrony between image and subtitle will be less of a concern in other audiovisual genres such as documentaries, especially in interviews with talking heads – i.e. a set-up in which there is a presenter or reporter on television who addresses the camera and is viewed in close up. Only synchrony with the spoken text will be of primordial importance here. An example of a programme that makes no use of visual information apart from gestures and facial expression is the *Hard Talk* series on BBC World, in which a BBC reporter interviews celebrities from the arts, science, sports or politics.

3.2.2 The multimodality of language

Another form of semiotic cohesion is at play in the interaction between speech and gesture. This is a feature of the so-called multimodality of language, of which film makes great use. Dialogue studies both in linguistics and anthropology make use of video recordings that allow scholars to complement their research into how dialogue works from a linguistic viewpoint, with the study of the interaction between word and movement. Luckmann (1990) writes that the full meaning of a statement in a dialogue is first produced by an adequate use of linguistic codes and the options of language, but he adds that these "options are chosen or routinely employed, by the speaker, along with body-postures, gestures and facial expressions which are laden with particular meanings" (ibid.:53-54). In film, which aims to tell a story, this interaction between words and gestures is always very purposeful, as is the positioning of the characters within a scene. Another form of cohesion is therefore at work here. Besides, like any form of iconography, body-postures and gestures communicate information non-vocally and are often culture-bound. They belong to what we can call the kinesic heritage of different communities. Some stereotypical differences in gestural meanings are well-known (e.g. shaking the head rather than nodding to signify 'yes' in Greek and Bulgarian), and though some works have been published on the topic (Poyatos 1997), much research is still needed in this area, particularly in the field of AVT. Still, even without worrying too much about culture-bound problems, movements, gestures, or a simple nod of the head can be quite challenging for the subtitler in themselves.

Example 3.3

In Anna Campion's film *Loaded* a group of students is spending the weekend at the house belonging to the aunt of one of the girls. The following exchange is taken from an early scene in the film. One of the guests asks: "Does your aunt mind us staying here?" and the girl replies, shaking her head, "No, she hasn't lived here since my uncle died". The subtitler cannot afford to contradict this movement, nor the clearly audible "no". The negative reply must therefore be retained in the subtitling, even if an affirmative reformulation is, theoretically, possible. If the subtitling were to opt for this latter alternative, the question would have to be phrased as "Is your aunt happy with us staying here?", for instance, which would then yield a reply along the lines of: "Yes, she moved out when my uncle died". However, if there is no obvious reason for changing an affirmative sentence into a negative one, or the other way around (e.g., because it is shorter), it is always advisable to retain synchrony not only with speech, but also with movement, as in this particular case.

Other terms used to refer to the movement and positioning of characters are proxemics and kinesics. Proxemics is the branch of knowledge that deals with the amount of space that people feel is necessary to set between themselves and others, whereas kinesics studies the way in which body movements and gestures convey meaning non-vocally. Within western cultures there is a great amount of uniformity in the degree of physical closeness that is acceptable between people in a certain situation. The challenge for the subtitler resides in the detection of coherence between movement or closeness and intonation, word choice, as well as other linguistic features that will, of course, be co-determined by the narrative situation and the scene as a whole.

3.2.3 Camera movement and editing

Camera movement can also require careful handling when its rhythm somehow conflicts with the linear succession of the subtitles, especially when there is a disruption in the synchrony between visual and acoustic channels (Cornu 1996:161-163).

A conversation between two people is often filmed with alternating shots (shot-reverse shot) of the two characters, usually over the opposite character's shoulder. This means that the camera sometimes focuses on the character speaking the lines, but that on other occasions it will direct the viewers' attention to the character who is listening in order to render their reaction (Reisz and Millar 1997:86). Theoretically, subtitlers have two options. Either the subtitles can follow the movement of the camera, which may be rather fast, or they can ignore the different camera positions, settling for a slower subtitling rhythm. This, however, may be equally disruptive if it does not match the rhythm of visual narration. In recent films the pace of editing has increased considerably; to such an extent that it is impossible and undesirable for the subtitles to follow the visual pace of the film, but in older, slower films the alternatives are worth considering.

In scenes filmed with alternating shots, the characters remain in one location. In other instances, editing may take the film to another place and/or time quite abruptly. Whereas, generally speaking, subtitles follow the rhythm of speech, but are allowed to linger slightly on the screen to offer viewers a more comfortable reading pace, in such cases they must respect the (visual) narrative structure of the film, and disappear with the cut to a new location.

Example 3.4

> *The Hours* takes place in three locations and at three different times: Richmond, England in 1923; Los Angeles in 1951; and Manhattan in 2001. It would obviously not do for a subtitle from one era to remain on screen in another, unless the voice provides a sound bridge or link between the scenes.

In any case, this kind of 'visual' timing is not only required for the sake of film aesthetics and narration, but also because of the technical features of DVD, for instance, which is divided into chapters. The issue of how to cue, spot or time subtitles is taken up in greater detail in §4.7.1.

3.2.4 A blessing in disguise

Despite the problems that may arise for the subtitler because of incongruities or overlap between image and sound, it will have become clear by now that the information the images convey can also be an asset in the translation process. Since subtitles are an ancillary translation that must be as unobtrusive as possible, subtitlers are actually under an obligation to make the most of the images' narrative function. They can and must rely on them to abbreviate text, leaving out redundant information and thereby allowing the film to tell its own story. In fact, it is often the very interaction of the film dialogue with the information given visually that allows for major deletions. This also explains why a print-out of subtitles, just like a dialogue list without scene descriptions, only very rarely makes any sense at all, and why it is essential for subtitlers to have the film at their disposal when they are translating.

Example 3.5

> In *Manhattan Murder Mystery* the following scene occurs. As Helen, actress and model in the film, comes down a dangerous-looking flight of stairs, she is warned: "Watch your step. It's very steep. Be careful". The subtitles can easily render this as 'Be careful!' in any language, without the need to refer to the step.

Example 3.6

> In another scene in the same film, a character is showing off his stamp collection and says: "Now, let me show you a mint nineteen thirty-three airmail". A translation stating "This is one from 1933" will do perfectly. Note, however, that film genre can sometimes have an impact on decision-making. If this scene were to occur in a documentary on postage stamps, the subtitle might have to be more detailed, depending on how the stamp in question is filmed.

Not only should visually conveyed information always be put to good use for the production of short, idiomatic and simple translation solutions, it can also help solve translation problems. The following scene from *The Grapes of Wrath*, the film based on John Steinbeck's novel of the same title, provides a good example.

Example 3.7

> The Joads, a poor peasant family from Oklahoma, are on their way to California. They have been chased from their land and are making the journey in a ramshackle lorry, joining an army of immigrants on the move. As they are about to embark on their crossing of the Death Valley desert, a bystander remarks: "Boy, but I'd hate to hit that desert in a jalopy like that!" Referring both to the desert crossing and the 'jalopy' (an old car in a dilapidated condition), one subtitler wrote:
>
> Ik zou niet graag met hen wisselen.
> [I'd hate to be in their place.]
>
> Another solution, which makes the most of the information provided by the images would be: "I'd hate to travel in one of those", using a deictic pronoun to replace to the 'jalopy', a word that may be rather difficult to translate concisely in most languages.

3.3 Subtitling, soundtrack, and text on screen

3.3.1 Subtitling's vulnerability

It is interesting to note that a relatively high number of people hold a rather negative opinion of the quality of subtitles, which is undoubtedly because the translated text is presented to the viewer at the same time as the original. This is a rather unusual state of affairs in translation and it sets subtitling apart. Indeed, the cohabitation of source and target text allows the viewers to immediately compare both messages, which consumers of other types of translations (e.g. dubbing or literary translation) cannot normally do. Although both languages also co-exist in interpreting and bilingual publications with parallel texts, the reception of the two messages is not as immediate as in the case of subtitling. While a translated novel or poem, or a dubbed programme, often obscures the original linguistic material, subtitles find themselves in the difficult position of being constantly accompanied by the film dialogue, giving rise to what in the professional world is known as the 'gossiping effect' (Törnqvist 1995:49) or 'feedback effect'. Especially now that DVDs are conquering our living-rooms, offering dubbing and subtitling side by side, as well as the possibility to stop the film, return to any previous shot, and freeze a subtitle on the screen for all to see and judge, this is an issue worth keeping in mind.

The coexistence of the two languages unavoidably has its repercussions on the translated programme. Thus, one common strategy is to transfer all those terms from the original that have strong phonetic or morphological similarities in both languages, and that the viewer may recognize in the original dialogue. Content-wise, the second translation of 'paranoid', below, works just as well, but the first option retains the link with what the audience actually hears.

Example 3.8

Listen, you're getting too paranoid.
Hé, je bent paranoïde.
[Hey, you're paranoid.]

versus

Overdrijf toch niet zo!
[Don't exaggerate!]

The non-appearance in the subtitles of recognizable lexical items audible in the soundtrack is a factor directly responsible for the criticisms that many viewers launch against subtitling. Many believe that the translator has 'forgotten' to translate such-and-such a word, which they have clearly heard on the soundtrack. In this respect, Karamitroglou (1998:6) writes that:

> Investigations in the psychology of viewing indicate that when such linguistic items are recognized by the viewers, the exact, literal, translationally equivalent items are expected to appear in the subtitles as well. This occurs because of the constant presence of an inherently operating checking mechanism in the brain of the viewers which raises the suspicions that the translation of the original text is not 'properly' or 'correctly' rendered in the subtitles, every time word-for-word translations for such items are not spotted.

In addition, it is just as important to try and maintain a close semantic and syntactic correlation between the dialogue of the film and the content of the subtitles. Maximum synchrony should be achieved whenever possible. Not only is it very frustrating to hear information that one has already read at the beginning of a subtitle, but it has to be borne in mind that listening to one text while reading another also slows down comprehension (Ivarsson and Carroll 1998:73).

Borrowing concepts initially proposed by House (1981), Gottlieb (1994:102) claims that "subtitling is an overt type of translation, retaining the original version, thus laying itself bare to criticism from everybody with the slightest knowledge of the source language". We would like to call subtitling an instance of 'vulnerable translation'. Not only must the subtitles respect space and time constraints, they must also stand up to the scrutiny of an audience that may have some knowledge of the original language.

This tends to be aggravated when the source language is English, or when the two languages have very similar linguistic roots. But also viewers who understand only a fraction of what is being said will have an idea of the output of a speaker. They may feel cheated when the aggressive or rude performance of an actor leads them to expect a certain type of vocabulary that is not relayed in the translation, when a laconic exchange becomes a lengthy subtitle, or when an actor who speaks in linguistic waterfalls is given very brief subtitles. They may then, rightly, start wondering what was 'lost in translation'. A great example from another branch in language transfer but with which subtitling has some affinities occurs in the film which carries that very title. The actor-protagonist Bob Harris must rely on consecutive interpretation to understand the wishes of his (fictional) film director, but whereas his employer's instructions are elaborate in Japanese, the English interpreter's version of them is so brief and simplistic that it elicits expressions of disbelief on Harris's part: "That's all he said?" This is the kind of criticism often heard when subtitling is discussed.

On the other hand, there is a limit to how far one can go in remaining faithful to the ST, not only because of technical limitations, but also because the target language cannot be infinitely stretched. Kriek (2002:276) uses the concept of *halve vertalingen* or 'half-way translations' for subtitles that render expressions or phrases from the source language almost literally. This is certainly not an example to be emulated, even though DVD subtitles tend to stay closer to the ST language than subtitles for television or the cinema. According to various professionals, this is because some of the clients for DVD – people from the film industry, for instance – are not subtitling specialists and have little experience with translation generally. They feel that the more literal a translation is, content-wise and formally, the better it is, claiming that this is also what the viewers prefer. Common sense dictates that in most cases a compromise will be required, but more research would certainly be welcome in the field of AVT reception.

Whatever the case may be, the use of explanatory notes to the translation, such as glosses, footnotes or a prologue, has always been anathema to subtitling. The translator may well have understood a particular play on words or recognized an obscure reference, but be unable to pass on the information because of the media's limitations. Worth mentioning are the new developments in the subtitling of some programmes for distribution on DVD, which do resort to the inclusion of translator's notes on the screen (Díaz Cintas 2005a and forthcoming; see also §5.4).

Chapter 7 offers a more in-depth analysis of the problems linked to the vulnerability of subtitling and looks at some of the strategies implemented by subtitlers to overcome them.

3.3.2 Multilingual films

Today quite a few films are shot in more than one language. This often happens in co-productions or in films that make use of the different languages spoken in the producing country; but the trend can also be seen as an attempt to reflect the pursuit of realism as part of the "'new wave' amongst filmmakers seeking to represent conditions of migrant and diasporic existence" (Wahl 2005).

Whatever the case may be, there is a lot of variation in the prominence of the second, or third language used in such films. The subtitler needs to be aware of this in order to decide what can and must be subtitled, and what need not or must not – unless the decision has been made by the client and is contained in the translation brief. If all languages recur regularly, all should be subtitled.

Example 3.9

Depuis qu'Otar est parti, is a French-Belgian co-production in Georgian, French, and Russian. The 'original' versions of multilingual films will themselves subtitle some of the languages they use. Indeed, the Georgian and Russian dialogues have French subtitles in the French-Belgian version of *Otar*. In the English version the three languages require subtitling, and the viewers have to rely on the narrative and its different locations to determine what language is spoken. In the case of Russian and Georgian the clues are not always forthcoming, and the purpose of the linguistic switches can only be derived from the social connotations they have. However, this problem is no different in the French version.

The solution may not be so simple if the second or even third language is spoken only occasionally, but for a particular purpose.

Example 3.10

In *Frasier*, a successful USA television comedy, both Spanish and French enter into the primary English discourse of the protagonists, with different representational and ideational implications. What options does the Spanish or French subtitler have in this case? In the Spanish subtitles both the English and French will be rendered, whereas in the French subtitles the English and the Spanish will be translated. However, the 'foreign touch' that these languages add to the original, including all their social implications, are lost, unless the viewer can rely on the sound track to some extent.

Example 3.11

> A slightly different problem occurs in the American feature film *Look Who's Talking*. The Hispanic nanny tells the mother, in Spanish, that a gentleman is waiting in the nursery. She replies, not having understood, that the cheque with the nanny's wages is in the mail. The Spanish dubbed version retains the comic effect by having the employee speak Portuguese. In the subtitles the effect is lost, and again, can only be recuperated by viewers who can put themselves in the position of the English-speaking character.

Example 3.12

> In the Belgian-Flemish film *Lijmen* some upper class characters speak French, resulting in scenes where the two national languages alternate depending on which character speaks. The Dutch speaker is subtitled in the French version on the DVD, and the Francophone character in the Dutch one.
> Pathway (French version): *DVD > Chapter 3 > Examples > Example 3.12 > French*
> Pathway (Dutch version): *DVD > Chapter 3 > Examples > Example 3.12 > Dutch*

Not all films in more than one language will cause problems, of course. If a film is mainly in English, and most of its characters speak English, but a few scenes take place in another country, e.g. Russia, there are likely to be at least some short exchanges in Russian. These will not always require translation. A few examples of this type of multilingualism occur in films such as *The Snows of Kilimanjaro*. However, even French people speak English most of the time in this film, with the occasional French repartees serving as little more than an exotic flourish.

Today, films whose stories travel or take place in multilingual environments tend to be more realistic in their use of language. Generally speaking, dialogue exchanges in a second – or third – language, which are merely part of the setting and have no narrative function, and which the audience will understand because of the context in which they occur, do not need to be subtitled.

Example 3.13

> In *Gazon maudit*, a French film, one of the protagonists Loli (Victoria Abril) occasionally lapses into her native Spanish in very specific instances, mostly in emotional or erotic scenes. These occurrences are not subtitled in the original, and need no translation in any other language since the context and the character's gestures make perfectly clear what is going on. A few linguistically comparable scenes in French also occur in the above-mentioned Belgian-Flemish film *Lijmen*. Short French exchanges or announcements are not subtitled in Dutch, whereas longer French scenes are.

Whether or not languages, or dialects, are subtitled in the ST and in the translated version, will also depend on the expectations one has of the average viewer in any particular country. Passages in Catalan in an English film will normally have to be subtitled for an English or Swedish audience, for instance, but subtitles may not be required for an Italian or Spanish public (§7.3).

3.3.3 Text on screen

Text on screen, inserts – as they are known in the profession – or the visual presentation of verbal signs in Delabastita's categorization (§3.1.1), can also present a challenge for the subtitler. Subtitles always give priority to dialogue over written text or songs (§7.5), although they must also try to cover any relevant information rendered visually. Given the causal, well-structured narration and mise-en-scène of most mainstream productions, there will probably be little or no interference from other semiotic channels whenever words do appear on screen. A classic example is the introductory on-screen narration in the *Star Wars* films. Something similar happens in the following example:

Example 3.14

In the opening scene of *The Man with the Golden Arm*, protagonist Frankie returns to town and walks past several neon lights and window signs that typify his neighbourhood, but there is no interference from film dialogue. Pathway: *DVD > Chapter 3 > Examples > Example 3.14 > City*

In other cases, e.g. when a letter or newspaper is filmed in close up, a character will often read the text out loud, causing visual verbal and acoustic-verbal channels to coincide.

However, if there is a conflict between the visual and verbal channels, and the information given aurally as well as visually is essential, various options remain. A concise summary can be given at the top of the screen, even if this means that not all viewers may have time to read it. This is also common practice in cartoons such as *The Simpsons*, where many an ironic comment is presented as an insert in the original, and in documentaries, when the subtitles risk covering up biographical information about the speaker. These data are usually moved to the top of the screen, or just above the biographical details of the speaker. Alternatively, the in-time of the subtitle rendering the source text may be slightly delayed. If written texts follow each other very quickly on screen, for instance in a shot using newspaper headlines to give information about a given period or event, the only solution is to abbreviate and cut, making sure the essence of the original message is preserved. Finally, if the words on screen are recognizable, because source and target language make use of words with the same roots, no translation is required, e.g. an insert like 'Paris, 1968'.

3.4 Change of medium

3.4.1 Speech to writing: a matter of compromise

Not only is subtitling an unusual form of translation because it is added to the ST, it also stands out as a unique translational genre because it renders speech in writing. This feature too determines the shape subtitles eventually take.

There are two basic types of speech in film: scripted and spontaneous speech. Scripted speech can be further subdivided into mimetic dialogue that imitates conversation, stylized dialogue of the type that may be used in period theatre, and speeches read from the page or teleprompters such as political speeches and television news.

Most of the film excerpts compiled on the accompanying DVD contain examples of supposedly mimetic scripted film dialogue. In some instances, exchanges sound more or less 'natural', but some scenes feature hard-boiled dialogue and stereotypical Hollywood one-liners, reminiscent of famous one-liners like "We'll always have Paris", from *Casablanca*, or "Are you talking to me?", from *Taxi Driver*. Many recent films, and especially films of the social-realist genre, such as films by Ken Loach or Mike Leigh, to name but a couple of examples, tend to have realistic-sounding dialogue. Ken Loach is also known for casting non-professional actors. Good examples of stylized theatre dialogue with some of its often poetic and rhetorical features would be any classical Shakespeare film adaptation, but subtitlers are also faced with them in modern feature films such as *Shakespeare in Love* (§7.3.1). Examples of the challenges presented by the unscripted speech that is so typical of live interviews will occur in almost any TV documentary.

The transition from oral to written mode obviously means that some of the typical features of spoken language will have to disappear, no matter what subgenre a dialogue belongs to. Then again, the oral features of spoken language in the cinema, on TV or any other medium, are relative since orality is co-determined by film's other semiotic systems and the function(s) the dialogue must fulfil (§3.1.2). This is a research area that has been covered by scholars like Chaume (2004), Díaz Cintas (2003), and Remael (2001) who take a look at it from a general AVT perspective. Assis Rosa (2001) offers a more specific account of some of the features of oral and written communication in Portuguese subtitling.

Whether scripted or spontaneous, conversation evolves sequentially. This means that as two interlocutors speak, they build on each other's interventions to move the dialogue forward. In other words, each and every intervention can take the conversation in a different direction. Speakers usually confirm they have understood what has been said before moving on the interaction, adding new information, giving comments etc. Each 'turn at talk', as such interventions are called in conversation analysis, is therefore context confirming and context renewing. Consider this short excerpt from the published script of *American Beauty* (Ball 2000:11-12), which comes after a scene at protagonist Lester's office. He has been told he will have to write a self-evaluation report if he wants to keep his job with the company he is currently working for. Carolyn is his wife.

Example 3.15

EXT. BURNHAM HOUSE – LATE AFTERNOON

A MOVING VAN is parked in front of the COLONIAL HOUSE next door to the Burnhams'. Movers carry furniture toward the house. The Mercedez-Benz pulls into the Burnham driveway. Carolyn drives, Lester is in the passenger seat.

CAROLYN:	–there is no decision, you just write the damn thing!
LESTER:	You don't think it's weird and kinda fascist?
CAROLYN:	Possibly. But you don't want to be unemployed.
LESTER:	Oh? Well, let's just all sell our souls and work for Satan, because it's more convenient that way.
CAROLYN:	Could you be just a little bit more dramatic, please, huh?

As they get out of the car, Carolyn scopes out the MOVERS next door.

CAROLYN:	So we've finally got new neighbours. You know, if the Lomans had let me represent them, instead of – (heavy disdain) – 'The real Estate King,' that house would never have sat on the market for six months.

She heads into the house, followed by Lester.

LESTER:	Well, they were still mad at you for cutting down their sycamore.
CAROLYN:	Their sycamore? C'mon! A substantial portion of the root structure was on our property. You know that. How can you call it their sycamore? I wouldn't have the heart to just cut down something that wasn't partially mine, which of course it was.

This bit of dialogue is clean-cut and well structured. The first line, which starts in mid-sentence, provides a sound bridge with the previous scene and relies on the viewer's memory of it to supply the information missing from its first half. When Carolyn says 'possibly', replying to Lester's 'you don't think it's weird and kinda fascist?', she confirms she has heard what Lester has just said, even agreeing with him to some extent. This is the context-confirming part of her utterance. Then she goes on to say 'but you don't want to be unemployed', which gives the conversation a whole new direction. This section of her turn is context renewing. The same happens in Lester's next turn, in which the exclamation 'oh' is context confirming and the remainder of his utterance is context-renewing. Real life conversations too are well-organized sequences, but on the surface they are much less clean-cut. Consider the following transcription, adapted from Goodwin (1979: 111-112):

Example 3.16

John:	I gave, I gave up smoking cigarettes ...
Don:	Yeah.
John:	I-uh, one – one week ago today, actually.
Ann:	Really? And you quit for good?

Not only does John hesitate a lot, he only finishes his sentence 'I gave up smoking cigarettes one week ago today, actually', after a prompt from Don ('yeah'). This is an example of the sequentiality and interactional nature of dialogue: it takes two to converse. Film dialogue does not render all the hesitations and false starts or requests for confirmation that are typical of conversation or speech in general. It only suggests these conversational features in as far as they have a narrative function. As we have seen in the scene from *American Beauty*, the characters do, but then again, do not really address each other; their words are meant for the viewers and must convey all the information they require about the story and the characters' psychology. Subtitling will usually take film dialogue's purposeful simplification one step further.

Indeed, the subtitler is limited to two lines of approximately 37 characters each for 5 to 6 seconds of speech. The actual lines available for the translation are calculated proportionally: a three-second intervention is normally rendered in one line (§4.7.1). The viewer will therefore have a very limited amount of time for reading and understanding the translation on screen. This is why subtitling has developed a style of its own that has an impact on grammar and register, as well as on the interactional and other oral features of dialogue. These features are signals speakers send to each other to convey they have understood an explanation, to underscore a mood or a connotation underlying their utterance, etc. At times they are no more than an interjection, but they are part and parcel of the sequential features of dialogue, even if they do not necessarily contribute to the propositional meaning of an utterance, as the 'oh' in Lester's turn in example 3.15.

Subtitling style will vary somewhat with genre, and customers will always have their say, but some basic subtitling guidelines are almost universal. Grammar and lexical items tend to be simplified and cleaned up, whereas interactional features and intonation are only maintained to some extent (e.g. through word order, rhetorical questions, occasional interjections, and incomplete sentences). In other words, not all the features of speech are lost, quite a few can be salvaged in writing, but rendering them all would lead to illegible and exceedingly long subtitles. Since subtitling focuses on those items that are informationally most relevant, often context renewing clauses are retained, whereas context confirming ones are dropped.

In documentary films, scripted speech can be challenging because of its heavy information load, but unscripted speech, with all the hesitations typical of oral discourse, can require quite a bit of interpretation and rewriting. Besides, there is the issue of whom the speaker is addressing. Interviews tend to be always introduced by journalists, who then also guide the interaction with the interviewee. Since the questions they ask determine topic and topic shifts, the interaction between journalists and respondents is different from real-life conversation, and from film dialogue, in that sense. Reid (1996) points out that in the case of such interviews, the subtitler may have to act as an intermediary between the interviewee and the audience. In the interview situation the person who is replying addresses the interviewer, and often counts on his/her expert knowledge when formulating answers. The subtitler may have to evaluate the knowledge of the broader target public of the subtitles and adapt both the form and content of the interviewees' interventions. The latter may speak poor English, leave their sentences unfinished, use specialized vocabulary, or rely on background knowledge that cannot be presupposed in the target audience. This may call for explicitation, explanation and even interpretation. What is more, in an interview situation, the images offer little help. The linguistic features of subtitling are taken up in greater detail in chapter 6.

3.5 Discussion points

3.5.1 Watch an episode of a TV series or a film using different languages and try to detect whether any stereotyping or form of prejudice lies at the bottom of this language variation. *Frasier* is a good example, and *Faulty Towers* another.

❶ Study how or if the subtitles try to solve this problem of multilingualism as a reflection of stereotypical characterization.

❷ If you have a DVD with both the dubbed and subtitled versions, compare the two and identify different translation strategies when dealing with multilingualism. What are the advantages/disadvantages of these two different forms of AVT in this respect?

3.5.2 Sometimes subtitles remain very close to the ST and in other cases the translation is a condensed paraphrase. Which do you prefer? What are the pros and cons of these two translation strategies? Might there be a connection between translation strategy and genre?

3.5.3 What would you do if you were to subtitle classics by authors such as

Molière or Shakespeare in which beautiful language is one of the attractions for the audience. Would you try to render the beauty and rhythm of the original or opt for a basic supporting translation? Motivate your choice.

3.5.4 Subtitling's vulnerability inevitably leads to criticism from viewers. If you were a member of a panel evaluating a TV channel's subtitles, what types of 'mistakes' or which kinds of 'deviations' would you penalize most? Discuss what factors you would reckon with when evaluating subtitles. What would your priorities be?

3.6 Exercises

Film analysis

3.6.1 Go to DVD > Chapter 3 > Exercises > Exercise 3.6.1 > *Beginning*
Watch the opening scene *Beginning,* from the film *The Snows of Kilimanjaro.*

❶ Summarize in about ten lines what happens in the scene (location, characters, action), using information from both the acoustic and visual channels.
❷ Identify which channel supplies which information. Is there any overlap?
❸ Discuss the narrative function of the music on the one hand, the close-up, medium, long shots, and editing (or cuts between shots) on the other.
❹ Try to predict which bits of information given in the dialogue will be of importance for the further development of the story. Write down a few key words and compare notes.

3.6.2 Go to DVD > Chapter 3 > Exercises > Exercise 3.6.2 > *Devlin*
Watch the scene *Devlin*, from *Mobutu, Roi du Zaïre*, featuring CIA Chief in the Congo Larry Devlin. Identify typical features of unscripted speech and discuss what kind of challenge they may pose for the subtitler.

Image, dialogue and subtitles

3.6.3 Go to DVD > Chapter 3 > Exercises > Exercise 3.6.3 > *Brawl*
Watch the clip *Brawl*. It is an excerpt from *The Last Time I Saw Paris*, depicting a quarrel between the two protagonists: Charles Wills who is a frustrated, unpublished writer at this point in the film, and Helen Ellsworth, his wife. The camera alternates between the two of them.

❶ Watch the entire scene and discuss how you would segment this passage, paying attention to subtitle synchrony with image as well as with speech.

❷ Consider the relationship between movement and speech in this scene: how does one reinforce the other? How do they collaborate to tell the story?

3.6.4 Go to DVD > Chapter 3 > Exercises > Exercise 3.6.4 > *Stamps*
Watch the scene *Stamps*, from *Charade*, and indicate in the dialogue list how you would segment the dialogue, taking into account the close ups of the stamps, which is the topic of the discussion between protagonist Reggie and Mr Felix, a stamp collector. Discuss how camera positions and the images more generally facilitate and/or complicate the subtitler's task in this instance, and how you would solve the brief instances in which the dialogue lapses into French.
[Pathway to dialogue list: *DVD > Chapter 3 > Exercise 3.6.4 > Transcription of Dialogue*]

Text on screen

3.6.5 In the film *About a Boy* the following notice appears on a supermarket door.

SPAT
Single Parents
Alone Together
Fridays at 2 p.m.

It is spotted by protagonist and eternal bachelor Will, who has just done his shopping and is wondering about the best way to meet single mums. There is no interference from music or dialogue.

❶ What would you subtitle if you were allowed one subtitle of 34 characters and spaces?

❷ Can you find an acronym to replace SPAT in your mother tongue?

3.6.6 Consider the following text that appears as a neon sign in *Taxi Driver*. The sign is positioned above the entrance to a sex club in an obviously sleazy Manhattan nightlife neighbourhood. We see the sign above the door as the protagonist Travis approaches and enters.

SHOW & TELL

Live Show ***XX-rated movies***

❶ Would you translate the sign?
❷ Imagine you have decided to translate: what would you translate and how, in a 27 character subtitling (including spaces)?

3.6.7 Go to DVD > Chapter 3 > Exercises > Exercise 3.6.7 > *Arrival* > English
Watch excerpt *Arrival*, from *The Stranger*, bearing in mind that the protagonist is a teacher at the local school.

❶ Determine which notices – text on screen – you would subtitle and which ones you would not.
❷ Try to reduce the text to short one-line versions of 37 characters maximum.
❸ Watch the two different versions in Spanish that have been commercialized on DVD, Spanish 1 and Spanish 2. Which one do you prefer? Why?

[Pathway to Spanish 1: *DVD > Chapter 3 > Exercises > Exercise 3.6.7 > Arrival > Spanish 1*]
[Pathway to Spanish 2: *DVD > Chapter 3 > Exercises > Exercise 3.6.7 > Arrival > Spanish 2*]

Subtitling's vulnerability

3.6.8 In the scene *Sunbathing*, from the film *The Broken Hearts Club*, three gay friends are having the following, trivial conversation:

Kevin:	I got one. Who would you kick out of bed: Morley Safer or Mike Wallace?
Patrick:	Okay, I believe this requires a daiquiri break.
Howie:	I'd say Safer.
Patrick:	Safer all the way. But, I would kick them both out of bed for Ed Bradley, circa 1980.
Kevin:	I'd kick Wallace. He always annoyed me.

❶ Bearing in mind what has been said about subtitling being an instance of vulnerable translation, what would you do with the different cultural referents being mentioned?
❷ Provide a translation for this text without taking into account the media limitations at this stage.
❸ Take a look at the translation done in Spanish, with a back translation into English, both for the dubbed and the subtitled versions. Which one do you prefer? Why?

[Pathway to Spanish translations: *DVD > Chapter 3 > Exercises > Exercise 3.6.8 > Sunbathing*]

Multilingualism

3.6.9 Go to DVD > Chapter 3 > Exercises > Exercise 3.6.9 > *Shooting* – English

Watch the scene *Shooting*, from the film *The Snows of Kilimanjaro.*

- ❶ How would you deal with this multilingual dialogue?
- ❷ What would you subtitle?
- ❸ What do you think of the strategy implemented in the Spanish subtitles?

[Pathway to Spanish version: *DVD > Chapter 3 >Exercises > Exercise 3.6.9 > Shooting – Spanish*]

4. Technical Considerations

4.0 Preliminary discussion

4.1 You can find the *Code of Good Subtitling Practice* proposed by Ivarsson and Carroll (1998) and approved by ESIST on any of the following websites:
www.esist.org/subtitling_code.html
www.transedit.se/code.htm
[You also have a copy of this document on: *DVD > Chapter 4 > Preliminary discussion > 4.1 code of Good Subtitling Practice*]

❶ Do you think it is positive, or even desirable, to have a set of guidelines that can be applied internationally? Or is it rather negative because it ignores and suppresses national idiosyncrasies?
❷ Could some standardization be reached at national level? At international level? Who should be in charge of it? How could it be reached?
❸ In the list offered by Ivarsson and Carroll, is there any recommendation that, in your opinion, may interfere unnecessarily with national subtitling practices?

In the initial section *Subtitle Spotting and Translation*:
❹ Comment on points 8 and 9.
❺ What do you think about points 11 and 13?
❻ Do you agree with point 12? Why?
❼ Can you think of any situation in which recommendation number 20 could not be implemented?
❽ What value does recommendation number 25 have?
❾ Would you propose any other recommendations?

4.2 Now compare the *Code of Good Subtitling Practice* with the *Set of Subtitling Standards in Europe* proposed by Karamitroglou (1998) that can be found on:
www.accurapid.com/journal/04stndrd.htm
[You also have a copy of this document on: *DVD > Chapter 4 > Preliminary discussion > 4.2 Proposed Set of Subtitling Standards in Europe*]

❶ Which one of the two sets do you think is most appropriate? Why?
❷ Can this set of standards be seen as complementary to the *Code of Good Subtitling*?
❸ Karamitroglou speaks about Europe. Can this limitation be justified? Could this set of standards also be applied in other countries and to other languages?

The aim of this chapter is to introduce the reader to some of the key concepts, tools and documents used in subtitling, from feet/frames and subtitling software programs to dialogue lists, without forgetting stylebooks and timecodes. This section also delves into the several spatial and temporal limitations that define this professional practice.

4.1 Subtitling programs

The computer has been one of the technological advances to have greatly changed the world of translation in general; and it could be argued that in the field of subtitling the impact has been even greater, with the launch of many computer programs designed exclusively for subtitling work. The first subtitling equipment was marketed in the second half of the 1970s and, over time, has been perfected to the generations that are available today (see appendix 2 for a comprehensive list).

Internet is the translator's other best friend. The wealth of information on the net seems to be endless. Dictionaries, glossaries, encyclopedias, specialized thematic websites, distribution groups, automatic translation tools, translators' forums, job offers, dialogue lists and scripts, compilations of subtitles, etc. are just a click away from anybody with a computer. We live in globalized times and, as Munday (2001:191) mentions, "the internet is also changing the status and visibility of translators and translation. Not only can professional translators now easily work transnationally via email, but the need for translation itself is also increasing". Appendix 3 offers a list of websites of interest to translators working in the field of audiovisual translation, although due to the temporary nature of some websites and their continually changing structure and content, we cannot guarantee that they will all be available at all times.

The recent breakthrough in the shift from analogue to digital technology with the possibility of digitizing images has also had a profound impact on the essence of this profession. The old VHS tape has virtually disappeared giving way to the DVD and to a better definition of the image. Workstations that only a few years ago required a computer, as well as an external video player and a television monitor – and even stopwatches in some cases – in order to undertake all the necessary stages of the work, are today obsolete and have been superseded by the computer alone equipped with software specifically designed for subtitling. Habitual practice ten or fifteen years ago in the spotting and simulation of subtitles has now become history. And what is today considered innovative and advanced may soon cease to be so.

Unless working with templates (§2.2), subtitlers these days usually require a computer, a subtitling program, and a digitized copy of the audiovisual programme to be subtitled. This equipment permits them to have simultaneously open on the computer monitor a word processor and a window to watch the programme, allowing them to spot the dialogue in the original, do the translation, use a spell checker, synchronize their own subtitles with the image on the screen, and simulate the final copy.

One of the most serious obstacles for the subtitler has traditionally been the prohibitive price of these subtitling programs. For the translator working only sporadically in this area, or for those who receive templates in English, the complete set of subtitling equipment is perhaps unnecessary. As mentioned previously, high prices have also had an adverse effect on the teaching of this discipline, as many universities find themselves unable to invest large sums of money in computer equipment.

A recent practice is to offer to the freelance subtitler a limited version of the subtitling program which, although not offering full functionality, is sufficient for the professional to undertake many of the tasks involved in subtitling. Because they have fewer functions, these freelancer versions are easier to use. On the one hand, they require less technical preparation on the part of the translators, and on the other they minimize the risk of the subtitler getting lost in the handling of often complicated programs.

The functionality of these programs is being constantly revised with a view to maximizing subtitlers' productivity and, as a result, reducing labour costs. Some programs incorporate a function that shows changes in soundtrack volume, making spotting and cueing of the original dialogue a lot easier, less time consuming, and more accurate. Text editing is also assisted with features such as spell checkers as well as error checking for subtitle length and timing. Shot changes can also be automatically detected these days, and voice recognition is another area in which much work is being done, having already borne some fruit in the preparation of live subtitles for the deaf and the hard-of-hearing.

Machine translation is another area that seems to be attracting lots of interest lately in our field. Given the economic importance of AVT in the audiovisual world it is hardly surprising that many researchers and companies have in recent years become interested in the subject and have started to investigate and invest in this area. But despite the fact that research in machine translation in general has been going on for quite some time, and that large sums of money have been invested in various projects, it appears that we are still years away from seeing it achieve adequate levels of linguistic quality that will entirely satisfy consumers of translations. A consensus has grown in AVT particularly that because of its specific characteristics, it does not lend itself much to automation.

A separate issue is that of developments in translation memory tools, which store previously translated sentences and allow the user to recall them as the basis for a new translation. Based on computational linguistic analysis at an advanced level, these tools have had a very important impact on translation practice, although again their value in AVT is questionable and still to be researched. At present, they appear to be more effective for working with documents characterized by a high level of lexical repetition. It is clear that the application of corpus studies to translation is an avenue of research that has yielded fruit in other areas such as technical and specialized translation, but which still appears not to have made its entry into the field of AVT.

Technology and computers have had a direct impact upon subtitling praxis and have made life easier for all those working in the field of subtitling. But it is also true that they have changed the professional profile expected of subtitlers. Linguistic competence and socio-cultural and subject knowledge are no longer sufficient in order to be able to operate effectively in this profession. It is now expected that they should be fully conversant with the information and communication technologies, and have the ability to quickly familiarize themselves with new programs and specifications, since they are more than likely to have to work with several different programs.

4.2 Feet and frames

When working for the cinema, a motion picture is measured using the Imperial units feet and frames, hence the term footage of a film. The maths are as follows: a film foot contains 16 frames, and for the viewer to believe that there is movement on the screen, 24 frames have to be shown every second on the cinema screen. Thus, a second of a film is equal to 1 foot and 8 frames (1.5 feet).

In order to guarantee a comfortable reading speed, it is a commonly accepted convention that a film foot (16 frames) should contain 10 characters (including letters, spaces and punctuation marks). In order words, a frame may contain 0.625 spaces or characters.

According to these values, and adapting the conversion table proposed by Castro Roig (2001:279), the following table of equivalences can be established:

Table 4.1 Equivalence between feet/frames and spaces

Feet : Frames	Spaces	Feet : Frames	Spaces	Feet : Frames	Spaces	Feet : Frames	Spaces
0:01	1	**1:01**	11	**2:01**	21	**3:01**	31
0:03	2	**1:03**	12	**2:03**	22	**3:03**	32
0:05	3	**1:05**	13	**2:05**	23	**3:05**	33
0:07	4	**1:07**	14	**2:07**	24	**3:07**	34
0:09	6	**1:09**	16	**2:09**	26	**3:09**	36
0:11	7	**1:11**	17	**2:11**	27	**3:11**	37
0:13	8	**1:13**	18	**2:13**	28	**3:13**	38
0:15	9	**1:15**	19	**2:15**	29	**3:15**	39
0:16 (=1:00)	10	**1:16 (=2:00)**	20	**2:16 (=3:00)**	30	**3:16 (=4:00)**	40
Feet : Frames	**Spaces**	**Feet : Frames**	**Spaces**	**Feet : Frames**	**Spaces**	**Feet : Frames**	**Spaces**
4:01	41	**5:01**	51	**6:01**	61	**7:01**	71
4:03	42	**5:03**	52	**6:03**	62	**7:03**	72
4:05	43	**5:05**	53	**6:05**	63	**7:05**	73
4:07	44	**5:07**	54	**6:07**	64	**7:07**	74
4:09	46	**5:09**	56	**6:09**	66	**7:09**	76
4:11	47	**5:11**	57	**6:11**	67	**7:11**	77
4:13	48	**5:13**	58	**6:13**	68	**7:13**	78
4:15	49	**5:15**	59	**6:15**	69	**7:15**	79
4:16 (=5:00)	50	**5:16 (=6:00)**	60	**6:16 (=7:00)**	70	**7:16 (=8:00)**	80

The following example, from the film *Manhattan Murder Mystery*, will help illustrate how to use these parameters when subtitling:

Example 4.1

Start	End	Total	Title
469.14	472.12	2.14	Did he seem a little too cheerful?
486.10	492.10	6.0	He sees himself as Humphrey Bogart in *Casablanca*.

The first utterance indicates that the actress starts her question in foot 469, frame 14, and finishes her sentence in foot 472, frame 12, which means that she has been talking for 2 feet and 14 frames. According to table 4.1 the subtitler will be allowed to write the translation in a subtitle of a maximum of 29 spaces. In the second example, the maximum number of characters available for the subtitle is 60. Exercise 4.8.4 has been designed to boost familiarization with this type of information.

4.3 Dialogue lists

The main aim of any translation is to reformulate a message originally produced in a source language in another language, avoiding at all costs any misunderstandings in the process. In other translation practices it might be easier to deal with some translational problems, since obscure cultural referents or difficult plays on words can be left out or drastically changed, without raising the receiver's suspicion. Even when there are errors in the translation, it is difficult for the consumers to spot them unless they have direct access to the original text, which is not always the case. But this camouflage is impossible in a translation practice as uniquely vulnerable as subtitling (§3.3.1), challenged by the concurrent presence of the original text at all times.

A good dialogue list is a key document that facilitates the task of the subtitler, helping to dispel potential comprehension mistakes. As far as terminology is concerned, there are many terms to refer to this type of document – among them screenplay, script, dialogue list, dialogue transcript, combined continuity, etc. – but, despite the minor differences among them, we will refer to them all under the umbrella term of dialogue lists.

A dialogue list is essentially the compilation of all the dialogue exchanges uttered in the film and it is a document usually supplied by the film distributor or producer of the film. Besides a verbatim transcription of all the dialogue, the ideal list also offers extra information on implicit socio-cultural connotations, explains plays on words or possible amphibologies, the meaning of colloquial and dialectal terms, gives the correct spelling of all proper names, clarifies implicit as well as explicit allusions, etc. Needless to say, they are not always this complete.

The European Broadcasting Union (EBU), resulting from the *Conference on Dubbing and Subtitling* that took place in Stockholm in 1987, launched a proposal with general guidelines aimed at homogenizing the production of these lists (Ivarsson and Carroll 1998:160). However, they are only recommendations, and have since fallen into oblivion. The reality is that these documents follow many different layouts and vary enormously from one to another.

Although dialogue lists are essential to carry out a good job, they are not very common in the profession, and this is why in many subtitling training courses students work directly from soundtrack alone, without any dialogue list. It may be somehow understandable that, due to time pressure, lists are not available for the subtitling of news programmes, but it is lamentable that they are not provided for the subtitling of films, which cost millions and are long term projects.

When working with old movies subtitlers do not usually have a list and are asked to transcribe the dialogue directly from the screen, a rather tedious task. In these cases, due care has to be taken, as poor sound quality, overlapping of dialogue, strong accents, and environmental noises can lead to misunderstandings of the source text and, therefore, to subtitles that are at odds with the original message. Things have improved considerably since the arrival of Internet and scripts with the dialogues of some films and popular TV series can be easily found on the net (see Appendix 3). They tend to be pre-production scripts that do not always coincide with what can be heard on screen, and a thorough checking should be carried out. The documents that come, if at all, with programmes to be broadcast on television or released on VHS or DVD tend to be mere transcriptions of the dialogue with no – or very little – additional information.

Dialogue lists for contemporary feature movies to be shown on cinema screens are the most detailed ones, particularly the lists for US movies. Big distribution companies are fully aware of the economic potential of their productions on the world market and provide these documents to smooth the translation process. The European cinema industry does not seem to realize the value of these documents and, when films do come accompanied with them, they tend to be rather basic and simplistic, with little information to help translators.

Translators allowed to do their own cueing may use dialogue lists for reference, but on some other occasions they may have to work from a spotting dialogue list, containing the dialogue already compressed into subtitle lengths in the original language. Translators then have to adhere to the cueing of these master subtitles and their translations have to render the content of the already pruned subtitles rather than the speech. Figure 1 is an example of a very detailed dialogue list of the film *Manhattan Murder Mystery*. You can find a digital copy of this document on DVD > Chapter 4 > Examples > Example 4.2.

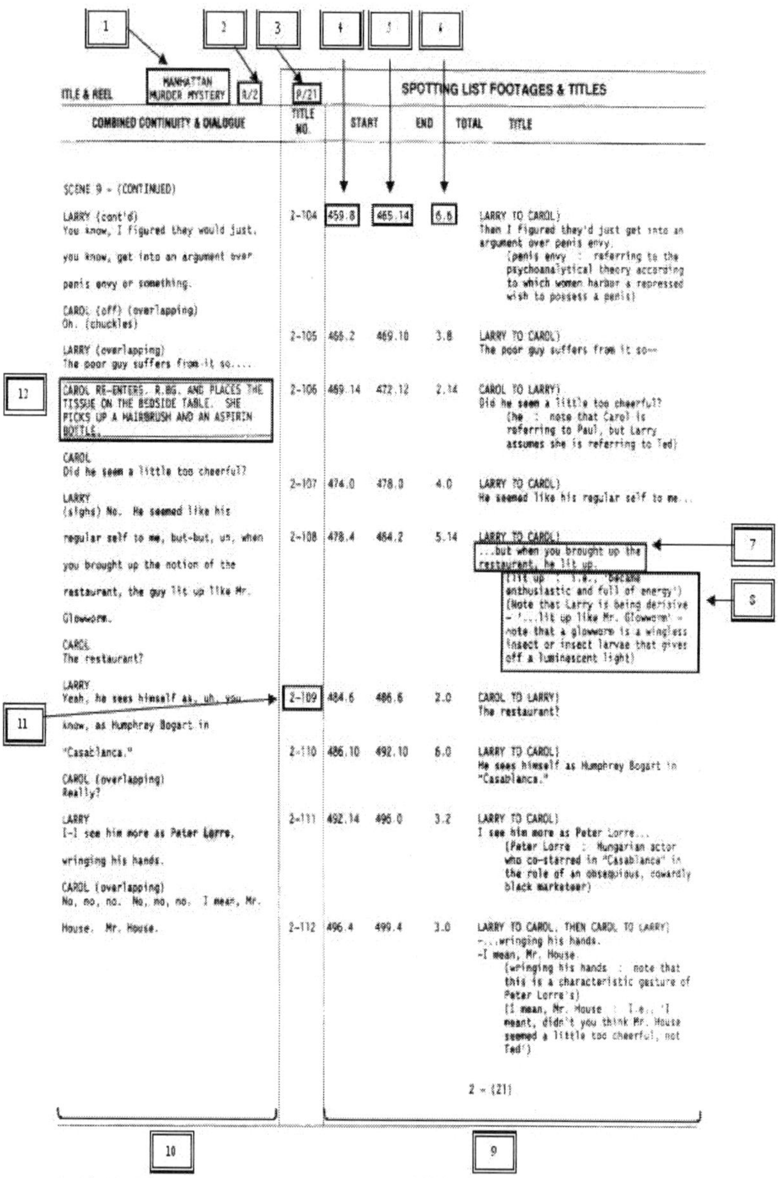

[ ] Title of the film.
[ ] *Reel*. A motion picture is divided in reels of some 1,000 feet (300 meters), lasting around 10 minutes each.
[ ] *Page*: 21 in this case.
[ ] Subtitle onset: foot 459, frame 8.
[ ] Subtitle outset: foot 465, frame 14.
[ ] Length of the subtitle: 6 feet and 6 frames.

[ ] *Master title*.
[ ] Additional information for the translator.
[ ] Column with the pruned dialogues to be subtitled.
[ ] Column with the complete and literal transcription of the dialogues, to be used for dubbing.
[ ] Subtitle number: number 109 in reel 2.
[ ] Additional information to contextualise the scene.

Figure 4.1 - Detailed dialogue list

This document is more precisely known as a combined continuity and subtitle/spotting list. On the left hand side of the page we find the combined continuity and dialogue, i.e. the detailed and faithful reproduction of what the actors say on screen, including repetitions, exclamations, redundancies, linguistic fillers, etc. together with the asides that help to contextualize the performance of the characters.

In the centre column, the subtitler is given the reel in which the speech is found and the sequential number of the subtitle.

On the right hand side of the page we find what in the profession are known as master subtitles, i.e. the dialogue already cut into chunks and pruned of 'irrelevant' information; the text that translators have to transfer into their target languages. It also incorporates lots of explanatory notes whose aim is to facilitate the translator's task. The three sets of figures preceding this material indicate the spotting of the subtitle, the precise place where it can be found in the footage of the film, and the length of the speech utterance.

On occasion, these annotations may seem rather insubstantial for the translation process. However, the asides as well as the explanatory notes may indeed fulfil another function. With all this information included in the dialogue list, the translator is asked sometimes to translate the film without having a copy of it, either because the actual copy of the film has not been finished yet, or because the distribution company does not want to release the film before its commercial launching in an attempt to frustrate illegal pirating, particularly important in the case of films that are preceded by big publicity campaigns that whet the appetite of future spectators.

What is relevant in the case of the compressed dialogue on the right hand side of the page is its greater rationalization and naturalization when compared with the 'gross' dialogue on the left. Hesitations, repetitions, false starters, etc. have all been neutralized into much more compact and logical, but at the same time more clinical and less colourful discourse, as can be appreciated in the following two examples from *Manhattan Murder Mystery*:

Example 4.3

You said she liked- She liked eating high cholesterol desserts. Is that what you said?	→	You said she liked eating high cholesterol desserts.
Yes, yes. Yeah, no, no, no, no, I-I-I-I understand. I, uh, yes, no.	→	Yes, no. I understand.

Somehow the translators' task has been lightened – the overlapping of dialogue, for instance, has been dealt with – but it could be argued that this is at the expense of their freedom, since they could have opted to segment the original dialogue in a different way. This opinion is shared by Smith (1998:144-145) when he states that "a ready-made spotting list would tend to encourage translators to divide their subtitles to fit it, even where better solutions could be found". Although a detailed standard list imposes some restrictions, it is our opinion that there should still exist some room for manoeuvre for the translator, who should have the latitude to refer to the soundtrack too. In the following example the original dialogue on the left column has been reduced to the master title on the right:

Example 4.4

You want to lie down for a while? We'll put a cold compress on your head, or a hot compress on your back, or--	→	You want to lie down? We'll put a cold compress on your head.

However, the subtitler has decided to depart from what has been recommended in the master title in order to create an impact in the translation that would have been lost otherwise:

Example 4.5

Túmbate, te pondré
compresas frías en la frente,
[Lie down, I'll put
cold compresses on your forefront,]

---

o calientes en la espalda. O…
[or hot ones on your back. Or…]

Here, the subtitler has preferred to transfer to Spanish a more complete version than the one proposed in the dialogue list, with the aim of reinforcing the nonsensical dimension of the English utterances. Had the subtitler blindly followed the instructions given in the master title, the humour of the original would have been irrevocably lost, since there is nothing strange in putting a cold compress on the forehead of someone ill or dizzy. It is the addition of the absurd element in the second half of the utterance – i.e. to put hot compresses on someone's back – that allows for a humorous reading of the text.

Dialogue lists, like dictionaries, are not infallible, and neither are their compilers. So, in the lucky event that one of these lists is provided by the distribution or production company, subtitlers ought to be careful since these documents usually forget to include texts that are not dialogue – i.e. newspapers, captions, songs, radio voices, and the like. On occasions they transcribe phonetically terms and expressions that have not been fully understood, and the spelling of loan words that come from a language different to the two in play can also be a source of problems.

Finally, a good dialogue list should be compiled by a professional with a flair for the sort of problems involved in linguistic transfer and should contain as many relevant details as possible. Some translators may, and in fact do, find these explanations irritating and often too basic, but it cannot be forgotten that the ultimate aim of the list is to be useful to as many translators as possible, in different countries, and from very different cultural backgrounds. So, when translating a US or French film, what may seem straightforward for a European audiovisual translator may not be so for a translator from an African or Asian country.

4.4 Style guides

In addition to a dialogue list of the programme to be translated, subtitlers also ought to receive a style guide, or equivalent, from the broadcasting or subtitling company, in which they can find the main parameters to be applied in their subtitles. Unfortunately, it is not a common occurrence in the profession and many translators are left to their own devices when producing subtitles.

Some companies do have their own guidelines, but they tend to be for internal use only and are not very detailed. Zabalbeascoa (1996:250) has been one of the first academics to call for a wider use of these documents in the profession. Although he is primarily concerned with the dubbing of television sitcoms, his call can be extended to the field of AVT in general:

> An essential part of the translator's reference material should be a specialized in-house **stylebook**, which could include all the information that the employer or firm can anticipate that the translator will need to know and use, including glossaries, television policies and translational norms [...] along with a considerable number of practical examples of problems and strategies.

On a more positive note, it is promising to see that these documents are becoming common currency in the profession and they are also being made more readily available to interested parties. Both the BBC (www.bbc.co.uk) and the Ofcom (www.ofcom.org.uk) in the UK have very detailed guidelines for subtitling for the deaf and the hard-of-hearing. In the case of the BBC the document is for internal use, whilst the Ofcom guidelines can be downloaded from their website. The Catalan public television broadcaster, Televisió de Catalunya, published in 1997 a book with a set of linguistic criteria for translating into Catalan. It can only be hoped that these developments will enhance the quality of subtitling.

4.5 Code of good subtitling practice

The consumption of just a few subtitled programmes brings home the realization that there is a general lack of consensus and harmonization when presenting subtitles on screen. Conventions are not always systematically applied and variations can be observed at a technical level as well as in the layout of the subtitles. A considerable range of styles has developed over time affecting the length and duration of lines, reading speeds, the use of typographical signs (§5.2 and §5.3), and line breaks, among others.

In the light of this situation, authors like Ivarsson and Carroll (1998:157-159) put forward a Code of Good Subtitling Practice in an attempt to offer general guidelines aimed at preserving and fostering quality in subtitling. The result of a common effort by a working group of professionals and academics within the European Association for Studies in Screen Translation (ESIST), these guidelines are widely regarded as standard in the profession. They are not binding, and companies and professionals alike can adhere to them if so they wish. The document is addressed not only to translators but to all professionals involved in the process of subtitling. The recommendations have been very fruitful, but changes brought about by digitization and new working routines now call for their revamping. Karamitroglou (1998) and Díaz Cintas (2003) have also worked in this direction, proposing guidelines at pan-European and Spanish levels respectively.

Although many regard this setting of parameters as a commendable effort, for others is nothing but a dogmatic catalogue of rules and regulations promoting unnecessary uniformity and erasing national idiosyncrasies. Subtitling conventions applied in many countries have come to be what they are after a long period. They have been socially sifted, are the result of a long tradition, and viewers are now familiar with them. From this perspective, it is understandable that some companies or television stations may look on these general recommendations with suspicion, as drawn up by professionals who might not have sufficient knowledge of specific local reality.

Some of these recommendations are easier to follow than others, and parameters governing the technical dimension are less exposed to criticism than guidelines about subtitle layout, which runs closer to the linguistic dimension of the target language and is more entrenched in the culture.

In our opinion, these guidelines should not be understood as an invasion on any country's or company's subtitling tradition, but rather a declaration of good intentions aspiring to set some minimum standards in the profession and to safeguard subtitlers' rights. These recommendations are not set in stone and they are, of course, all open to debate, changes and modifications. The most important issue here, however, is to use them as a trigger to stimulate debate and reflection. Here, they have been grouped under three categories: spatial dimension, temporal dimension, and punctuation and other conventions. The latter is, without a doubt, the most extensive of the three and is dealt with separately in chapter 5.

4.6 Spatial dimension

In this section we will limit ourselves to some purely formal layout issues and other spatial aspects of subtitling, even though these are inevitably linked to the distribution of text on the screen, and therefore to linguistic matters. Linguistic considerations, the core business of subtitling from a translational point of view, are the topic of chapters 6 and 7. Here we touch on issues of a more technical nature or related to particular house styles, where decisions tend to be taken by technicians, producers, distributors, and project managers rather than subtitlers. Still, subtitlers are a link in a chain, and it is good to have an overall view of the process and to know what happens with a programme before and after the actual translation.

Even though there is no absolute uniformity in the way subtitles are positioned on the screen, there certainly are a number of trends. Today, the situation is one of variation within generally accepted practice. The initial diversity was due to the more or less independent, gradual development of subtitling and subtitling guidelines in different countries, based on individual preference, national literary or cinematic/broadcasting traditions, and the evolution of technology. The development of subtitling for new media has no doubt also been a determining factor in the emergence of formal guidelines. The fact that the most prominent new medium, i.e. the DVD, usually contains several subtitling tracks in different languages, has actually led to more rather than less uniformity, whereas television subtitling remains less uniform. DVD does, however, also appear to be having an influence on TV norms (cf. below). We will be considering subtitling as it appears on TV, on cinema screens, on videotapes, and DVD. Newer forms like subtitling for Internet, fansubs, and computer games, usually derive their guidelines from existing styles, just as surtitling for the theatre and the opera initially turned to open subtitling for guidance. It usually is not the subtitler who makes the final decision in these matters; however, future subtitlers should above all try to be flexible in their approach, gain an insight into the advantages and disadvantages of different practices, and be consistent when applying the conventions proposed by a particular subtitling company.

In each of the sections below, we will indicate what guidelines are to be followed when carrying out the exercises contained on the DVD.

4.6.1 Maximum number of lines and position on the screen

For many cinema professionals and film buffs subtitles are a blemish on the film screen and we do not really wish to contradict them. We have stated above that subtitling is a type of translation that should not attract attention to itself. This holds for its formal as well as its linguistic features. That is why, generally speaking, interlingual subtitling is limited to two lines, which occupy no more than two twelfths of the screen. In this, subtitling for a hearing public differs from (teletext) subtitling for the deaf and the hearing impaired, which often makes use of three or even four lines. Bilingual subtitles may also resort to four-line subtitles sporadically.

In the world of digital video, any picture is made up of individual dots known as pixels – literally picture elements. Each frame of the video is a picture 720 pixels wide and 576 pixels high, known in the profession as broadcast resolution. Written text and graphics shown on screen may get distorted if they appear too close to the edges because TV manufacturers deal with the screen edges differently. This is why all text must be centrally positioned within a safe area. This safe area is usually 10% with each frame edge, e.g. 72 pixels in from the right and left edges and 57 pixels from the top and bottom. By default, the following standard parameters are applied by WinCAPS in regards to the safe area: top 32, left 56, right 56, and bottom 32. They should always be respected when working with this subtitling program.

The standard position for subtitles is horizontal at the bottom of the screen since this limits the obstruction of the image, and this part of the screen is usually of lesser importance to the action. Some languages, like Japanese, have a long history of placing subtitles vertically on the right-hand side of the screen, especially for theatrical releases. With the arrival of video and DVD, horizontal subtitles have become more common than ever before, although both approaches still co-exist.

The positioning of a two-line subtitle at the bottom of the screen does not offer any options since both lines are in use. The situation is different when dealing with one-line subtitles, with some companies using the first – i.e. top – line and some others preferring the second line. This traditional variation in the placement of one-line subtitles is giving way to a more uniform approach these days with most one-liners habitually appearing on the second – i.e. bottom – line, keeping clear of the image as best they can.

WinCAPS

One-line subtitles should be written on the second, bottom line.

Technology regarding DVDs and cinema projection is evolving constantly and extremely quickly, which means that new methods of projecting and engraving subtitles keep appearing on the market. Technical advances have made it possible to place the subtitles, either both lines or just the bottom one, immediately below the image. Pollution of the original photography is obviously reduced, but more research ought to be carried out to establish whether this aesthetic change has any negative impact on overall appreciation of the programme, since the eye has to move across a wider screen area in order to scan all the information available.

Subtitles can be moved from the bottom of the screen to another position if the need arises. Such a move can occur if:

- ❑ The background at the bottom of the screen is so light that the subtitles are illegible.
- ❑ Some important action is taking place at the bottom of the screen.
- ❑ Some essential data are displayed at the bottom of the screen while dialogue continues and must therefore be subtitled (examples are: other subtitles, inserts with dates or information about a speaker, or the broadcaster's logo).

When the decision is taken to displace the subtitles in a film, they are then placed at the top – most common practice – or in the middle of the screen, but this is extremely rare. An example occurs in the classic *Taxi Driver*. Protagonist taxi driver Travis takes the woman he would like to be his partner to a porn movie. The film is Swedish and subtitled in English. On the French subtitled DVD, the French subtitles appear at the top of the screen each time the English 'cinema' subtitles appear at the bottom.

In the case of TV documentaries or interviews, it is often the inserts with details about the speaker or interviewee that are moved to the top of the screen, whereas the subtitles remain in their usual position. However, if the original inserts cannot be edited and changed, subtitles tend to be moved to the middle of the screen, just above the text appearing on screen. If the decision goes against re-positioning the subtitles, one of the strategies implemented consists in encasing them in a grey or black box that covers up (part of) the original data.

Since viewers expect subtitles to appear at the bottom of the screen it is better not to move them around unnecessarily. Besides, there are a limited number of alternative solutions to avoid collisions with other textually rendered information. A one-line subtitle, placed on the top or bottom subtitle line, may not obstruct anything at all. Alternatively, the position of the subtitle can also be shifted horizontally, to the right or left, so that it does not cover up the inserts or the logos. But this accumulation of different bits of original and translated information may be confusing to the viewer, considering the limited exposure time available. In fact, the same problem arises when data appear both at the top and the bottom of the screen. In these cases, the exposure time of the subtitle has to be reconsidered and the translation left a bit longer on the screen if possible. The subtitle could also be made to appear slightly earlier or later, if this does not disturb synchrony exceedingly. Each particular instance will require an ad hoc solution, and it must be remembered that all these suggestions are emergency measures of sorts.

4.6.2 Font type and number of characters per line

Today, most subtitles are white, although occasionally yellow is used when subtitling black and white films, so that the contrast between image and text is sharper. Fonts without serifs are preferred (Arial, Helvetica, Times New Roman) and the size varies.

WinCAPS

The font we recommend to use is Arial 32. Please note that 32 refers to pixels, not points.

The characters are almost always shadowed or black contoured, which solves legibility problems, even if the letters appear against a very light background. Should this not do the trick, when the subtitles appear against a very light background, one of the solutions may be to encase them in a grey or black box. The boxes are standard in subtitling software and can be made to appear throughout the film or simply whenever they are required in concrete subtitles. They are partly transparent and the shade of grey can be adapted (rendered lighter or darker) depending on whether or not the background must remain visible to some extent. If the only purpose of the box is to improve legibility, a grey box is preferable because it stands out less on the screen than a black one and is therefore less obtrusive.

Bearing in mind what has been said about the screen safe area (§4.6.1), for the Roman alphabet the maximum number of characters allowed on a one line TV subtitle is usually 37, including blank spaces and typographical signs, which all take up one space. Occasionally, clients will ask for a maximum of 33 or 35 characters per line, or allow up to 39 to 41 characters depending on their guidelines and software used. Exceptionally, some film festivals will go as high as 43 characters per line. For cinema and DVD a maximum of 40 characters seems to be the norm, whereas for VHS this used to be between 33 and 35. The evolution seems to be upwards, probably due to higher quality projection or engraving of the subtitles on the one hand, and increased viewing experience on the other. In any case, the concept of characters per line is somewhat being blurred when working with digital technology, as pixels are fast becoming the way of measuring text on screen. As the basic unit of the composition of an image on a television screen, computer monitor, or similar display, they allow for greater rationalization of the space available for subtitles. The syllable 'mo' takes clearly more space than 'li', and whereas under characters per line they both count as two letters, using pixels they will allow for a varying number of letters in a line, depending on the actual space they occupy.

Still, a higher number of characters per line often results in more image being covered by text, or in a smaller font being selected, which again hampers legibility, and viewers who have to read more have less time to scan the film's other information channels. More research into the relative importance of these various channels for information would certainly be welcome. In practice, subtitlers get instructions as to how many characters they can use, either from their customers or from the subtitling company they are working for. Once the number is known, the software preferences are set accordingly and the program takes care of the counting. The cursor normally moves down to the second line when the first one is full and programs usually have a function or a checker, which tells the subtitler when the maximum number of characters has been exceeded. Each program has its own warning system, usually a symbol that changes colour.

The maximum number of characters per line varies according to alphabets, and it is normal to allow 35 for Cyrillic languages like Bulgarian, Macedonian and Russian, 34 to 36 for Greek and Arabic, 12 to 14 for Japanese and Korean and between 14 and 16 for Chinese.

WinCAPS

> To carry out the exercises in WinCAPS, we recommend using a maximum of 39 characters per line. The total for a two-liner is, therefore, 78 characters.

There is no fixed rule as to the minimum number of characters a subtitle must have, but subtitles counting less than 4 to 5 characters are rare. Any subtitle should ideally remain on screen for at least one second so that the eye of the viewer can register its presence, although it is not uncommon to come across subtitles that stay on screen for as little as 21 or 22 frames.

Subtitles that are kept on screen for a shorter period of time risk appearing and disappearing like a flash and therefore not being read by the viewer. On the other hand, if a very short subtitle remains on the screen too long, the viewers will have time to read it repeatedly, which is equally irritating and can break the reading rhythm. In other words, extremely short subtitles must be used for a good reason and timed carefully. In some cases, a one-word subtitle can just as well be incorporated into the preceding or following one (§4.7.1).

4.6.3 One-liners and two-liners

The ideal number of lines and their positioning on screen is an issue a bit closer to the jurisdiction of the subtitlers. Is a single line subtitle always the preferred solution? Are two short lines of equal length better? Should one go for a short first line and a longer second line? Opinions again vary, but some consensus does exist. Choices regarding the physical distribution of text always try to balance between issues connected with the linguistics of subtitling, since respecting syntactic and semantic units promotes legibility, and more purely visual aesthetic matters. In addition, ideal line length also depends on the screen safe area and on the positioning of the subtitle, i.e. left-aligned versus centred.

The general rule is: if a relatively short subtitle fits into one line, do not use two. There is no need to make eyes travel from one line to the next when all the information can be presented in a single line that viewers can read at a glance. Theoretically, this is a rule that can be applied, at least, in the case of left-aligned subtitles. However, especially in the cinema and if the subtitles are centred, some subtitling companies do prefer for aesthetic reasons to have two shorter lines of equal length rather than one exceedingly long one – i.e. one that would use up the maximum of 39 or 40 characters and spaces. But then again, grammatical considerations also come into play (§6.4).

Extremely long subtitles also force the eye to travel, if only from left to right (or right to left depending on the language), particularly on large cinema screens. Sometimes, this is unavoidable, especially when bilingual subtitles are required, but in other cases one option should be given priority against the other. Some sentences, composed of clauses, lend themselves more easily to two-line subtitles than others. Besides, a sentence break can help render intonation. In short, if a one-liner is divided over two lines, this is usually done because the one-line subtitle would be very long and/or the break helps to underscore syntax and/or intonation. Compare, for instance, the following alternatives. In the film dialogue, there is a brief pause after 'up there':

Example 4.6

<table>
<tr><td colspan="2">ST: Can you see the light up there, in the window?</td></tr>
<tr><td>Can you see the light in the window?</td><td>Can you see the light?
In the window?</td></tr>
</table>

As we have mentioned, when dealing with one-liners, a decision has to be taken on whether to place them on the first/top line or on the second/bottom line of the screen. Some companies give preference to subtitle placement on the bottom line since this way the written text is pushed to the edge of the screen and hence interferes less with the image. Other studios give priority to the top line. The reasoning behind this is that they prefer the consistency of starting the subtitles always at the same height on the screen. This way, the eye can get used to it and goes automatically to the same place on the screen every time a new subtitle pops up. This second option does not make much sense when working for small screens and may be more productive in cinema subtitling where the dimensions of the screen are bigger and the eye has to travel more.

With two-liners, a recommendation based on aesthetics is to keep the top line shorter whenever possible in order not to pollute the image. However, sense blocks and readability ought to be the most influential aspects in subtitle positioning. In the two-liner in the example given above, the first line is longer than the second, which could not be avoided due to the way the utterance is structured syntactically. Let us compare the four versions of the same subtitle, below:

Example 4.7

My whole life, I've been followed by loneliness.
My whole life, I've been followed by loneliness.
My whole life, I've been followed by loneliness.
My whole life, I've been followed by loneliness.

We are only considering layout at this point; and from this perspective the second and third examples are the best solutions, in the sense that they both apply the general rule of keeping the top line shorter. Not only are they aesthetically more pleasing, but in the case of left-aligned subtitles this means the eye has to cover less of a distance to read the second line.

In any event, the overriding factor when presenting two-liners on screen is to secure line-breaks which are appropriate syntactically, respecting and reflecting the logic of the sentence. In this sense, solutions one and four above ought to be avoided. Priority has to be given to a subtitle that is easy to read, rather than to a convoluted subtitle that is symmetrically perfect, obstructs the image less, but is difficult to read.

4.6.4 Centred and left-aligned

In the past, TV subtitles were often left-aligned, and some TV channels still left-align subtitles in countries like The Netherlands, although televised feature films often have centred subtitles. By contrast, subtitles are nearly always centred on DVD and this approach appears also to be gaining ground on TV, where more variation can be detected these days. One of the main reasons why subtitles are being centred on television is because broadcaster logos are sometimes placed in the lower left-hand corner of the screen, thus blocking the first couple of characters and hampering legibility. Even though most TV stations tend to have their logos in the upper left or right corners, the risk remains when a programme is sold.

In the cinema, subtitles have always appeared in the middle of the screen: in a large movie theatre left-centred subtitles would be too far removed from spectators sitting on the far right. Another reason in favour of centring subtitles has to do with the fact that the action tends to happen in the middle of the screen. Thus, if the subtitles are also positioned in the centre, the eye has to travel less from the image to the text.

As far as reading is concerned, if the subtitles are left-aligned and start always at the same point on the screen, the eye gets used to it and goes to the same spot when a new subtitle is due to appear. If, on the other hand, subtitles are centred they will always appear at different points on the screen and it will be impossible for the eye to anticipate the location of the subtitle.

The trend appears to be increasingly in favour of centring subtitles for all media. On occasion, however, and rather inexplicably, some companies mix the two approaches and use centred subtitles throughout the programme, except for dialogue subtitles in which the lines are left-aligned and preceded by a dash.

WinCAPS

All subtitles, including dialogue subtitles, should be centred on the screen.

4.7 Temporal dimension

4.7.1 Spotting and duration of subtitles

Also known as timing or cueing, this consists of determining the in and out times of subtitles, i.e. the exact moment when a subtitle should appear on screen and when it should disappear, according to a series of spatial and temporal parameters.

The spotting of the dialogue has to mirror the rhythm of the film and the performance of the actors, and be mindful of pauses, interruptions, and other prosodic features that characterize the original speech. Long sentences might have to be split over several subtitles and short sentences combined to avoid telegraphic style.

The golden rule for ideal spotting is that subtitles should keep temporal synchrony with the utterances. If possible, a subtitle should appear at the precise moment the person starts speaking, and should disappear when the person stops speaking. Thanks to an eight-digit timecode, the exact cues are accurately defined in hours, minutes, seconds and frames (§4.7.7).

Studies show that when a subtitle remains on screen longer than the time the viewer actually needs to read it, there is a tendency to read it again. To avoid this unnecessary second reading, six seconds is the recommended maximum exposure time to keep a full two-liner on screen. Thus, since the limit of what can be written on screen is dictated by the physical length of the lines – i.e. two lines of some 37 to 39 characters – keeping 74 to 78 characters' worth of information beyond six seconds is never recommended in subtitling because it can lead to re-reading. Therefore, when spotting a dialogue, periods longer than six seconds should be reconsidered and split into smaller units. If it is the same person who is talking for more than six seconds, we should look into dividing the utterance when a natural pause crops up in the delivery, or at a point where the logic of the sentence allows for it (§6.4). According to Ivarsson and Carroll (1998:82), in connected speech speakers tend to make a slight pause either to breathe or to signal grammatical or logical units, at intervals that vary between five and eight seconds, thus facilitating the spotting task. Let us consider the following utterance from the film *The French Lieutenant's Woman*:

> At a time when the male population of London of all ages was one and a quarter million, the prostitutes were receiving clients at a rate of two million per week.

It lasts 8 seconds and 23 frames. When cued all together, the subtitle will have to condense the original information dramatically if it is to fit in a two-liner of some 74 characters, and it will exceed the six seconds. A much better option is to spot the utterance in two different subtitles, taking into account the logic of the sentence and the fact that the actress makes a slight pause half way through. A few frames, usually two or three, will have to be left between the two subtitles:

Example 4.8

Subtitle 1:	04:19
At a time when the male population of London of all ages was one and a quarter million,	
Subtitle 2:	03:18
the prostitutes were receiving clients at a rate of two million per week.	

At the other end of the scale, to avoid flashing subtitles on screen and guarantee that viewers have enough time to read the content, the ideal minimum exposure time for a subtitle is commonly agreed at one second – i.e. 24 or 25 frames – although some companies might set it as low as 21 frames, even with short subtitles that could leave the screen earlier. If the timing of a particular brief utterance falls under this category of less than one second, there are two possible strategies. If another person is speaking immediately before or after, consideration should be given to the possibility of using a dialogue subtitle presenting both persons in the same projection. If the utterance is preceded and followed by pauses, the subtitler should consider allowing for a certain margin of asynchrony at the onset and the outset of the subtitle (§4.6.1).

4.7.2 Synchronization

Temporal synchronization between subtitle and soundtrack is arguably the main factor affecting the viewer's appreciation of the quality of a translated programme. Poor timing, with subtitles that come in too early or too late, or leave the screen without following the original soundtrack are confusing, detract from enjoying a programme, and have the potential of ruining what may otherwise be an excellent linguistic transfer. Accurate timing is crucial for optimal subtitling since it reinforces the internal cohesion of the translated programme and plays the essential role of helping the viewer identify who is saying what in the programme.

To ease the task, many subtitling programs have these days a sound recognition application that detects the point at which speech begins and its duration, offering a graphical representation of the actual speech. Whereas it can be difficult, via headphones, to discern audibly the precise moment of speech onset, this display aid is very valuable in timing subtitles and making them coincide with the spoken word.

Example 4.9

> You can see what a program with this function looks like by going to:
>
> *DVD > Chapter 4 > Examples > Example 4.9a > FAB*
> *DVD > Chapter 4 > Examples > Example 4.9b > WinCAPS*

However, perfect synchronization may not always be attainable and a certain degree of flexibility can be observed in the professional practice. In concrete instances, when the original dialogue is semantically dense and it is very difficult to condense or delete information without compromising the message, a certain degree of asynchrony is allowed in the presentation of the subtitles. In these cases, they can appear a few frames before the actual dialogue is uttered and leave the screen a fraction of a second after the speaker has actually finished talking. This strategy is frequently used in SDH, when the spotting needs to follow the image more closely than the soundtrack, but restraint is advised when working in interlingual subtitling. Its sporadic application may be of great value to the subtitler, but if used too often it may be easily interpreted as lousy timing.

4.7.3 Multiple voices

As opposed to oral speech, written texts, including subtitles, are sequential and can only present dialogue exchanges one after the other. This makes the spotting of overlapping dialogue particularly tricky. When there is more than one person speaking at the same time the spotter has to make the difficult decision of deciding which information will make it to the target language and which will have to be deleted. In addition, the timing will have to be done in as clear a way as possible so as not to confuse the viewer, who can hear several voices at the same time and may not know who is saying what. In these cases, good layout of the subtitles is also essential.

When spotting, the faster the pace of the dialogue exchanges, the more challenging the task becomes. This is particularly true when, as Ivarsson (1992:49) mentions, "several people are involved in a series of rapid exchanges, especially if they are having an argument or are seen in different places, for example talking on the telephone", and the subtitler will have to be on the alert when these circumstances come together in a scene.

4.7.4 Shot changes

Although not always possible to comply with, another golden rule in spotting recommends that a subtitle should not be maintained over a cut. The subtitle should leave the screen just before the cut occurs and a new subtitle spotted after the cut, which functions as a dividing frontier between subtitles. This recommendation is based in studies on eye movement that have shown that if a subtitle is kept on screen when there is a cut change, the viewer is led to believe that a change of subtitle has also taken place and starts re-reading the same onscreen text. From a film studies perspective, Cornu (1996) also insists that cut and shot changes must be respected, arguing that the editing of the film itself dictates the editing of the translated text.

There is some controversy as to when to time the subtitles before the shot change. For some professionals it is common practice to avoid displaying a subtitle precisely as a shot change takes place, arguing that this can distract the viewer from the visual content of the video and is somewhat disturbing to the eye; others prefer to use the exact moment when the cut happens to cue the subtitle out.

Some of today's subtitling programs come with an additional shot change detector that automatically analyzes a video file and identifies the shot changes within it, making the whole process much easier.

Respecting cuts has become more of an issue as some of today's fast moving films rely on editing techniques where cuts are frequent as a means to contribute to the dynamism of the action. Besides, actors may still be speaking whilst the shot changes, providing what is known as a sound bridge. It is difficult, not to say impossible, not to break this rule, and the number of occasions when a subtitle has to cross a cut will vary from production to production. The distribution format also has an impact and films to be screened in the cinema tend to adhere to this rule in a much stricter way than programmes to be broadcast on television or commercialized on DVD. Priorities have to be set and, whilst soft cuts pose less of a problem, hard cuts should be respected as much as possible.

One way of avoiding crossing an excessive number of cuts is to accelerate the spotting, which results in a larger number of short subtitles, sometimes lasting less than one second.

Although at first glance spotting can be perceived as a complex and difficult task for the untrained, present day software subtitling programs have facilitated it enormously, and given a bit of training and some exposure anybody can do a good job.

4.7.5 Delay function between subtitles

A slight, clear pause has to exist between two consecutive subtitles if the viewer is to register that a change of written material has taken place on screen. If a subtitle is immediately followed by another one without leaving any frames between the two, the eye finds it difficult to realize that new information has been presented. The chances of this mishap occurring are greater when the two subtitles share a similar layout.

To avoid this potential problem, many subtitling programs have an automatic delay function that creates a small pause immediately after the out-time of every subtitle, before the next one can be cued in. This delay function can be manipulated and various values can be selected, but in order to be effective a minimum of two or three frames are needed.

WinCAPS

For the exercises contained on the DVD, it is recommended that a minimum gap of two frames be left between consecutive subtitles.

4.7.6 One or two lines?

Studies on the reading speed of viewers seem to indicate that the greater the number of words in one subtitle, the less time is then spent reading each one of these words. That is, viewers need proportionally more time to read short subtitles than longer ones (Ivarsson and Carroll 1998:64). According to Brondeel (1994:28):

> Average latency (0.35 sec.) in perception seems to make two-line subtitles possibly less demanding of the viewer than e.g. two successive one-liners, which require two onsets. Consequently the overall "reading time" in two-liners seems to offer the viewer more "reading comfort".

Given these findings, it would seem more appropriate in general to resort to two-liners whenever possible; obvious exceptions being cases when the original utterances are very short themselves, or when a cut has to be respected.

However, authors like Lomheim (1999:192) prefer the use of one-liners as he believes that they are easier to read than two-line subtitles; even he, however, shows some caution in this respect, adding that "if one-liners contain greatly condensed information, coupled with a high degree of implied information, it is quite conceivable that they may be more difficult to interpret than two-liners".

Once more, arguments can be found in favour of two apparently opposing approaches. In our opinion, the subtitler has to be aware of this controversy and consider the appropriateness of resorting to both types of subtitles throughout the programme to be translated.

4.7.7 Timecodes

The introduction of timecodes in the subtitling process brought about changes that have altered virtually all stages in the profession, from the timing of the subtitles to their engraving or projection on screen, including the way they can be archived, revised, and amended. The first timecodes made their appearance in the 1970s although they only became indispensable in subtitling in the mid-1980s. Before their arrival, stopwatches were used to do the cueing.

A timecode generator assigns an 8-digit figure to every single frame of the film or programme. It is a sort of identity sign unique to each frame, making it very easy for any professional to identify a particular frame within the whole programme. The code is engraved at the top or the bottom of the working copy, where a TCR – Time Code Reader – indicates the hours, minutes, seconds and frames, as can be seen in figures 2 and 3:

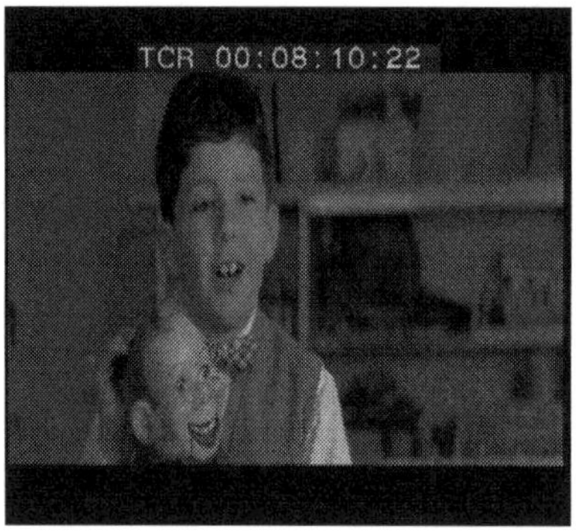

Figure 4.2 – Frame with timecode

Figure 4.3 – Frame with timecode

In figure 2, the value 00: 08: 10: 22 (which is sometimes expressed as 10: 08: 10: 22 as some software programs have difficulty in recognizing figures starting with 00) indicates that this frame can be found at the beginning of the film (hour 0), 8 minutes (of a total of 60), 10 seconds (of a total of 60), and 22 frames (of a total of 24 in cinema, 25 in television and video in PAL system, and 30 in television and video in NTSC system).

To indicate that the programme has moved past the first hour, the following code will appear: 01: 08: 10: 22, although the first two digits could also be changed to 11 if the second option is followed. The most common formats for creating timecodes are the Longitudinal Time Code (LTC) and the Vertical Interval Time Code (VITC).

Timecodes are an essential tool not only for subtitling, but also for the rest of AVT modes such as dubbing, voice-over and audio description. They allow quick and easy location of scenes and frames, and perfect synchronization between soundtrack and written subtitles. To illustrate the value of timecodes, let us consider the following dialogue exchange:

Example 4.10

001: 00:37:22:19 00:37:26:01

Isn't it all down to genes?
- Don't know.

002: 00:37:26:17 00:37:31:16

If they could control that,
they could create two-footed players.

In the first example, the numbers mean the following:

001	subtitle number
00:37:22:19	in-time
00:37:26:01	out-time

From this information it can be calculated how long the first exchange has lasted, by working out the time that has lapsed between the in and out cues: 3 seconds and 7 frames. There is then a silence of 16 frames until the first speaker starts talking again in subtitle 002. This time, the sentence lasts slightly longer than in the previous example: 4 seconds and 24 frames.

Once we know the period of time the speakers have spoken and the reading speed that can be applied to the subtitles, we can then proceed to assign these exchanges a maximum number of characters that subtitlers will have to respect when writing their translation (see tables 4.2 and 4.3). In most cases, the subtitling program does the calculation automatically, and timecode checkers warn of any inconsistencies in the allocation of times.

Although the results are basically the same, two main approaches can be followed, depending on the parameters applied: words per minute or characters per second. Calculations done in words per minute are based on the English language, and assume that the average length for an English word is five letters.

4.7.8 Reading time

As mentioned previously, two of the basic principles in subtitling dictate that the subtitle has to appear and disappear in synchrony with the original dialogue, and that its exposure time on screen has to be sufficient for the viewer to read the content comfortably. The time a subtitle remains on screen depends therefore on the delivery of the original dialogue and the assumed reading speed of the target viewers. When the original text is uttered at a slow pace the subtitler will not encounter major hurdles to transfer the information to the target language in its entirety. The problem arises when people on screen speak too fast for the target viewer to be able to read it in translation.

It is very frustrating and disconcerting to see how the subtitle disappears from the screen when we have not yet finished reading it, or to end up with a feeling of stress because we have been forced to read too fast and have not had the time to enjoy the images: the typical occasion on which we feel that we have 'read' rather than 'watched' the film.

To address this challenge, the two parameters that can be manipulated are the degree of condensation that we are willing to apply to the original dialogue, and the speed at which the information is to be presented. In this last issue, it is always difficult to generalize and agree on a reading speed that is comfortable for 'all' viewers, since the audience is potentially very heterogeneous in factors like age and educational background.

When deciding the audience's average reading speed it has to be taken into account that not only does the written text of the subtitles have to be read, but viewers have to be given ample time to be able to scan the images and 'read' the photography. Consuming subtitles is not a mere reading exercise, as the message has to be fully assimilated and understood in a very short span of time. As mentioned by Derasse (1987:12), "the reading time cannot be assessed on an absolute basis. It is conditioned by such factors as vocabulary and the presence or absence of action". Indeed, the use of convoluted and tortuous syntax, or obscure vocabulary may well affect viewers' reading speed, by making them lose concentration and slow down. The degree of familiarity that viewers can be assumed to have with the source language and with subtitling are also factors that have an impact on the final decision.

The distribution channel is another consideration to be taken into account and many professionals and companies believe that subtitles ought to be kept on the television screen for longer than in the cinema or the DVD, or allow for fewer lexical units in the same time span. The reason behind this is that the television has to address a wider spectrum of viewers who are usually at home, as opposed to the cinema or the DVD which imply an active approach, in the sense that viewers have made a conscious decision to go and pay to watch a subtitled movie at the theatre or to buy it on DVD. In general terms, the profile of the average cinemagoer is usually perceived as more cultivated than that of the television viewer. Besides, the cinema allows for greater concentration, and the DVD can be paused or rewound if needed. All these arguments have led to the current situation in which subtitling reading speeds tend to be considerably higher for the cinema and the DVD than for the television.

4.7.9 Six-second rule

As we mention above, seconds and frames are the measurement units used when working for the television, and subtitling in this medium has traditionally been based on what is known in the profession as the six-second rule (D'Ydewalle *et al.* 1987; Brondeel 1994). According to this rule, an average viewer can comfortably read in six seconds the text written on two full subtitle lines, when each line contains a maximum of some 37 characters, i.e. a total of 74 characters.

The mathematical reasoning behind the six-second rule is as follows. Two frames allow for a subtitle space. Given that the cinema illusion requires the projection of 24 frames per second (and 25 in television), this means that subtitlers can enjoy 12 subtitling spaces per second. In six seconds, then, the total will be 72, which becomes 74 in companies using 37-character lines. This calculation implies a rather low reading speed of some 140 to 150 words per minute or about 2.5 words per second.

If we apply these parameters, scaling them with the formula used by WinCAPS, we come up with the maximum number of spaces available for any time period, as shown in table 4.2 below:

Table 4.2 Equivalence between seconds/frames and spaces

145 words per minute		**Seconds : frames**	**Spaces**	**Seconds : frames**	**Spaces**
		01:00	16	02:00	29
		01:04	17	02:04	32
		01:08	18	02:08	34
		01:12	20	02:12	36
		01:16	23	02:16	38
		01:20	25	02:20	40
Seconds : frames	**Spaces**	**Seconds : frames**	**Spaces**	**Seconds : frames**	**Spaces**
03:00	44	04:00	58	05:00	70
03:04	46	04:04	60	05:04	71
03:08	48	04:08	62	05:08	72
03:12	50	04:12	64	05:12	73
03:16	52	04:16	65	05:16	73
03:20	54	04:20	67	05:20	74
				06:00	74

With the help of this table, we can now estimate the approximate number of characters that can be used to translate any dialogue. So, if an actor speaks during 4 seconds and 24 frames as in the example above, the subtitler can make use of some 69 spaces to translate the content into the target language.

According to these figures too, and provided the editing of the scene and the delivery of the original allow it, a one-liner of some 7 or 8 words should not stay on screen more than 3 seconds, and a two-liner containing between 14 and 16 words ought to remain on screen a maximum of 6 seconds. One exception to this rule is the subtitling of songs, in which case the subtitle can be left hanging on screen beyond the six seconds if the rhythm requires it.

As mentioned above, these are the approximate values that have been traditionally applied when subtitling for television, but it does not mean that they are set in stone. A degree of flexibility can be observed in the profession with some broadcasters following them more closely than others. In any case, these figures have to be understood as general guidelines that help to maintain consistency in the overall approach but are also open to changes and alterations. In fact, some television stations decide to depart from these guidelines slightly. Arguing that regular exposure to subtitles has the benefit of increasing viewers' reading speed, some broadcasters rely these days on reading speeds of around 160 words per minute, using lines of 39 spaces.

Table 4.3 Equivalence between seconds/frames and spaces

160 words per minute		**Seconds : frames**	**Spaces**	**Seconds : frames**	**Spaces**
		01:00	17	02:00	31
		01:04	18	02:04	34
		01:08	20	02:08	37
		01:12	23	02:12	40
		01:16	26	02:16	42
		01:20	28	02:20	44
Seconds : frames	**Spaces**	**Seconds : frames**	**Spaces**	**Seconds : frames**	**Spaces**
03:00	48	04:00	63	05:00	75
03:04	50	04:04	65	05:04	75
03:08	53	04:08	67	05:08	76
03:12	56	04:12	69	05:12	76
03:16	58	04:16	71	05:16	77
03:20	60	04:20	73	05:20	77
				06:00	78

In some instances, this higher speed comes with a reduction in the maximum exposure time for subtitles, with five seconds becoming the new limit as opposed to the traditional six. According to Becquemont (1996:147), this is the evolution that has taken place in France, where in the 1980s subtitles would stay up to six seconds on screen, and by the 1990s this duration was considered excessive by some professionals and shortened to five or even four and a half.

4.7.10 DVD reading speed

Norms and conventions evolve quickly in subtitling and the advent of the DVD has been one of the major catalysts in the profession. As far as reading speed is concerned, 180 words per minute is increasingly becoming the norm in this new medium, with some companies applying even higher rates.

Unless otherwise indicated in individual exercises, the assumed reading speed to be applied when working on the clips included on the DVD is 180 words per minute, which roughly translate into the following characters per seconds and frames:

Table 4.4 Equivalence between seconds/frames and spaces

180 words per minute		Seconds : frames	Spaces	Seconds : frames	Spaces
		01:00	17	02:00	35
		01:04	20	02:04	37
		01:08	23	02:08	39
		01:12	26	02:12	43
		01:16	28	02:16	45
		01:20	30	02:20	49
Seconds: frames	**Spaces**	**Seconds : frames**	**Spaces**	**Seconds : frames**	**Spaces**
03:00	53	04:00	70	05:00	78
03:04	55	04:04	73	05:04	78
03:08	57	04:08	76	05:08	78
03:12	62	04:12	76	05:12	78
03:16	65	04:16	77	05:16	78
03:20	68	04:20	77	05:20	78
				06:00	78

WinCAPS

The minimum and maximum exposure time of subtitles on screen are 1 and 6 seconds respectively, unless otherwise stated.

The automatic reading speed checks can confirm whether the amount of text used in given time durations is consistent with the reading speed selected.

4.8 Exercises

Dialogue lists

4.8.1 Go to DVD > Chapter 4 > Exercises > Exercise 4.8.1
Here you find a sample of several dialogue lists and scripts from different films and documentaries in different languages.
- ❶ Discuss the similarities and differences between them, especially regarding the layout and the information included in each one of them.
- ❷ Is there any particular one that you prefer?
- ❸ Is there any information that you would add or delete?

4.8.2 Go to DVD > Chapter 4 > Exercises > Exercise 4.8.2
Here you find five pages of the dialogue list that was first sent to the translator of the film *The Broken Hearts Club*.

[Pathway to the key*: DVD > Chapter 4 > Exercises > Exercise 4.8.2 > Key to exercise 4.8.2,* where you can find the revised pages that were finally sent to the translator]

❶ Look for any discrepancies between the information on the footage and subtitle column on the right and the dialogue on the left.

❷ Pay special attention to the different cultural referents mentioned by the characters, and check if the explanations provided about them are correct. If not, make the necessary changes.

4.8.3 Find on Internet the scripts or dialogue lists of the following films and television series:
[Pathway to the key*: DVD > Chapter 4 > Exercises > Exercise 4.8.3 > Key to exercise 4.8.3*]

- ❑ Blue Velvet (David Lynch, 1996)
- ❑ Bowling for Columbine (Michael Moore, 2002)
- ❑ Rich and Famous (George Cukor, 1981)
- ❑ Friends (David Crane and Marta Kauffman, 1994-2004)

4.8.4 You have a page of a very detailed dialogue list from the film *Manhattan Murder Mystery* in Figure 1 above (§4.3), and also on DVD > chapter 4 > Examples > Example 4.2. Using table 4.1 for equivalence between feet/frames and spaces, work out the maximum number of spaces that you could use for the translation of the master titles already spotted in the column on the right-hand side of the page, Spotting List Footages & Titles.
[Pathway to the key: *DVD > Chapter 4 > Exercises > Exercise 4.8.4 > Key to exercise 4.8.4*]

Timecodes

4.8.5 Go to DVD > Chapter 4 > Exercises > Exercise 4.8.5
You will find an exercise that will help you to familiarize yourself with reading timecodes, and with getting a general idea of how much information can be written on screen depending on the duration of the utterances. There is a list of 15 subtitles with their in and out times. First, you need to find out the duration of each subtitle. Once you know the seconds and frames, work out the number of characters that can be used in the translation by using the information contained in table 4.3 (160 words per minute). Remember that there are 25 frames per second.
[Pathway to the key: *DVD > Chapter 4 > Exercises > Exercise 4.8.5 > Key to exercise 4.8.5*]

Subtitling

4.8.6 Go to DVD > Chapter 4 > Exercises > Exercise 4.8.6
Here you find several pages of the dialogue list for the scene *Poker*,

from the film *Manhattan Murder Mystery*. Translate the master titles into your working language, applying the parameters indicated in table 4.1 above.

4.8.7 Go to DVD > Chapter 4 > Exercises > Exercise 4.8.7
Here you find several pages of the dialogue list for the scene *Neighbours*, from the film *Manhattan Murder Mystery*. Translate the master titles into your working language, applying the parameters indicated in table 4.1 above.

4.8.8 Go to DVD > Chapter 4 > Exercises > Exercise 4.8.8
Here you find several pages of the dialogue list for the scene *Kitchen*, from the film *Stuart Little*. Translate the master titles into your working language, applying the parameters indicated in table 4.1 above.

5. Punctuation and Other Conventions

5.0 Preliminary discussion

Watch some 3 or 4 programmes subtitled into one of the languages you know and which have been commercialized by different companies, or broadcast by different television stations.

5.1 In the material you have watched, have you noticed any differences in the formal layout in which subtitles are presented? Which differences? Make a list of some three main areas of disparity that have called your attention.

5.2 What do you think are the reasons for these differences in the presentation of the subtitles? Aesthetic, commercial?

5.3 In the programmes you have watched, is there any one way of presenting the subtitles that you prefer above the rest? Why?

5.4 Would you discard some of the conventions you have seen on screen? Which one/s? Why?

5.5 Would you propose any other conventions to enhance the layout of subtitles? Why?

5.6 In your opinion, what sort of impact could a lack of harmonization have on the industry? And on the audience?

5.7 Do you consider the subtitling done in your country to be of 'good' or 'bad' quality in general? Why?

5.8 Do you believe the quality of subtitling varies according to the means of distribution (cinema, television or DVD)? Or to the language from which the translation is done?

Subtitling can be considered a specific type of discourse presenting a series of lexical, syntactical, and typographical characteristics that help to define it. However, we do not need to watch too many programmes to realize that professional practice is rather heterogeneous and the conventions applied can vary substantially from one audiovisual programme to another, from one company to another, and from one country to another.

This chapter deals with typographical syntax, also known as orthotypography, the field that defines the meaning and correct usage of typographical signs, notably punctuation marks and various elements of layout that are used for separating, highlighting and clarifying written text. Our intention in this chapter is to offer an overview of the main issues that affect the formal presentation of subtitles, and to provide a set of guidelines that enjoy professional recognition and will allow the reader to complete the exercises in this book and on the DVD.

5.1 In search of conventions

Despite the many different ways of tackling subtitles, their formal presentation on screen is not fortuitous and subtitles follow some form of conventions that the translator has to be aware of when subtitling. One of the main problems, however, is the lack of harmonization due, amongst other things, to the fact that many subtitling companies, television broadcasters, and DVD distributors do not always have a stylebook with specific instructions. But the absence of these books does not mean that conventions do not exist. People have grown used to consuming subtitled programmes and, as Cerón (2001:173) mentions, "whenever movie and TV viewers are watching a subtitled film, they are deciphering a whole set of codes. They may be unaware of it, but they will react immediately to a departure from the norm".

Subtitling follows a set of typographical rules that are not radically new, but part and parcel of the grammar of a language, so that when viewers watch a subtitled programme they do not have to learn a whole new body of norms. Subtitles are ultimately an instance of written text and they tend to follow the standard rules that govern punctuation. However, the direct application to subtitling of conventions that have been designed for the delivery of other discursive practices less subject to media limitations can lead to errors.

Contrary to the way we consume a written text on a page, the compulsory segmentation of subtitles gives them a fragmentary nature that complicates their reading. Each subtitle is an isolated unit, disconnected physically from the preceding and the following subtitles. Reading subtitles that appear and disappear at a given speed, that come accompanied by images and by a soundtrack in another language is a more demanding task than reading a novel or the newspaper. It is rather difficult, not to say impossible like in the cinema, to go back and read again what we have not fully understood but has just gone off the screen. The images and the soundtrack are the immediate co-text of the subtitles. The translation has to compete with the original dialogues whilst complementing them at semiotic (§3) and linguistic levels (§6). The job of the subtitlers is to facilitate this reading exercise for the viewers, and in so doing they have to revisit some of the standard punctuation rules and give them a new twist. The conflict between what is considered standard punctuation and what is actually required in subtitling has led to a rather specific usage of certain punctuation marks that we are going to see in this chapter.

We have already considered the space and time limitations that govern the structure and texture of subtitles (§4). In previous pages we have offered some general recommendations that can be followed, in principle, by any language community. The debate is open, though, as to whether these guidelines should actually vary among countries to better suit cultural idiosyncrasies, or whether subtitling could aspire to a certain degree of harmonization at a global level

– at least on the technical side. But then again many issues would need to be properly addressed, not least deciding who should have the responsibility for putting forward those rules and conventions. In any case, the orthotypographical dimension is bound to be the most difficult to standardize since it impinges directly upon the essence of the language. Interferences from other languages have traditionally provoked heated arguments and strong reactions because of their invasive and polluting nature. At European level at least, it is evident that different national subtitling practices share some of the same conventions, and this should be perceived as an added bonus. However, dialogue and consensus rather than imposition should lie at the base of any changes or new proposals.

Globalization made its entrance in the audiovisual translation world thanks to developments like satellite and cable television, and more recently the DVD. Convergence processes seem to be, in fact, the way forward for some players in the search for the Holy Grail in subtitling (Georgakopoulou, forth.), although the new glocalization forces are starting to come to the fore too, demanding that local voices and interests be heard and respected. The collision between these seemingly opposing forces may be seen as responsible for the present state of affairs, where practice is varied and diverse.

5.2 Punctuation conventions

In this climate, attempting to offer a fixed and unequivocal set of guidelines is certainly a daunting task. While some of the rules followed in subtitling today seem to be backed by logic, many are probably applied arbitrarily and may be difficult to justify over others. In addition, the conventions applied in the profession are not homogeneous, and many major subtitling companies maintain their own, unique in-house guides of punctuation rules which they apply as part of their stylebooks and which are sometimes diametrically opposed to the conventions applied by competing companies. Any attempt to draw up a list of conventions that can be applied universally could even be considered conceited and presumptuous, and nothing could be further away from our aim. We try here to focus on generally accepted practice, while identifying current points of contention and keeping an eye on different possibilities. We have taken a close look at the guidelines followed by several companies and have tried to synthesize them to reach conventions with widespread validity in the profession. In some cases it is clearly impossible to assess whether some conventions are 'better' than others. They are simply different. As is nearly always the case in translation, subjectivity plays a big role.

However, in these pages we do 'recommend' some rules over others so that we have a number of common parameters that can be applied when carrying out the activities proposed in the book and on the DVD. If all approaches were to be equally acceptable, we would run the risk of anarchy in the teaching and learning environment. Readers interested in doing the exercises contained in this multimedia project are expected to follow the guidelines favoured in the book. In those cases in which professional practice is not fully harmonized, the convention recommended by the authors of this book is clearly stated in a box with the heading WinCAPS.

Some examples are preceded by the symbol [×], which does not mean that they are 'wrong' in the traditional sense of the word, but rather that they do not comply with the conventions put forward by the authors. The other graphic device used in the examples is a grey line [________________], which indicates the boundary between two different subtitles.

Given the nature of this book, all our examples are in English and follow the conventions that are appropriate for the English language. However, common sense ought to prevail when creating subtitles in other languages, and the basic grammatical conventions used in those languages should be respected. Punctuation rules in other languages can differ greatly to English ones, and subtitlers ought to avoid aping the punctuation used in the English template files or the dialogue lists provided by the clients. Anybody working in subtitling, or translation for that matter, should master their working language and know all its nuances: accents, diacritic signs, writing of figures, etc. Spelling in the target language must be perfect, spotless. Equally important is being fully aware of the requirements of the company, and applying their guidelines consistently.

Great care has been taken to illustrate our points with real examples from a variety of audiovisual programmes and films that have been broadcast on television and commercialized in the cinema, on VHS and DVD. To avoid confusion, some of the examples quoted have been adapted where necessary to follow the presentation rules advocated in this book.

5.2.1 Commas (,) and semi-colons (;)

The comma is possibly the most flexible of all the punctuation marks, and it is impossible to sum up all its uses here. Its role is primarily to show the structure of a sentence, dividing it in sections to make the text more easily understood. Both commas and semi-colons separate parts that are related to each other in the same statement, and their usage signals a slight pause in the reading. They are written immediately after a word, and leave a space before the following word.

The appearance and disappearance of subtitles on screen dictate the reading speed for the viewer and commas must be used in the appropriate way in order to facilitate this process. The use of commas in subtitling does not necessarily fully comply with grammar rules. Commas must be used whenever there is a risk for misunderstanding what the original is saying. There are instances where the comma is contrastive and its use has to follow the prosody of the speech. Note the difference between the following two subtitles:

✓ You know he's bought a car.	✓ You know, he's bought a car.

Words used as vocatives require commas:

✓ Marilyn, come with us to the beach.	✓ Don't do it, dad, or it'll get worse.

Commas are also needed to mark off phrases and clauses inserted in the main sentence, although, whenever possible, these enclosed phrases should be moved to the beginning or the end of the subtitle, as in the example on the right:

✓ His attitude was, in my opinion, very unpleasant.	✓ In my opinion, his attitude was very unpleasant.

Using commas at the end of a subtitle that continues in the next one should be kept to a minimum, since they may be confused with a full stop and lead the viewers to believe that they have reached the syntactical conclusion of the sentence. In some cases, the change of subtitle can be considered a substitute for the comma which may otherwise be necessary in a standard written text. The actual physical disappearance of the written text from the screen imposes a pause in the reading pattern that many consider has the same value as the use of a comma. If no punctuation mark appears at the end of a subtitle line, this automatically signals that the sentence runs on. Given the general agreement that subtitles ought to be semantically and syntactically self-contained, subtitlers have to be cautious when using commas and semi-colons that will tend to lengthen a sentence, and try to finish the idea within the same subtitle projection. Subtitles should not be overburdened with too many punctuation marks that may hinder their reading. In some cases, it may be more appropriate to try and split the original sentence in several smaller ones in the subtitle or subtitles.

The use of the semi-colon is very rare in subtitling and it should be avoided as it is easily confused with the colon.

5.2.2 Full stops (.)

The full stop at the end of a subtitle is an unequivocal indication that the sentence is finished. Its presence on the screen tells the viewers that there is no continuation to the subtitle and sends them back to the image. The full stop follows the word without a space, and the next line or subtitle starts in upper case:

✓	The lady's not coming today. The bottle calls. I'm on my way.
✓	Zaza, your fans are waiting for you, and my dinner is going cold. ——— Please be reasonable.

Some companies do not make use of the full stop at the end of a subtitle, which "creates the most confusing and even irritating situation of all, as it may mean two contradictory things: either that the sequence stops there or that it goes on. Needless to say, this makes subtitles following this style very difficult to read" (Cerón 2001:176).

5.2.3 Colons (:)

A colon is normally used in subtitling with the same functions it has in standard grammar. It signals a small pause and takes the reader's interest forward by announcing or introducing what is to come. Some companies leave a blank space immediately before the colon, arguing that this way it stands out more visibly on screen. This is particular of some languages like French and is also common practice in teletext subtitling. However, our recommendation is that a colon follows the preceding word without any space and leaves one space before the following word.

x	He used to say : "Never say never".	✓	He used to say: "Never say never".

A colon is used to introduce a list, an enumeration, or an explanation. A small letter should follow the use of the colon in these cases:

✓	They took everything: sandals, towels, swimming trunks, and goggles.

A colon is never followed by a capital letter, except when the following word is a proper noun or the first part in the quotation of somebody else's words, as in the following example.

x	And then he said: "she doesn't live here anymore".	✓	And then he said: "She doesn't live here anymore".

The viewer's expectation is to find further information after a colon. So, in the following example the subtitle on the right is more appropriate when the person whistles a sound that does not require subtitling and the viewer is expected to finish the sentence with the information contained in the soundtrack:

×	And she whistled like this:	✓	And she whistled like this…

5.2.4 Parentheses ( ) and brackets [ ]

Round parentheses and square brackets serve to set apart relevant but supplementary information that could be dropped without changing the meaning of the sentence. They are effective only in very restricted contexts and this is one of the main reasons why they are not very common at all in subtitling. Besides, given the constrained nature of subtitling and the need for condensation, explanations and repetitions tend to be the parts of the discourse to disappear first in the translation. Thus, the use of parentheses is very limited, whilst square brackets are virtually never employed in subtitling.

Although parenthesized and bracketed material is rather more distanced from the sentence proper than material within commas, the natural tendency in subtitling is to eliminate the parenthesis and brackets and reconstruct the sentence using commas and, if necessary, adding a connector:

×	What happens in this clip (nearly 30 actors in total) ——— is that there's too much activity going on all the time.	✓	What happens in this clip, with nearly 30 actors in total, ——— is that there's too much activity going on all the time.

In certain cases, like in the example below, parentheses are used in the translation to replicate the parentheses appearing in the written insert that viewers can see on screen. In the opening scene of the film *The Broken Hearts Club*, the viewer can read an insert with the pronunciation and definition of the term 'meanwhile', which in the film is used in a rather cryptic way by some of the characters. In the Spanish subtitle, the first set of parentheses, along with the phonetic pronunciation of the word, are lost. The rest of the information has been transferred as:

Meanwhile (mēn´hwīl) *noun* A red alert amongst friends signalling them to take immediate notice of a passing stranger (usually attractive).

Mientras tanto: *sustantivo*. Señal entre amigos para advertirse que tomen [Meanwhile: substantive. Signal among friends to alert each other to take] ______________ nota de los extraños que pasan (normalmente atractivos) [notice of passing strangers (normally attractive)]

5.2.5 Exclamation marks (!) and question marks (?)

Exclamation marks show in writing something that is normally said loudly or strongly in speech, with a certain prosodic pattern to convey anger, scorn, surprise, happiness, and disgust. They are also used to indicate irony, to underline insults and expletives, and to command. As with the colon, some companies leave a blank space immediately before the exclamation and the question mark, arguing that this way it is easier to see them on screen. In this book, the rule is that both signs are written immediately after the word that precedes them, without any blank space in between, and separated with a space from the word that follows them:

×	Nice car ! Where did you buy it ?	✓	Nice car! Where did you buy it?

It is an error to add a period after an exclamation or question mark, since they already have one:

×	I cannot believe he said it!.	✓	I cannot believe he said it!

When the exclamation or question mark coincides with the end of a subtitle, it tells the viewer that the query is complete and does not carry on to the following projection. Unless clearly rhetorical, the viewer will then expect an answer to the question:

✓	Were you having dinner? Can you reheat it? ______________ Don't worry. I'm not hungry anymore.

As with all emotional punctuation marks, there is a danger of overusing them in subtitling. Subtitles should not be overloaded with unnecessary punctuation that does not bring in any information, is pleonastic and only uses up space. If scattered throughout the subtitles, they lose their force and become tiresome for the viewer. Exclamation marks convey intensity to a written text and need to be used sparsely since part of that intensity may also be retrievable from the soundtrack or the gestures. On some occasions, mainly when translating directly from the dialogue list or from templates, there is a risk of copycatting in the subtitles the same amount of punctuation as in the working documents. The subtitler may fall into the trap of overusing exclamation marks to reflect a nervous or histrionic performance. However, it has to be stressed that subtitles are only a part of the audiovisual programme. Viewers are also watching the images and listening to the original soundtrack and they can apprehend certain emotions directly from the original: surprise, sadness, anger, happiness, and the like. This is why it is recommended not to rely on the script when deciding whether to use exclamation marks and to listen to the actual speech and the way it is delivered orally. It would not be appropriate, therefore, to constantly use exclamation marks to indicate, for instance, that a character is shouting.

The use of several independent exclamation marks within the same subtitle should be avoided if possible:

×	Come on! We're all waiting!	✓	Come on, we're waiting!

Double or multiple exclamation or question marks should be avoided in all cases:

×	Did they really?? I don't believe it!!

Some sentences resemble questions in their structure, but are used as exclamations. They are exclamatory questions and in normal writing can usually end with both a question and an exclamation mark, in this order. However, this approach should be avoided in subtitling. If no answer is put forward, the exclamation mark should take precedence. On the contrary, if the statement receives a reply, then the question mark should be given the priority:

×	Isn't she clever?!	✓	Isn't she clever!
×	Isn't she clever?! - Of course she is.	✓	Isn't she clever? - Of course she is.

Obvious rhetorical questions that do not expect an answer should not end in a question mark, and an exclamation sign is more appropriate:

✓	And I'm supposed to be the oldest!

5.2.6 Dashes (–) and hyphens (-)

Although strictly speaking they are different signs and dashes are slightly longer than hyphens, we shall consider both the same sign for subtitling purposes, stick to the smaller of the two (-), and refer to them as dashes. Their general function is to link compound words or to create new adjectival groups:

✓	They were in quiet, contemplative, in-between-tour, writing-records modes.

A dash to divide words at the end of a line may be common in written language, but it is never used in subtitling since it makes reading more difficult:

×	Those are cops and fire- men from Marseille.	✓	Those are cops and firemen from Marseille.

The parenthetical dash, used as an alternative to brackets, is discouraged in subtitling:

×	What happens in this clip - nearly 30 actors in total -	✓	What happens in this clip, with nearly 30 actors in total,

In subtitling, dashes have a much more specific function than in standard written language and are used to indicate that the text appearing in one subtitle belongs to two different people. Dialogue subtitles always consist of two lines. The first line is reserved for the speaker we hear first in our spotting, and the second line for the second speaker. A way of indicating that this is a dialogue turn is to present each line preceded by a dash, with a space left between the dash and the first letter, although some companies prefer not to leave a space after the dash:

×	- I couldn't move her. - Be firm, for goodness' sake!	×	-I couldn't move her. -Be firm, for goodness' sake!

This convention of using two dashes can be considered traditional and seems to be most frequent in cinema subtitling. A new approach, however, appears to be gaining ground in the profession. In an attempt to rationalize the space available in each line, this convention resorts to the use of a dash in the second line only, leaving a space between the dash and the letter, as in the following example:

✓	I couldn't move her. - Be firm, for goodness' sake!

Although possible, it is considered incorrect to include more than one character on a line. In the following subtitle, either the first statement or the second question need to be moved to the previous or following subtitle, depending on the spotting that we think is most suitable:

×	- What am I going to do? - Put it under the rug. - It's a wall-to-wall carpet.	✓	What am I going to do? ——— Put it under the rug. - It's a wall-to-wall carpet.
		✓	What am I going to do? - Put it under the rug. ——— It's a wall-to-wall carpet.

WinCAPS

To indicate a dialogue exchange, a dash is only used at the beginning of the second line, and a blank space is left between the dash and the first letter.

5.2.7 Triple dots (...)

As mentioned previously, each subtitle appears on screen as an individual and isolated item. To facilitate reading, when a sentence is not finished in one subtitle and needs to be carried over to the next subtitle or subtitles, continuation dots have generally been used as a bridge at the end of the first subtitle and the beginning of the following one to alert the viewer visually of this connexion. This use of the three dots is unique to subtitling. No spaces are left between the dots and the words or punctuation marks that precede or follow them. Note that the word following the dots is written in lower case, as it is a continuation from the previous subtitle:

×	Your friend called. He's taking me to dinner . . . ——— . . . at some Mafia joint next week.	×	Your friend called. He's taking me to dinner... ——— ...at some Mafia joint next week.

To save a space, some companies use three and two dots respectively to indicate sentence continuation:

×	Your friend called. He's taking me to dinner… ———— ..at some Mafia joint next week.

Nonetheless, using the dots with this function seems a rather uneconomical way of conveying information in a professional practice where space is at a premium. The trend nowadays is to act by default. That is, if the subtitle does not have a full stop at the end of the line, then it means that the sentence is not finished and continues into the following subtitle. The absence of the stop, together with the fact that the next subtitle starts with a word in lower case, are sufficient pointers to understand that the second subtitle projection must be the continuation of the previous line:

✓	Your friend called. He's taking me to dinner ———— at some Mafia joint next week.

Even though the recommendation in this book is to avoid the use of the continuation dots between subtitles, there are occasions when using them helps internal cohesion and boosts the viewer's understanding of the written subtitles. This is particularly true in the case of songs, when the spotting of the lyrics can be tricky and the time allocated for the translation of one or two words can be very long. Nino Matas (personal communication), the subtitler into Spanish of *Moulin Rouge*, comments that in the film:

> most of the subtitles are the lyrics of the songs, and the time gap between subtitles was so long that, if we didn't put the continuation dots at the beginning of the subtitles, it was very difficult to relate the content with the previous subtitle. In many cases, the vowel at the end of a verse could still be heard when the following subtitle had already been cued in, and sometimes the subtitle was a single word, or two. Without the continuation dots the word was "isolated" for too long, lacking temporal connexion with the previous and the next subtitles. (our translation)

Another function attached to the three dots is the same as in other written texts, i.e. to indicate prosodic features like pauses and hesitations in the way speakers deliver their utterances. A blank space is always left after the dots but not before, as in the following example:

✓	You mean that... you won't do it?
✓	It... It's not true, is it, Renato?

When a sentence is carried over to the next subtitle because of the presence of a lengthy pause that calls for two different subtitles, suspension dots are then used at the end of the first subtitle but not at the beginning of the next one:

✓	You mean that... ——— you won't do it?

When there is a clear interruption, usually followed by a new sentence that marks a change of direction in the thread of the conversation, a space is also left after the dots and before the next word, which is spelt with a capital letter:

✓	I knew he'd... But it doesn't matter now.

Some authors, like Ivarsson and Carroll (1998:113), recommend not to leave a space after the dots in the case of hesitations and to leave a space when they indicate interruption. However, the convention in this book is to allow always for a space after the dots since both the context and the spelling are clear indicators of the value of the three dots in any particular case.

Triple dots are also used to account for an ellipsis at the beginning of a subtitle, when the start of the original sentence is inaudible or missing in the soundtrack:

✓	...and he never played it again.

They are also used when conveying that a sentence or idea has been left unfinished in the original too:

✓	Come in. - Do you like cho...?

When a character finishes a sentence that has been started by another person:

✓	A cake. On top, I want you to write… - "To Lolo. From Auntie", as always.

When a list of items is deliberately not completed:

✓	She took books, records, DVDs…

And when it is felt absolutely necessary to emphasize a stutter in the diction of some character. In this case, the reduplication of a letter together with the use of the dots is usually sufficient. No spaces are left between the dots and the previous and following letters:

✓	We d…d…don't want to go.

Triple dots are also used to link subtitles that can be perceived as being too far from each other, as in the case of overlapping dialogue, when a second speaker intervenes, interrupting the utterance of the first speaker. In these cases, the continuation should be signalled with the three dots at the end and the beginning of the subtitles affected (example on the left). The dots are not required, however, when the subtitles follow each other (example on the right):

✓	We have been travelling since… - We are all tired here. …the early hours.	✓	We are all tired here. - We have been travelling since the early hours.

Although a certain degree of surprise can be emphasized in written form by using the three dots at the end of a statement and before an exclamation or question mark, their use with this function is not recommended in subtitling:

x	Am I the oldest…?
x	Working so early in the morning…!

It is worth remembering here that subtitles are consumed in conjunction with the image and the soundtrack of the original. Viewers can hear how a particular person is talking, and apprehend whether the delivery is choked, hesitant, or straightforward. Subtitlers should resort to the suspension dots sparingly, and only when there is a good reason for their use. They should use them as a stylistic tool to pepper the subtitles, but avoiding a potential pleonastic or redundant conflict with the original.

The three dots should never be used to transmit to the viewer that the actors are saying a lot more than can actually be fitted in the subtitles.

WinCAPS

> Three dots are never used as continuation dots, unless there is a long pause that forces the cueing of two subtitles. Otherwise, the absence of a full stop at the end of a subtitle is sufficient to indicate that it is unfinished and must therefore be continued in the following subtitle.

5.2.8 Asterisks (*)

The asterisk is mainly used in a written text to signify that a letter or letters have been intentionally omitted from what can be considered by many as an objectionable word. Though a total stranger to all types of subtitling in the past, asterisks seem to be creeping in as an answer to the ever more frequent bleeps that punctuate some television programmes in certain countries. This new prudery that has gripped the media is responsible for the fact that some of Helen Mirren's lines as Detective Superintendent in the British TV series *Prime Suspect* have been bleeped out when broadcast on American public television. The extent of the manipulation goes to rather extreme and unsophisticated lengths, blurring and obscuring the investigator's mouth every time she loses her temper, so that her expletives cannot be lip read either (Baxter 2004). When captioned for the deaf and the hard-of-hearing, these words are edited out completely unless their obliteration has an impact on the syntax of the sentence. If, on the other hand, deletion leads to a grammatical conflict, some broadcasters write the initial letter followed by a set of asterisks, as in the (in)famous case of the play *Shopping and F***ing*, by Mark Ravenhill.

5.2.9 Slashes (/)

This punctuation mark, also called 'stroke' and 'forward slash', has a very concrete and limited use, with many guidelines recommending its avoidance in subtitling. When found in subtitles, it is normally as part of a symbol to abbreviate the message and comply with the medium limitations. Only well known cases in the given language ought to be used, such as c/o (care of), km/hr (kilometres per hour) or 1/3 (one third) in English. They tend to make more of an appearance in films and programmes where scientific jargon is of the essence:

✓	Pulse 88. BP 140/95. It's a bit elevated.

5.2.10 Other symbols

Mathematical symbols of the type + (plus), > (bigger than), and = (equal to) should normally be avoided in subtitling. However, there is a limited number of symbols with which audiences are familiar, depending on the cultures and languages, and that can be used sporadically without much problem:

# number	% percentage, per cent
$ dollars	¢ cents
€ euros	£ (sterling) pounds
¥ yens	& and

In any case, the full expression ought to be the first choice if the limitations allow it, and the symbols only used as a last resort:

✓	Besides, he's got an 80 per cent stake in the club.

Whether references to foreign currencies ought to be translated has to be considered case by case. Within Europe, matters have been greatly simplified, of course, with the introduction of the euro. Before deciding whether pound sterling or dollars have to be translated into, say, euros or rupees, or the other way round, we need to consider how well acquainted our target audience is with the foreign currency and how important it is that the viewer has an exact translation of the amount mentioned or just a rough idea of whether it is very much or very little. The spelling of the currency ought to be checked too, as this can vary substantially from language to language.

Having said all this, normal practice tends to avoid converting foreign currencies into local ones. Whenever possible, the general rule is to use the full name rather than the symbol:

✓	What's his stake? - I'd say 10,000 pesos.

If the limitations do not allow for this, then the symbol can be used. In English, the symbol precedes the amount and is joined to it without a space, whereas in other languages it tends to be placed after the number:

×	After a long conversation we paid them £ 7,000 in cash.	✓	After a long conversation we paid them £7,000 in cash.

If the context is sufficiently clear, the reference to the currency can be deleted in the translation:

Would you like to try our new bacon and egg sandwich for one dollar twenty-nine only?	→	Would you like to try our new sandwich for 1.29 only?

5.2.11 Capital letters

Capital letters should be used in subtitling in exactly the same way as they are used in standard writing, i.e. at the beginning of proper names, and to start a new sentence after a full stop, a question mark or an exclamation mark.

In the past, capital letters were used to render shouting. Nowadays, their use is more limited, and their sporadic presence confers them more expressiveness. Subtitles should never dominate the screen and, therefore, the use of capitalized subtitles should be avoided. Not only do capital letters occupy more space than small letters, they are also more difficult to read. If used, they are always full caps and never small caps. These subtitles do not normally have a full stop at the end of the line. The following instances may call for the use of upper case:

- The title of the film or programme:

SPLENDOUR IN THE GRASS

- Road signs, graffiti, newspaper headlines, banners, writing on clothes, messages on computer monitors, and inserts that are relatively short and written in upper case themselves. The following example is part of the decoration on a celebration cake:

20 YEARS OF HAPPINESS

- When it is felt that the situation needs extra emphasis, such as a big banner in a political march or street demonstration:

ALEJO CRUZ FOR DEPUTY

FAMILIES OF THOSE MISSING FOR POLITICAL REASONS

- ❑ On some occasions, capital and small letters share the subtitle to reflect the different font sizes visible on screen:

TO THEIR LEGITIMATE FAMILIES The grandmothers of the Plaza

5.2.12 Quotation marks or inverted commas ("..."), ("…"), ('…')

When emphasis is needed to foreground certain words or expressions, subtitling is relatively limited in the number of typographical effects that it can accommodate. Although they are technologically possible and easy to produce, effects like bold, underline, or change of colours are virtually never used in traditional, interlingual subtitling. The only two main devices that subtitlers can exploit are quotation marks and italics (§5.3.1).

The use of quotation marks is a rather murky area since they are not deployed in a very systematic way in subtitling and their value can sometimes overlap that of italics, depending on the companies. The mere fact that quotation marks take up more space than italics on occasion inclines the balance in favour of italics, even though this might go against standard practice. All in all, however, quotation marks are more frequent in subtitling than italics, one of the reasons being that italics do not show up sharply on screen and pass unnoticed for some viewers.

Quotation marks are often called inverted commas, or quotes for short. They differ in shape depending on the language, but some, like the Spanish or French ones («…»), are not possible in most subtitling programmes, and English quotes tend to be used instead. Two kinds of quotation marks can be distinguished in English: single ('…') and double ("…"), ("…"). Double quotation marks are the most frequently used in subtitling and, although both types can be found in subtitles, the straight ones seem to be the most common.

Quotation marks are mainly used to indicate direct speech. They also enclose the exact words of a quotation from a particular source, such as a book, a film, or a newspaper. They are used when a person is reading a text out loud, or quoting literally what somebody else has said:

✓	He should tell her: "Get out, you fat cow!"

✓	You have to say to yourself, calmly: "Albin, you broke it".

When the characters of a movie play the role of actors within the film – i.e. they stage a play – the use of the quotation marks is debatable. In these cases, it is obvious that the actors are 'quoting' from a play that they have learnt by heart, but if the play is long there is a risk of burdening the subtitles with far too many quotes. Discretion must be shown in these instances.

If a citation has to continue over several subtitles, different approaches are possible. Following the general convention applied in normal written texts, the inverted commas are used only at the beginning and the end of the quote. However, given that the viewer can only see one subtitle at a time, some companies prefer to use opening and closing quotation marks in every subtitle, arguing that the viewer needs to be reminded that a quote continues:

×	"Sergeant Chirino, terrified, hides behind the well. ——— Moreira escapes over the fence. He fires his pistol at the sergeant ——— who is badly hurt in the left arm."	×	"Sergeant Chirino, terrified, hides behind the well." ——— "Moreira escapes over the fence. He fires his pistol at the sergeant" ——— "who is badly hurt in the left arm."

An intermediate solution, recommended here, consists of opening the quotation marks at the beginning of each subtitle to remind the viewer of the citation, and closing them only in the last subtitle of the series:

✓	"Sergeant Chirino, terrified, hides behind the well. ——— "Moreira escapes over the fence. He fires his pistol at the sergeant ——— "who is badly hurt in the left arm."

There is, however, one exception to this rule. When the entire quote spans two subtitles only, it is recommended, for aesthetic reasons, that the inverted commas be used at the beginning and the end of the quote, as in the example below:

✗	"Hotel needs holiday reps. ——— "Smart appearance, imagination and language skills required."	✓	"Hotel needs holiday reps. ——— Smart appearance, imagination and language skills required."

When the citation encompasses the whole subtitle(s), and a full stop or triple dots are used at the end of the last subtitle, because of a pause or hesitation, the punctuation marks are considered to be part of the actual quote and should be inserted before closing the quotation marks, as in the following example:

✓	"But there's no harm done. It's not the end of the world."

However, when the quotation only runs for part of the subtitle, the full stop should go outside the inverted commas:

✓	And then he said: "It was her fault".

Note, though, that exclamation and question marks at the end of a subtitle behave differently:

✓	And then he shouted. "Leave me alone!"

A quotation can be separated from the speaker by a colon, as in the previous examples, or by a comma when the order is reversed, although this structure is discouraged:

✓	"It was her fault", he said.

Quotation marks within quotations should be avoided if at all possible, since they are hard to distinguish on the screen. Where necessary, single inverted commas should be used:

✓	"The last words uttered by Berthier were: 'Don't forget my little gift'."

Quotation marks can be also used to fulfil several other functions which can be covered by italics as well, but quotes seem to be favoured on the whole by companies. For example, inverted commas indicate that a word or expression is being used with a metalinguistic value, i.e. to speak about language itself:

✓	Then an adverbial, "sedjem-en-ef".

Quotation marks are used to denote that we are dealing with words or expressions that have been made up by the actors, are grammatically or phonetically incorrect, are in the process of being coined, or belong to a very marginal register. With colloquialisms, subtitlers have to decide how likely they are to be accepted and understood by the target audience. If the term is relatively frequent in daily speech, then the inverted commas may not be necessary:

✓	He says "Geiby" instead of Gaby.
✓	Mlle Corre, in the leader's speech replace the word "scum" with "lout".

Quotation marks are sometimes used with names of restaurants, cinemas, hotels, wines and other brand names that are left in the original language in the subtitles – even though they may not be widely known by the viewers – because the context elucidates their nature. This translation strategy contributes to creating a foreign atmosphere, reinforcing the feeling of otherness in the target text. It is difficult to give a set of straightforward rules on how to act in these cases but subtitlers are advised to weigh up the context and to resort to inverted commas when attempting to add special emphasis, to refer to something that can actually be seen on screen, or to dispel any possible confusion or misunderstanding:

✓	Are you taking her to "Vincent's"?
✓	I always liked my "Bentley".

However, inverted commas are not normally used with proper names, names of cities or other places, celebrations and events that are sufficiently well known by the target public, or clear in the programme, and do not pose any comprehension problem:

✓	A visit to the Sagrada Familia should do the trick.

✓	Where are you going? - To confess. __________ There are confessors in Albacete!

Lexical items that refer to concepts or ideas that are somehow special and should not be taken at face value also call for quotes. Words and expressions under this category tend to be pronounced with special intonation or prosodic emphasis:

✓	You can disguise it all you want under your "Patrick's good advice".
✓	This kind of "right" is gonna put us in the toilet.
✓	By saying your "son" you mean Enrique, don't you?

Quotation marks are also used to stress the value of nicknames, to underline plays on words, or to signal that a word or expression is being used ironically:

✓	At least I don't call him "fruitcake" like the other kids.
✓	You do the whole "hip, dope-smoking homo" act __________ and now it's my fault?

The diegetic value of short dialogue exchanges, conversations, and whole interventions in a different language has to be weighed up before proceeding to translate (§3.3.2). When somebody speaks a second language – say Spanish or French – in an English spoken film, these interventions are not normally subtitled when translating for the Hispanic and Francophone markets, since they coincide with the language spoken by the target audience and can therefore be understood directly from the original soundtrack. However, when these exchanges or words are in a third language, other than the main one spoken in the film and the one spoken by the viewers – e.g. the same film for a Croatian audience – a decision has to be made. The general rule of thumb is to follow the same strategy that has been implemented in the original thus respecting the director's wishes. If the final decision is to translate the dialogue, some professionals recommend enclosing them within inverted commas (Ivarsson and Carroll, 1998:114-115), but current practice seems to favour the use of italics.

5.3 Other conventions

In this section, we move on to discuss some of the other typographical conventions that can also be found in subtitling.

5.3.1 Italics

Italics, which incidentally are not available in teletext technology and cannot be used in captioning or subtitling for the deaf and the hard-of-hearing, have a wide variety of uses in interlingual subtitling. In addition to quotation marks, they are the other major typographical effect available to the subtitler to call attention to certain elements of the text. This printing type slops to the right (*italics*) and has the great advantage of putting emphasis on a word or phrase in a subtitle without taking up any extra space. The downside is that it does not stand out prominently on a television or cinema screen, and can sometimes be hard to distinguish from the rest of the text.

One of the innovations of subtitling discourse is the use that it makes of italics to serve new purposes. Thus, one of italics' unique functions in subtitling is to account for voices and cries that can be heard in the distance, for utterances spoken by characters that are off-screen and sound far away, and for speech that is heard at the other side of a closed door, for instance. In short, they account for human voices originating from a source that is not visible on-screen.

Italics are also used to represent voices that can be heard through a machine, whether on or off screen: voices heard from the other end of a door interphone, and voices coming from a radio, a television set, a computer, or a loudspeaker, as in the following example where a voice from a TV set can be heard in the room:

✓	*It is too bad that* *some news media abuse their rights.*

However, italics are not used if the speaker is not in shot but shares the same space or is physically near the rest of actors on-screen, i.e. in the same room, or just outside an open door or a window.

Italics are also used to translate the interventions of a person who is at the other end of the telephone line, whom the viewer can hear but not see at any point during the conversation. If, however, the editing of the film resorts to the typical shot-reverse shot – i.e. the camera moving alternatively from one speaker to the other – in such a way that the viewer has the opportunity of seeing both actors, it is advisable not to italicize any of the subtitles. It can be confusing, and arbitrary to some extent, to see how the utterances of the two actors keep changing their printing type and italics are assigned to both of the characters. The confusion is accentuated when the shot changes are fast and some of the subtitles have to stay on-screen despite the cuts.

Italics are also useful to represent voices from within, e.g. thoughts, voices that are in a character's mind, interior monologues, voices that are heard in dreams, and the like. In all these cases, the voices are usually off-screen.

Another use attached to italics is to particularize a word or phrase by stressing it. An example can be found in Woody Allen's film *Manhattan Murder Mystery*. The dialogue list gives the express instruction to the subtitler to write the noun *Waldron* in italics. This indication is not superfluous since the term plays an important part in the development of the plot and the resolution of the mystery. The intention behind it is to render the term unfathomable and wrap it in secrecy. The total lack of context leads the protagonist to believe that it must be somebody's name, only to discover later in the film that it is in fact the name of a hotel. After the discovery, the noun is never again italicized.

When dealing with lexical borrowings and neologisms from other languages the profession seems to be divided as to whether to use inverted commas or italics. Our recommendation is to transcribe single foreign words or expressions in italics if they are considered not to be fully integrated in the vocabulary of the target audience:

✓	And you're a *jamona.*

Or when it is a clear attempt at adding flavour to the translation:

✓	*Oh là là!* The white master is in a bad mood!

But no italics are called for when the term is well known and has been adopted by the target community, or when it occurs very often in the same programme:

✓	And don't bring croissants tomorrow.

✓	My father was a connoisseur. He loved art and bric-a-brac.

Literary and bibliographical references; titles of publications, and books; as well as titles of films, other audiovisual programmes, shows, operas, songs, and names of record albums also go in italics:

✓	Who's that? - Albert, from the *Little House.*
✓	I want Renato to take you through *The Queen of Broadway.*
✓	*You're So Vain,* that's Carly Simon.

However, italics should not be used for names of pop groups, sports teams, restaurants, companies, drinks, or food that are reasonably well known by the target community:

✓	U2 recorded it a few years ago.
✓	They've been eating at McDonalds.

A special case requiring the use of italics is when another foreign language, unfamiliar to the target audience, can be heard in the film or programme. If the decision is to translate this information into the target language, all the exchanges in the more marginal language in the film ought to be italicized. The Australian film *Head On* stars a young man caught between his Greek heritage and the world of music, sex and drugs in the city of Melbourne. Although English is the main language throughout the film, Greek exchanges are also very frequent in his conversations with members of his family. It is obvious that Greek has been subtitled in the original film for the Australian audiences and the strategy followed in the Spanish subtitled version has been to translate and italicize all conversations conducted in Greek and to use plain letters for the translation of the English dialogue.

Chanting by crowds taking part in street demonstrations and parties is also translated using italics, as in the following slogans from the film *The Official Story*:

✓	*It will end. It will end.* *This habit of killing.*
✓	*Let them tell us where* *those kidnapped babies are!*

When a word or expression needs to be highlighted with italics but they are already being used in the same sentence, inverted commas can be used for the emphasis. The following subtitle is the translation of an utterance that can be heard from a television set in the scene:

✓	*Friends, stay with us* *for more surprises on "People Today".*

Italics are also favoured by most companies – and this is the use we also recommend in this book – in the following instances:

- ❑ To indicate that the translation belongs to an off-screen narrator's voice, unless this is the only voice heard in the programme, as may be the case with film documentaries.
- ❑ To translate the lyrics of songs.
- ❑ To translate certain written messages, letters and inserts appearing on the programme or film (§5.3.1.2). This usage competes, however, with upper case (§5.2.11). If the text on the screen is short and written in big letters, the subtitles tend to go in capital letters, not italics. If, on the contrary, the size of the letters is small and the text relatively long, italics are used in the subtitles.

5.3.1.1 Songs

As far as presentation on screen is concerned, several strategies are applied when dealing with songs. In countries like Portugal, for instance, the traditional approach consists of using the same font as in the rest of subtitles, and displacing the text to the left-hand side of the screen. But most languages prefer to italicize the content of the subtitles and put them in the same place in the screen as the other subtitles.

In the case of some companies, song subtitles are punctuated following the conventions of poetry: each line starts with a capital letter and no full stops are used at the end of a line. However, our recommendation is to apply the same punctuation rules as in the rest of subtitles, since we believe that this way the task of reading the text is facilitated. All songs should go in italics:

✗		✓	
	A kiss may be grand *But it won't pay the rental*		*A kiss may be grand* *but it won't pay the rental*
	On your humble flat *Or help you feed your pussycat*		*on your humble flat,* *or help you feed your pussycat.*
	Men grow cold *As girls grow old*		*Men grow cold* *as girls grow old.*
	And we all lose our charms in the end		*And we all lose our charms in the end.*
	But square cut or pear-shaped *These rocks don't lose their shape*		*But square cut or pear-shaped,* *these rocks don't lose their shape.*
	Diamonds are a girl's best friend		*Diamonds are a girl's best friend.*

Songs usually permit a lot more flexibility in the presentation of subtitles than dialogue exchanges. Depending on the rhythm and the lyrics, the cueing of some songs can be problematic and have an impact on the actual translation. Sometimes, subtitles will have to be left on screen a bit longer than strictly necessary. In other cases, the syntax of the target text might have to be manipulated if we do not want to give information away too soon. In the previous example, the content and syntax of the last line of the song are relatively simple and should not give rise to particular problems when translated into other languages, like Spanish:

✓	
	Un diamante es *el mejor amigo de la mujer.* *[A diamond is* *the best friend of the woman.]*

What at first glance might look relatively straightforward may become complicated on screen. In the film *Moulin Rouge* the Spanish translation above is used whenever Nicole Kidman sings the refrain at a normal pace. However, at the very end of the song she slows down and creates long pauses in the delivery of this line. There is also the intervention of another character whilst she is still singing. In an attempt to keep synchrony with the soundtrack, the end result is the spotting of four subtitles instead of one, the use of triple dots to link the subtitles, and a target text with rather twisted syntax, verging on ungrammaticality:

✓	*Un diamante...* *[A diamond...]* ——— *...es, de la mujer,...* *[...is, of the woman,...]* ——— *....el mejor...* *[...the best...]* ——— *...amigo.* *[...friend.]*

5.3.1.2 Letters and written documents

The translation of text from letters and other written documents depends on the way they are presented in the programme. Sometimes, the letter can be seen on screen and it is up to the viewer to read it. Another cinema strategy is to make the actor read the letter out loud so that the viewer hears the content.

When the original letter or note has to be read from the screen, the subtitles ought to go in normal font, i.e. no italics. If appropriate, the translation should imitate the original in terms of size. Long letters will call for lower case, but a ransom letter with little text on it and all in capitals can be rendered in a subtitle in upper case:

✓	HE'LL BE KILLED

In the case of letters that viewers do not have to read since the information is conveyed aurally in the soundtrack, there are several possibilities. Adapting the recommendations put forward by Ivarsson and Carroll (1998:119), we advise writing the content of the subtitles in inverted commas, since this can be considered a case of citation. Only when the text is too long can the quotation marks be dispensed with. As for the font style to be used, it should be normal font in the following instances:

- ❑ When the person writing the letter repeats the content out loud whilst writing it.
- ❑ When the fictional writer reads the content of the letter aloud once it has been written.
- ❑ When the addressee reads the letter out loud.

Italics are called for when:

- ❑ The voice of the person writing the letter can be heard in off, as an interior monologue, whilst writing the actual text.

- We hear the voice in off of the person who has written the letter, whilst we see the addressee reading it on screen.
- We see the addressee on screen reading the text whilst we hear his/her voice in off, as an interior monologue.

5.3.2 Colours

One of the main differences between interlingual and intralingual subtitles is their different approach to the use of colours. Most teletext subtitling for the deaf and hard-of-hearing tends to rely on the use of different colours to identify the various characters that take part in the programme and to add emphasis to certain words and expressions. Given that hearing viewers can retrieve this information effortlessly from the original soundtrack, the use of polychrome features has been deemed irrelevant in interlingual subtitling, in which historically just one colour has been used throughout the entire programme. Besides, colours can be perceived as calling undue attention to the subtitles and detracting from the photography.

The two main colours used in our profession are white and yellow. In cinema, subtitles are mostly white simply because they have been laser engraved on the celluloid and they are an integral part of the film copy. Thus, when they are projected on a big white screen we see them white. If the screen were pink, we would see them pink. On some occasions, they are yellow, which means that the subtitles are not engraved on the copy of the film but electronically projected onto it so as not to damage the copy. Electronic subtitling allows for a wide spectrum of colours in which subtitles can be beamed. However, only yellow and white are normally used.

Unless the copy is the same as the one released for the cinema, productions broadcast on television or distributed on video, DVD or Internet usually resort to subtitles that are projected onto the programme rather than engraved. The colour can then be chosen, and once again only yellow and white are employed.

No alternation of colours is allowed in interlingual subtitling for hearers, and once a colour has been selected, be it yellow or white, it is maintained during the whole programme.

5.3.3 Abbreviations

Abbreviation is a general term used to refer to a shortened form of a word or phrase. It may be made up of one or several letters and is normally used because its occupies less space than the word or phrase it replaces. There are four main ways of shortening a word in English, giving us four different types of abbreviations: clippings, acronyms, contractions, and blends.

1) ***Clippings*** or ***shortenings***: omitting syllables, as in 'fab' (fabulous), 'mo' (moment), 'flu' (influenza), 'plane' (aeroplane), and 'celeb' (celebrity). They behave like proper words and are written in lower case, unless they start a sentence or follow a full stop, in which case they take upper case. When using them in subtitling, translators have to be aware that they are usually quite informal and add a colloquial tang to the speech. Using them in a translation into English simply because they are shorter than the actual word or phrase can turn out to be an erroneous strategy, bringing in undesired nuances to the register of the translation. When translating them from English into other languages, the same considerations should be borne in mind.

2) ***Acronyms***: can be formed in various ways. The most common is using the first letter of each word, as in 'FBI', 'BBC', 'UNESCO', and 'EU'. They are written without full stops between the letters. If real, some of these abbreviations stand for organizations and bodies that tend to have an equivalent in the rest of languages, and are thus easy to translate. If made up for the film or programme, they can be used as in the original:

×	I'll try to get my old job back at E.U.R.E.S.C.O., I suppose.	✓	I'll try to get my old job back At EURESCO, I suppose.

There is a rather new breed of acronyms in English that are growing fast and making it to everyday language: 'pto' (please turn over), 'fyi/FYI' (for your information), 'ott/OTT' (over the top), or 'btw' (by the way). As before, subtitlers into English need to carefully assess whether the register of the original dialogue justifies the use of these abbreviations, and should avoid using them simply because they save space.

The English language is very prone to using and creating new words like acronyms and clippings, which can become a source of major challenges for subtitlers working into other languages where this linguistic phenomenon is not so widespread. Given the media limitations we encounter in subtitling, the translation of 'pro' (professional), 'ad' (advertisement), 'asap/ASAP' (as soon as possible), and 'blt/BLT' (sandwich of bacon, lettuce and tomato) can prove very problematic when the target language cannot clip the words in the same way and needs to spell them out in the subtitles.

Acronyms are also created by using the initial letters of words that become words in their own right, as in 'radar' (RAdio Detection And Ranging), 'laser' (Light Amplification by Stimulated Emission of Radiation) or 'aids' (Acquired Immune Deficiency Syndrome). When they are fully lexicalized they tend to be written in lower case.

3) ***Contractions***: leaving part of the word out, usually the middle, as in 'Dr', 'Mlle', or 'km'.

4) ***Blends***: joining parts of two words together to become a new word, as in 'Interpol' (International Police), 'Eurovision' (European Television) or 'heliport' (helicopter + airport). These are only rarely written in all capitals:

×	Your husband was tailed by EUROPOL.	✓	Your husband was tailed by Europol.

The rules governing the punctuation of abbreviations vary enormously from language to language and subtitlers ought to be aware of the rules that apply in their own languages. In English, full stops have been used traditionally to shorten words, names and places. The purpose of the full stop is to show that a group of letters is other than a normal word. As abbreviations become more and more familiar, so it becomes more and more usual to omit the full stops. They are being abandoned in favour of speed, economy and cleaner typography. We recommend writing abbreviations without full stops or spaces between letters:

×	I don't give a damn about your M P.	✓	I don't give a damn about your MP.
×	I am H.I.V. positive. It's different. - So what?	✓	I am HIV positive. It's different. - So what?
×	My mom's not even 50 and she's right out of W.W.I.	✓	My mom's not even 50 and she's right out of WWI.

Abbreviations of the type 'km' (kilometre/s), 'cm' (centimetre/s), 'kg' (kilogram/s), and 'm' (million/s) should be used sparingly and priority given to the full spelling of the nouns. If used, they are always written immediately after the numbers, and separated by a space:

×	After having driven 70km, we decided to go back home.	✓	After having driven 70·km, we decided to go back home.

The use of abbreviations in subtitles is perfectly legitimate as long as they are widely known by the target audience or do not cause any confusion. However, it is recommended not to use them very frequently and to avoid them whenever possible, unless the nature of the programme or film calls for them, as in documentaries or factual programmes.

As for their translation, subtitlers, like any other translators, must be careful when transferring abbreviations to their working language since sometimes they remain the same, but in other cases they change radically or can be confused with other abbreviations better known in the target language. In some cases the abbreviation of a similar institution in the target culture can be used in the translation, but in other instances the best strategy is to spell out the abbreviation or to replace it with an explanation:

Police! Civic authorities! ASPCA! ASAP! (ASPCA: American Society for the Prevention of Cruelty to Animals)	→	Police! Protection civile! SPA! Vite! [Police! Civic Protection! SPA! Quick!] (SPA: Société Protectrice des Animaux)
I called EMS and they got here as soon as they could, but they were too late. (EMS: Emergency Medical Services)	→	He llamado a urgencias, pero han llegado tarde. [I've called emergencies but they have arrived late]

Special attention must be paid to the literal calque of abbreviations that might not be common in the target language or should be written differently, like OK, or the following example in Spanish:

Do you watch TV every day? - I don't watch TV!			
×	¿Ves la TV todos los días? - ¡Yo no veo la TV! [Do you watch the TV every day? - I don't watch the TV!]	✓	¿Ves la tele todos los días? - Yo no veo la tele. [Do you watch the telly every day? - I don't watch the telly.]

When a rather obscure or made-up abbreviation has an important role in the programme or film and recurs with certain frequency, one of the possible strategies, if the limitations allow it, is to present the actual abbreviation accompanied by a translation explaining it the first time it appears. After that, the abbreviation can be used in its original form every time it appears in the subtitles.

Very informal abbreviations of the type being used in chats and mobile phone text messaging such as 'b4' (before), 'c u l8r' (see you later), or '2nite' (tonight) are not acceptable in current subtitling. They can be seen as the new textual type for the new millennium, in a society immersed in the veneration of audiovisual culture. Strong similarities can be found between these new forms of communication and subtitling. Messages are constrained by space limitations, condensed to convey the essence of the information, and consumed via screens. Very few other instances illustrate better the phenomenon of language economy discussed by linguists. It can be argued that these points of contact could lead in the (not so distant) future to a process of hybridization in which some of the features could migrate to subtitles. But only time will tell.

5.3.4 Numbers

A general stylistic rule, applicable to other languages and text types, recommends that whenever possible a subtitle or new sentence should not start with a figure written in digits.

5.3.4.1 Cardinals

Provided there is space available, the general rule is that cardinal numbers up to ten (included) are normally written in letters. From eleven onwards they are written in digits.

×	There are only 2 entrances to the house.	✓	There are only two entrances to the house.
×	It's almost twenty years Since you saw the boy.	✓	It's almost 20 years since you saw the boy.

Exceptions to this rule are the numbers of houses, flats, apartments and hotel rooms, always written in digits, as well as the days of the month in some languages:

×	Don't go to apartment eight it's always full of strange people.	✓	Don't go to apartment 8 it's always full of strange people.

Numbers up to ten are also presented as digits if they are next to abbreviated units of weight and measurement. In these instances, the symbol is written after the figure with a space:

×	They were caught in the cinema with seven kg of drugs.	✓	They were caught in the cinema with 7 kg of drugs.

But when weights and measures are not abbreviated, the numbers should be in letters:

×	She ran 3 kilometres until the nearest beach.	✓	She ran three kilometres until the nearest beach.

The usual division of figures runs in groups of three starting to count from the right. Some authors like Ivarsson and Carroll (1998:119) discourage the use of commas or periods between the digits and prefer to leave a blank space. However, our recommendation is to write these long numbers with a comma in English, since this helps reading them on screen. Please note that this practice varies a lot and most languages use a full stop in this position:

×	That dog was worth at least 20 000 pesos.	✓	That dog was worth at least 20,000 pesos.
×	I guess there must be as many as 5 000 people.	✓	I guess there must be as many as 5,000 people.

When dealing with years, commas are not normally used and no blank space is left:

×	I'll show you one from 1,933.	✓	I'll show you one from 1933.
×	I'll show you one from 1 933.		

Decimals are always written in digits, with a period separating both parts in English:

×	She scored six point five in the text.		
×	She scored 6,5 in the test.	✓	She scored 6.5 in the test.
×	She scored 6'5 in the test.		
×	She scored 6 5 in the test.		

If possible, avoid writing all the digits of very large figures like millions and billions, since lots of numbers in the same line make it difficult to read. It is better to write a smaller number followed by the noun instead. When appropriate, the number can be rounded up or down:

×	3,000,000 inhabitants.	✓	Three million inhabitants.
×	19,715,900 inhabitants.	✓	19.7 million inhabitants.

Due care has to be taken with the word 'billion'. A billion in British English used to mean a million million (1,000,000,000,000) but these days it refers to a thousand million (1,000,000,000). In many other languages, the old value is still in place for the word 'billion':

ST: Four and a half million, I…I…I can understand, but four and a half billion?			
×	Si fueran 4,5 millones lo entendería, pero, ¿4,5 billones? [If there were 4,5 millions I would understand it, but, 4,5 billion?]	✓	Si fueran 4,5 millones lo entendería, pero, ¿4,500 millones? [If there were 4,5 millions I would understand it, but, 4,500 millions?]

Approximate quantities, along with set phrases or idioms involving figures, are usually written in letters:

×	It won't work in 1,000,000 years.	✓	It won't work in a million years.

5.3.4.2 Ordinals

There are no strict rules as to how to present ordinal numbers on the screen. Given their length, it is most common to find them abbreviated and written in digits. Depending on the subtitling programme, the English 'st', 'nd' or 'th' endings may appear in normal font or superscript, although the first option is more common:

✓	On our twentieth, I bought her some lovely handkerchiefs.	✓	On our 20th, I bought her some lovely handkerchiefs.
		✓	On our 20th, I bought her some lovely handkerchiefs.

The ordinal ending is normally omitted when dealing with dates:

×	It appeared in *La Gaceta*, Buenos Aires, June 5th, 1880.	✓	It appeared in *La Gaceta*, Buenos Aires, June 5, 1880.

When more than one number appears in the same subtitle, there is a tendency to write only one of them in digits:

×	It's only the 2nd time in 20 years.	✓	It's only the second time in 20 years.

If the enumeration is random, normally used with a hyperbolic function, ordinal numbers tend to be written with letters:

×	I'll tell you for the 30th time.	✓	I'll tell you for the thirtieth time.

Overall, there is a high degree of flexibility when dealing with numbers in subtitling. If the limitations are severe and the text of the subtitle cannot be condensed or reduced any more without compromising the content, then numbers below ten can be written in digits:

x	They'll pay five million for the two cars.	✓	They'll pay 5 million for the 2 cars.

Subtitlers have to be careful when dealing with numbers, since these strategies imply a certain manipulation of the reading speed. They condense the text physically but not semantically. The actual reading of a number – say 739 – takes longer than the three spaces used on screen might lead us to believe, and the use of digits forces viewers to read faster. In isolated subtitles the problem does not arise, but if many figures appear in successive subtitles it may become an issue. One way of facilitating the reading process is to allow for the subtitles to stay a bit longer on screen, but without going beyond the six seconds.

5.3.4.3 Time

When dealing with the time, whether using the 12 or the 24-hour system, the numbers are separated with a colon or a period, but never with a comma or a blank space. The use of the colon is becoming more common because it replicates more closely the way digital clocks show the hour.

x	Where was he at 7'30?	✓	Where was he at 7:30?
x	Where was he at 7,30?	✓	Where was he at 7.30?
x	Where was he at 7 30?		

This presentation of the time is not unique to English, and is spreading to other languages that have traditionally used a comma in these cases, but the conventions applied in the target language must be respected. Due care also has to be taken with the use of the abbreviations 'am' and 'pm' since they may not be appropriate in some languages. If used, a space is left between the number and the abbreviation.

5.3.4.4 Measurements and weights

Although we may come across subtitles like the one below, the tendency nowadays when subtitling into English is that metric measurement units are not converted into the imperial system:

Pesaba 4 kilos al nacer, ¿no es increíble? [He weighed four kilos at birth, isn't it unbelievable?]	→	He weighed 9 pounds at birth!

However, when translating from English into other languages the normal practice is to convert imperial measurements into metric for the benefit of the target audience. If viewers are not used to references such as 'she's six foot ten', they do not even know whether the woman in question is tall or short, which is the point the speaker is making. Someone who is used to the metric system will know the woman is very tall when they read she is 'about two metres'. The typical conversions are feet and inches into meters and centimetres for length, pounds and stones to grams and kilograms for weight, and Fahrenheit to Celsius for temperature.

Whether the exact translation with digits needs to be given or not depends on the context. When the intention of the original is to give a general idea of the physical features of people, or to indicate broadly the distance that separates two cities, it is perfectly legitimate to offer an approximation and round the figure obtained after the conversion up or down to the nearest full number. In a science programme an exact translation may be required. Let us take a look at the following English statement:

I got an APB on a Caucasian male. Brown hair and eyes. 160 pounds, 5 feet 11.

Whilst the unit used to inform us about the weight of the person is perfectly clear, i.e. pounds, the height may not be so. More knowledge of the culture is needed to know that the element missing here is the elliptical 'inches' that goes with the number 11. Once all the information is clear, and with the help of one of the many conversion calculators available on the net (http://convert.french-property.co.uk), we discover that the man weighs 72.576 kilograms and is 1.8034 meters tall. However, these figures are far too precise for what is needed in this particular context, and of the following two subtitles, the one on the right made it to the screen in Spanish:

x	He pillado a un hombre blanco. Pelo y ojos castaños. 72,576 kg, 1,8034 m. [I have caught a white man. Hair and eyes brown.72,576 kg, 1,8034 m.]	✓	He pillado a un hombre blanco. Pelo y ojos castaños. 70 kg, 1,80 m. [I have caught a white man. Hair and eyes brown. 70 kg, 1,80 m.]

The use of fractions is not very common in subtitling and is only justified when the topic and nature of the programme make them appropriate, e.g. a documentary on maths or a science-fiction film. In normal speech, the fractions should be written in full, and only abbreviated to digits in exceptional cases, when the media constraints are very strict. Depending on the subtitling program used, fractions (3/4) might be replaced by fraction characters (¾):

×	Only 1/3 of the population managed to escape the fire.	✓	Only a third of the population managed to escape the fire.

5.4 A glimpse of the future?

We are living a period characterized by an extraordinarily dynamic and creative activity in the world of subtitling in general, and DVD subtitling in particular (Díaz Cintas, forthcoming). With the arrival of DVD it is clear that not only is professional practice changing but the very essence of subtitling and the conventions applied are also in flux. The reasons are manifold. Of the various AVT modes, subtitling has experienced the fastest and greatest growth in the market and it will continue to do so for the foreseeable future. The development and spread of digital technology, fuelled by our society's cult of the image, have accelerated the flow and exchange of audiovisual materials, and subtitling is rapidly becoming the preferred AVT mode on the Internet. This exponential growth has allowed for the emergence of new voices – voices of dissent that subvert conventions traditionally considered standard in the delivery of subtitles.

The overwhelmingly upheld idea that the best subtitles are those that are not noticed by viewers is certainly partly responsible for this state of affairs. Subtitles are text added *a posteriori* and were never intended to be an integral part of the artwork. They are not an artistic creation but a necessary evil (Marleau 1982) that we have to cope with in order to gain access to programmes in other languages. The less attention they call to themselves, the less we notice them, and therefore the better they are.

The number of typographical devices available to the interlingual subtitler has traditionally been very limited, with underline, bold, square brackets, and colours for instance, out of the question. There has always been a certain fear of venturing into daring strategies that would be at odds with tradition. Interlingual subtitling remains, on the whole, conservative in essence, and is governed by a relatively small range of conventions, as opposed to other similar discursive practices like SDH and fansubs.

However, new conventions that diverge acutely from what has been considered standard practice in interlingual subtitling up until now have started to crop up in subtitled programmes commercialized on DVD.

When two actors speak in the same subtitle, new practice departs from tradition and aesthetics to adopt criteria more concerned with lexical density: the priority is to include as much information as possible in the subtitle, and so the dialogue uttered by the second speaker immediately follows the first speaker, starting on the very same line and preceded by a dash:

x	Do I know you? - Colonel Jack O'Neil, from General West's office.

Another convention being subverted is the number of speakers encountered in the same subtitle. Tradition has dictated that a maximum of two actors and two turn-takings share the same subtitle. A new subtitle needs to be cued in when a third speaker, or speech turn, is to be translated. Following a pattern similar to the one seen above, we also find instances in which three turn-takings are fitted into one subtitle in order to make the most of the space and time available:

x	How'd he get like that? - His kid accidentally shot himself. - Jesus.

The number of lines available for writing subtitles is also being challenged, and three-liners are starting to appear.

Some films like the Japanese *Zatoichi's Pilgrimage* and *Baby Cart in the Land of Demons* make an unprecedented use of colours when subtitled into English, resorting to a palette of five different colours throughout the same film: white, yellow, green, blue, and red.

According to tradition, when two speakers appear in the same subtitle, each one is allocated a line and both appear at the same time on the screen. SDH also makes sporadic use of what is known as cumulative subtitles (BBC 1998:9) or 'add-ons' to allow two – exceptionally three – turns to appear in the same subtitle but not at the very same time. The first speaker is cued alone, and the subtitle is written in yellow:

x	Hey, Hokuro... shield me!

The second part of the text appears in synch with the second speaker's turn and is added to the first part, while this first utterance remains on screen. The colour of this second line is green:

x	Hey, Hokuro... shield me! Yes, sis!

All parts leave the screen at the same time. This technique is applied when delaying part of the information is important for dramatic considerations, such as keeping punch lines separate, or to follow the rhythm of a song. Aping

SDH, interlingual subtitling is also resorting to this strategy, as can be seen in the example above.

The interference and presence of the translator through metatextual interventions in the film itself, be it in the form of footnotes or glosses, has always been out of the question in subtitling. The imperative of having to synchronize original dialogues and subtitles, the need to stay within a maximum of two lines per subtitle, and the widespread belief that the best subtitles are those that go unnoticed, seem to confirm the idea that it is actually impossible to add any extra information alongside the translation. Once again, subtitling for DVD appears to be breaking old taboos and offering a wide range of new opportunities. The following two-line subtitle comes from the Japanese film *Zatoichi's Pilgrimage*:

> I'll take your jitte.
> (jitte: staff of office)

The original term 'jitte' is left in the translation and immediately explained in the line below by means of a gloss. The explanation is given between brackets and in a different colour (white) to the subtitle (yellow). The same strategy of leaving and explaining foreign terms is applied in the Japanese film *Baby Cart in the Land of Demons*, albeit in a much more disruptive and innovative way. The following four lines of information appear on screen at the same time. The first two lines appear at the very top of the screen, i.e. above the image, and in white. The other two lines are presented at the bottom of the screen, i.e. below the image, and in yellow:

> "Genpuku Ceremony:" celebration of boys
> reaching adulthood, at ages 12-16.
>
> ...was deferred until her
> Genpuku Ceremony.

This subtitle is left on screen just below four seconds, which is very little time for the average viewer to read all four lines of text. Besides, the actual reading of this information takes on a full new twist, at odds with normal practice. Against habit, viewers are here meant to read first the information that appears at the bottom of the screen and then raise their eyes to the top of the screen to start reading the metatextual information about the translation, in what we could call a 'headnote' or 'topnote'. From a translational perspective, this approach questions preconceived ideas about the visibility or invisibility of the subtitler. In a rather bold and unconventional way, translators make an unequivocal appearance on the screen, and their colour is white.

Interlingual subtitles have traditionally been a lot more conventional than SDH and that is why they offer the subtitler more scope to be creative. Where can this creativity drive be traced? All these new changes in interlingual subtitling – use of colours, cumulative subtitles, explicative glosses and headnotes – could be considered the fruit of the contemporary agitation that welcomes the advent of a new breakthrough in mass communication: the digital era. Digital technology offers a great deal of technical potential for the development of new conventions in subtitling, both interlingual and SDH. It has also changed our perception of audiovisual materials and offered us greater choice. DVD has altered the way in which audiovisual programmes are consumed, giving viewers an unusual degree of control as to the language combination in which they wish to watch a programme. We are dealing with an active rather than passive viewer. The average viewer is increasingly immersed in the world of the image and is more familiar with new technologies. Never before has there been such a close relationship between films and computers as we see now, with most computers equipped with DVD readers and burners. The television and the computer appear to be converging into one and the same screen offering very similar functions. They seem to be interchangeable. Today, we can watch the television on our PC or laptop and use the television set as a computer. Interactivity is a buzzword and its potential enormous.

Despite their apparently innovative nature, these conventions are not so much 'new' as 'borrowed' from other instances where subtitles are also used, notably video games and fansubs. In this respect, interlingual subtitling on DVD seems to be leading the way to change, ahead of cinema and television, in all likelihood because of its digital nature. As yet, it is difficult to tell whether the solutions seen here, or some of them, will spread to other media. As far as languages are concerned, the most innovative approaches occur when subtitling from Japanese to English. Are they the trademark of just a few DVD authoring companies? Will they migrate to other language combinations? The current situation is not clearly defined and should give us food for thought. We seem to be witnessing a process of hybridization where different subtitling approaches and strategies are competing and merging. Subtitling conventions are not set in stone and only time will tell whether these conventions are just a mere fleeting fashion or whether they are the seed of a new type of subtitling for a new distribution format.

5.5 Discussion points

5.5.1 Some people argue that deviating from the standard use of punctuation and conventions for the sake of subtitling's technical specificities is not advisable under any circumstances. Why would some professionals hold this view? What is your opinion on the matter?

5.5.2 What do you think about the use in subtitling of abbreviations that are common in chats and texts messages?

5.5.3 Take a look at any of the websites on smileys and emoticons (e.g. www.clicksmilies.com). What do you think of their use in subtitling? Are these devices too intrusive or could they be justified?

5.6 Exercises

5.6.1. Go to DVD > Chapter 5 > Exercises > Exercise 5.6.1
Here you find a list of subtitles whose punctuation could be improved in order to comply with the conventions proposed in chapter 5.
[Pathway to the key: *DVD > Chapter 5 > Exercises > Exercise 5.6.1 > Key to exercise 5.6.1*]

5.6.2. Translate the following text into two subtitles, bearing in mind the limitations specified within square brackets.
[Pathway to the key: *DVD > Chapter 5 > Exercises > Exercise 5.6.2 > Key to exercise 5.6.2*]

At 25 stone and 6ft 4, the agency's heaviest model	[max. length – 53 spaces]
is part-time heavy, Jonathan Emmanuel.	[max. length – 36 spaces]

5.6.3 Go to DVD > Chapter 5 > Exercises > Exercise 5.6.3
Punctuate the text correcting any misspellings and bad grammar, and capitalizing letters where appropriate.
[Pathway to the key: *DVD > Chapter 5 > Exercises > Exercise 5.6.3 > Key to exercise 5.6.3*]

5.6.4 Go to DVD > Chapter 5 > Exercises > Exercise 5.6.4
Proofread the subtitles you find in this document.
[Pathway to the key: *DVD > Chapter 5 > Exercises > Exercise 5.6.4 > Key to exercise 5.6.4*]

6. The Linguistics of Subtitling

6.0 Preliminary discussion

Subtitling is sometimes accused of being an impoverished language form because of the linguistic straightjacket imposed on it. Others say that creativity can overcome all obstacles, even in subtitling, because faithful translation is a relative or even useless concept.

❶ Discuss what the above-mentioned concepts might refer to: 'impoverished language', 'linguistic straightjacket', and the relativity of faithful translation.

❷ Then try to determine where you stand on these issues, and draw up a list of five items that you expect will be a challenge in subtitling, from a linguistic point of view.

❸ What do you think of the following quote from Myers (1973:58)?

> One can only come to the conclusion that subtitling is adequate only for those who have mastered speed-reading or those who are only interested in looking at pretty shots.

6.1 Subtitling: translation as rewriting

Translation Studies has long moved away from the idea of any translation being a faithful rendering of its source text (ST). In the 1980s, the interest of translation scholars gradually moved away from a fixation on the ST as a determining factor in the transfer from one language and culture to another, to an interest in the target text (TT) and its function at the receiving end. That is, from the process to the product. As films and TV programmes are made, sold, re-edited, translated, remade, re-translated, and re-distributed in different formats for different media, and by many different people, both the notions of 'original text' and 'author' indeed seem to evaporate. Having said this, STs continue to be translated into TTs, and there is no denying that translation remains a linguistic act as well as a cultural one. However, as texts are translated or rewritten (Lefevere 1987) their links with previous texts, the functions they will fulfil in their new target environments, and how they will be received, can in no way be taken for granted, especially since texts are travelling further and further afield.

Besides, in today's globalized world, source and target texts become confused in yet another way: through fusions of cultures producing hybrid cultural artefacts. Originally, hybridity may have been a feature of postcolonial texts (Bhaba 1994; Mehrez 1992), but today it is central to our global age.

European cinema, for instance, is characterized by co-productions and by films in which characters speak more than one language (§3.3.2), or in which they use hybrid, mixed or 'impure' language variants. In other words, the ST to be translated is physically present, of course, but is heterogeneous in form. To the problems of linguistic translation and that of rendering intralinguistic and extralinguistic cultural elements from one language and culture into another, the challenge of rendering hybrid forms or multilingualism is added (Delabastita and Grutman 2005).

This awareness of the complexity of the ST and its sometimes ambiguous nature has contributed to an increased focus on the creative component in any form of translation (Remael 2003). All texts are written within and bound by certain constraints that writers or translators somehow must overcome. AVT in general, and subtitling in particular, are no different, even though early scholars in the field (Titford 1982) defined subtitling in terms of spatial and temporal 'constraints' that supposedly did not apply to other forms of translation. Even today, the technicalities of space and time (§4) with which the subtitler must indeed reckon, are often referred to in order to point out the limitations of this particular form of AVT. And yet, many of the constraints subtitlers work within are not typical of subtitling only: translated poetry must deal with issues of layout and rhythm, and translated theatre with performance-bound constraints (Zabalbeascoa 2001). Limitations of space and time, the particularity of rendering speech in writing, the presence of the image and the presence of the ST are some of the challenges that subtitlers must face, but all forms of translation pose challenges and all translated texts are the result of reading, interpretation and choice. Mayoral Asensio, Kelly and Gallardo (1988) offer a detailed analysis of the impact that the existence of more than one communication channel has on the translation process. Whether a translation solution is a 'good' or 'bad' one always depends on a host of factors, and cannot be judged out of context. The apparent simplicity of subtitles does not make them ineffective as a translation.

6.2 Text reduction

The written version of speech in subtitles is nearly always a reduced form of the oral ST. Indeed, subtitling can never be a complete and detailed rendering. And neither should it, for that matter. Since the verbal subtitle sign interacts with the visual and oral signs and codes of the film, a complete translation is, in fact, not required. This does not mean, however, that the viewers do not have a right to a qualitatively high-standard translation that will fill in the foreign language gaps for them. Quantity and quality are hardly the same. The concrete causes of the inevitable quantitative reduction in text and content are given below.

Why text reduction?

1) Viewers/listeners can absorb speech more quickly than they can read, so subtitles must give them enough time to register and understand what is written at the bottom of the screen.
2) Viewers must also watch the action on screen and listen to the sound track, so they must be given sufficient time to combine reading with watching and listening.
3) Subtitles are limited to a maximum of two lines. How much text they contain depends on the time available, the subtitling reading speed applied, and the speed at which the ST is actually pronounced.

There are two types of text reduction: partial and total reduction. Partial reduction is achieved through condensation and a more concise rendering of the ST. Total reduction is achieved though deletion or omission of lexical items. Very often both processes are combined, leading to the rewriting that is so typical of subtitling. In other words, having assessed how much time and space are available for a given translation, and having ascertained that some form of text reduction is required, the subtitler then proceeds to:

- eliminate what is not relevant for the comprehension of the message, and/or
- reformulate what is relevant in as concise a form as is possible or required.

Very often both processes are at work, as in the example below. A man and a woman who have contacted each other through the personals meet for the first time. This is part of their conversation.

Example 6.1

Man : Quoi? Vous avez déjà fait ça ? Rencontrer des hommes par annonce pour… ? [What? You've done this before? Meet men through an ad to…?]	→	What? You've done this before? You've met men through ads to...
Woman: Non, non - je voulais dire: j'ai déjà rencontré des hommes, qui me plaisaient, enfin, je croyais qu'ils me plaisaient, puis, après, je voyais que non, en fait, je m'étais trompée, ils me plaisaient pas… pas du tout, vous comprenez ?		No, I mean I've met men I liked... ——— Well, I thought I did then realised I didn't ——— I didn't like them at all.

[No, no... I mean, I have met men before that I liked, well, I thought I liked them, but then, later on, I realised that I didn't, in fact, I was wrong, I didn't like them... not at all, you see?]

In the first subtitle nothing has been deleted or abbreviated. The translation is rather literal. It is good to keep in mind that this happens regularly and that the subtitler therefore should not abbreviate the original unless this is absolutely necessary. In fact, something has been added to this subtitle: a repetition of the personal pronoun plus the short form of the auxiliary verb 'have' for *vous avez*.

The subsequent subtitles cover the woman's reply. She speaks too quickly and says too much for her reply to be contained in just one subtitle. Her intervention has therefore been segmented, and in each subtitle something has been either deleted, or reformulated more concisely, or both. And yet, the woman's description of her experience comes across perfectly.

In the second subtitle one *non* has been deleted and the adverb *déjà* [before] has also been eliminated. The third subtitle resorts to a typical feature of English grammar with its use of 'I thought I did', reinforcing internal cohesion by referring back to the previous subtitle 'I've met men I liked'. In other words, the subtitler uses the form and content of the preceding subtitle to build on in the present one, and to reformulate without actually omitting much. The adverbs *puis* [then] and *après* [later on] have been joined in the single 'then', which is the obvious solution since this is a ST repetition if not in form, at least in content. The most far-reaching instance of condensation occurs in the second line of the third subtitle. First of all, the personal pronoun 'I' is not repeated. Since repetition is not required in this case in English, that is fine. Secondly 'realised I didn't' is a reformulation and condensation of *je voyais que non, en fait, je m'étais trompée* [I realized that I didn't, in fact, I was wrong]; whereas *en fait* [in fact], used for emphasis only in the original, has been omitted in the translation.

The last subtitle again omits and reformulates while condensing. The sentence *ils me plaisaient pas... pas du tout, vous comprenez* [I didn't like them... not at all, you see] is rendered as 'I didn't like them at all'. When choosing between the negative *pas* [not] versus *pas du tout* [not at all], the stronger expression is the obvious choice, since the character corrects herself while speaking and it is the corrected version that is rendered. To conclude, *vous comprenez* [you see] does not add anything to the propositional content of the sentence – even if it does contribute to interpersonal interaction – and so, it can be omitted.

The above self-contained scene is rather straightforward and it is therefore relatively easy to determine what must be included, what must be rewritten, and what must be omitted, given pre-established space limitations. However, this may not always be the case, and foolproof reduction or omission rules do not exist.

In general terms, one could say that the subtitler must act on the principle of relevance. What is relevant is "connected or appropriate to the matter at hand" (NOED 1998), but there is more to this concept. It was Gutt (1991) who first applied the theory of relevance, itself largely the work of Sperber and Wilson (1986), to the theory of translation. Kovačič (1994) later tested its value for the study of subtitling. We cannot possibly go into relevance theory here, not even into its application to AVT, but it basically claims that communication works on a principle which operates in terms of a balance between processing effort and pay off. This is known as the 'mini-max effect', i.e. achieving a maximum effect with a minimum effort. Kovačič found the approach was quite useful for analyzing and explaining the logic of subtitling omissions, which cannot simply be put down to linguistic factors. It is the balance between the effort required by the viewer to process an item, and its relevance for the understanding of the film narrative that determines whether or not it is to be included in the translation. This means that subtitlers should view a film in its entirety before embarking on a subtitling assignment, even if professionals rarely have the time or opportunity to do this: what may appear to be a simple detail no doubt has a function in the larger scheme of the script (§3.1). Even an inconsequential greeting like 'good morning', cannot automatically be rendered as the much shorter 'hi' or 'hello'. Disregarding matters of style, the ST expression also contains a time reference, whereas neither 'hi' nor 'hello' do. Having seen the entire film gives the subtitler a better outlook on what is and is not redundant. Within the context of one particular scene, the question to be asked in case of doubt is: what requires more effort on the part of the viewer? A shorter subtitle with less information (quicker reading, more thinking)? Or a slightly longer subtitle with more information (slower reading, less thinking)?

The question of how much has to be deleted or otherwise reduced also needs to be looked at in context because it will vary from film to film, and from scene to scene. When people argue, for instance, they not only tend to speak louder, but also more quickly. Díaz Cintas (2003:202) counts a reduction of 40% in the Spanish subtitles of Woody Allen's *Manhattan Murder Mystery* but points out that even that percentage is rather high. Woody Allen's films are notoriously talkative and the speed of delivery is no doubt a determining factor. Lomheim (1995:203) did the count for three episodes of quite different TV series – thriller, comedy, and sci-fi – and came up with 22%, 24% and 37% respectively. The most important thing to remember from this, rather than the percentages in themselves, is that some cutting is usually required even though this may be quite frustrating, and that the amount of cutting/reformulating will vary with genre, context, speed of delivery, etc. (Georgakopoulou 2003). A positive way of looking at this subtitling feature is to regard it as a way of freeing oneself from the ST and achieving a translation that is tuned to the needs of the target audience. The practical details of judicious reduction are discussed below.

Whether rephrasing or omission, or a combination of the two, is the best solution, must be ascertained in each instance. One factor that may be decisive is the combination of genre and rhetorical function. In a scene depicting a lovers' quarrel – for instance, an emotionally rather than referentially significant scene – leaving out details and following the rhythm of speech may be better than rephrasing and thereby losing the parallelism with the ST. When subtitling off-screen commentators in a documentary film, rendering all they say may be more important, and therefore a reformulation that allows the subtitler to condense without losing information may be a better option. The subtitles below are from a scene of a feature film in which the characters are having an argument. Rendering some of the rhetorical features of their interventions is therefore important. The first subtitle combines omission and condensation, while maintaining the rhetorical build-up of the dialogue. Even the repetition of the affirmative 'OK' has not been omitted, although it could easily have been left out. The second subtitle translates the entire turn.

Example 6.2

Woman: Ok, on n'habitait pas dans un palace, ok, je bossais beaucoup, mais on s'en sortait ! On était heureux ! [Ok, we did not live in a palace, ok I worked a lot, but we did manage! We were happy!]	→	OK, the place was small. OK, I worked a lot, but we were happy.
Man: Qu'est-ce que t'en sais qu'elle était heureuse ? Elle te l'avait dit ? [How do you know she was happy? Did she tell you?]		How do you know she was happy? Did she tell you?

No rules can be given as to when to condense and reformulate, or when to omit. Studying existing subtitles is the best way to learn from professionals, though not much research has been conducted in this area in a systematic way. Some of their choices may be more appropriate than others, but nobody is perfect. In addition to the technical constraints of time and space, both the co-text and the larger context in which a scene occurs are decisive, its connections with what went before and what is still to come, its formal linguistic and rhetorical-stylistic features, its informative significance, its interaction with visually and orally rendered information, etc. Details may be lost, since subtitles tend to go for what is essential, focusing on the propositional dimension – i.e. the content – of an utterance and making sure the build-up of the programme or narrative comes across. But then again, most of the losses tend to be compensated by the information conveyed through the other filmic channels. Subtitlers must also bear in mind that they are translating for a target audience that can be more (children's programmes) or less (a talk show) defined. In fact, subtitling makes watching a programme just that bit more of an active undertaking. Some more concentration may be required and viewers can be expected to appeal to their general knowledge to fill in some of the gaps. A good knowledge of the source and target cultures, as well as information (or a very educated guess) about the target audience, should allow the subtitler to judge how familiar the audience might be with the producing culture. Long subtitles under a speaker who says very little, and short subtitles under a speaker who just keeps rattling on, will both have a disturbing effect. In the first case the viewers have too much reading to do, and in the other they may feel cheated out of information.

6.2.1 Condensation and reformulation

How one should condense and rephrase depends on what 'can' be done as much as on what really 'needs' to be done. Besides, some changes are due to linguistic differences between the language pairs involved. In any case, subtitlers must use the target language's intrinsic possibilities to the full, which is why a native or at least near-native command of the target language is absolutely essential. It is of the utmost importance that all reformulations are idiomatic, i.e. that they sound natural and do not contain calques. An English phrase like 'What do you think?' could be replaced by various alternatives in French, depending on the scene. It does not have to be the fairly literal *Qu'est-ce que t'en penses ?*, an alternative might be *Ça vous va ?*

The examples below illustrate some of the strategies subtitlers use, but should not be read as instructions. They are no more than suggestions of ways to go about reducing text without losing too much content, and they are in no way exhaustive. Moreover, some of the examples will fit under several headings, because different subtitling 'tricks' are often used in combination. Discussing them one by one is therefore a bit artificial. In fact, subtitling 'tricks' do not really exist: subtitlers come up with solutions whenever they are confronted with a challenging dialogue or scene and some of the challenges appear to recur. That is as far as the generalization goes.

6.2.1.1 Condensation and reformulation at word level

- ❑ ***Simplifying verbal periphrases.*** Colloquial language, especially English, often uses verbal periphrases that can be lengthy and therefore use up valuable space. That is why subtitlers tend to replace them with much shorter verb forms, if the target language allows:

Example 6.3

I'm gonna have this place fixed up…then I'm gonna sell it.	→	Reformaré este local y lo venderé. [I'll fix this place and I'll sell it.]
I should really be going actually.	→	Je dois partir. [I have to leave.]
He is gonna be just the same.	→	Il ne changera pas. [He won't change.]

- ❑ ***Generalizing enumerations.*** Occasionally, generalizations will replace enumerations, and although they modify the style of the speaker, they can help to save space, as in the following example:

Example 6.4

You lied to us, son. Your own mother and father.	→	Tu nous as menti, à nous, tes parents. [You lied to us, to us, your parents.]

- ❑ ***Using a shorter near-synonym or equivalent expression.*** One obvious strategy to reduce subtitle length would seem to use shorter synonyms, and this is sometimes done. Why not write 'I feel' rather than 'I have the feeling', or 'we need to talk' rather than 'I have to tell you something'? However, one must keep in mind that:

a) Synonyms are almost always near-synonyms rather than exact equivalents.
b) Synonyms can belong to different registers and can therefore be less appropriate in a particular context.
c) Function words make for slower reading than content words – i.e. 'his' as opposed to 'the butcher's' – because they require more cognitive processing on the part of the viewer.

In the examples below, the trick seems to work, even though 'be good to' in the first subtitle is not a literal translation of the French ST *être correct avec*.

However, the scene as a whole makes clear what is meant. The translational shift becomes less striking, and textual cohesion is maintained when the dialogue is heard, and read, in context. The second example is quite unproblematic.

Example 6.5

QUOI ! J'ai toujours été correct avec elle ! [WHAT! I've always treated her right!]	→	What? I was good to her.
He's got lots of money.	→	Il est riche. [He is rich.]

- ***Using simple rather than compound tenses***. The next example is almost a classic because in certain contexts a simple past can easily replace a past perfect, that is, if there is no need to state explicitly that one past action occurred before another. Simple tenses obviously take up less space than compound forms.

Example 6.6

Son père l'avait foutue à la porte ! [Her father had thrown her out!]	→	Her father threw her out.

Sometimes, a change in tense is inevitable, like in the example below, where English takes a simple past tense and French requires a *passé composé*, a complex tense. A more literal verbal tense, 'I have stopped', would not be grammatically correct in the sentence.

Example 6.7

J'ai arrêté de fumer il y a exactement 134 jours… [I have stopped smoking exactly 134 days ago…]	→	I stopped smoking exactly 134 days ago…

In other cases, the subtitler may have a choice, but tenses can only be adapted when the target language is sufficiently flexible and the change does not lead to grammatically incorrect sentences or calques.

- ***Changing word classes.*** Very often a change in word class can offer shorter alternatives, for instance, turning a verb into a noun, an adjective into a verb, a verb into an adverb, an adjective into a noun or vice versa.

Example 6.8

Verb into noun	Je me suis mis à travailler ! [I started working!]	→	I found a job.
Verb into noun	When General Pinochet was arrested in London…	→	Na de arrestatie van Pinochet… [After the arrest of Pinochet...]
Adjective into verb	That's an expensive weapon!	→	Ça coûte cher ! [That costs a lot!]
Adjective into adverb	I was in a deep sleep.	→	Je dormais profondément. [I slept soundly.]
Adjective into noun	I don't want it to be too transparent.	→	Je ne veux pas de transparence. [I don't want transparency.]

- ***Short forms and contractions.*** Most languages will allow some kind of abbreviation and/or contraction in set words. When translating into English, short verb forms like 'it'll' or 'I'd' will come in handy, and in Dutch pronouns like *hij* [he], *haar* [her], and *het* [it] can occasionally be replaced by *ie*, *'r*, and *'t* respectively. French and Spanish, for instance, make use of pronominal enclitic forms, but these can entail a change in register, as polite requests might sometimes be turned into more direct forms of address when using the imperative tense. The subtitle below offers an example.

Example 6.9

Would you like to share it with me?	→	Compartámoslo. [Let's share it.]

Still, an accumulation of such contracted forms may hinder comprehension, whereas in other instances the style of a formal-sounding speaker may require a formal subtitling style, in which case short forms should not be used. The two subtitles below are fine, since they recreate informal exchanges. Note that in the first one, the auxiliary 'will' has been omitted altogether, which means the subtitle adopts a feature of spoken language.

Example 6.10

Je dois y aller, je te rappellerai. [I must go, I will call you back.]	→	I've got to go, call you later.

Quoi, il y a quelque chose qui ne va pas? [What, is there something that is a problem?]	→	What's up? What's the problem?

6.2.1.2 *Condensation and reformulation at clause/sentence level*

- ***Changing negations or questions into affirmative sentences or assertions, indirect questions into direct questions, etc.*** Sometimes changing the mode of a sentence can have the added benefit of reducing its length. The negative sentence below has become an affirmative one: a phrase with 'not', such as 'not large', would obviously have been longer than the present one with 'small', but another change has occurred as well. It is clear from the context that the speaker is discussing the house he used to live in with his wife. The subtitler can therefore use 'place' rather than 'palace' without causing confusion.

Example 6.11

Ok, on n'habitait pas dans un palace... [Ok, we did not live in a palace...]	→	Ok, the place was small...

In the next example, the more or less rhetorical question, which was meant to be informative in any case, has become a statement. This allows for the introductory verb, the one formulating the question, to be deleted and the compound sentence to become a simple one.

Example 6.12

Did I tell you there's a party Friday?	→	Er is 'n feestje vrijdag. [There's a party Friday.]

Below, the first question, which actually doubles as an admonishment, has become an imperative, and the second question is also turned into an imperative.

Example 6.13

What are you making a face for?	→	No ponga esta cara. [Don't pull that face]
Can't you hear the difference?	→	Ecoutez donc ! [Listen!]

- ***Simplifying indicators of modality***. Modal auxiliaries and other markers of modality indicate degrees of uncertainty, possibility, probability etc. and are very common in formulaic forms of address or polite requests. Omitting or simplifying clauses that contain them can save space, but must be undertaken with care since the omission may result in a translation shift. It can make a character come across as more abrupt, more decisive, or less polite.

  In the first example, the modal auxiliary 'could' in the subtitle, combines the 'if you like' and 'can' from the ST.

Example 6.14

Wij zijn ook zo klaar. Als u wilt, dan kunnen wij u thuis afzetten. [We'll be ready in a minute too. If you like, we can drop you off at home.]	→	We'll be ready in a minute. We could give you a lift.

In the second example the modal auxiliary 'may' has been left out altogether, which does modify the statement, especially since the cautious introductory clause 'I understand' has also been deleted.

Example 6.15

I understand that it may be the best result, politically, that can be delivered just at the moment.	→	Dat is de beste politieke oplossing op dit moment. [That is the best political solution right now.]

By contrast, in the example below the omission of 'can' does not matter, it simply saves space. The speaker is not really asking a question about the other character's 'ability' to see the light in the window.

Example 6.16

Can you see the light up there in the window?	→	Vous voyez cette lumière, là-haut ? [You see the light, up there?]

Finally, in the last example, the omission of modal 'would' breaks no bones either. The hierarchy between nurse and doctor is well established and the nurses' tone is very submissive.

Example 6.17

You wouldn't have time for a cup of tea, doctor?	→	Een kopje thee, dokter? [A cup of tea, doctor?]

- ❑ ***Turning direct speech into indirect speech.*** This 'trick' also allows subtitlers to get rid of the presentative verb that normally introduces the words of a speaker, but appears to be less common. Below, the verb phrase *souvent, je me dis* has been reduced to 'sometimes'. Note that the personal pronoun has been moved back. *Je* [I], originally the subject of *me dis* [tell myself] in the first clause, is now the subject of 'am glad'.

Example 6.18

Souvent, je me dis: "Tant mieux qu'elle soit partie, comme ça, on est soulagés". [I often tell myself: "Good thing she went, we're more at ease like this".]	→	Sometimes I'm glad she went. It makes things easier.

- ❑ ***Changing the subject of a sentence or phrase.*** This operation of necessity goes hand in hand with a change in sentence structure, but does not necessarily involve major translation shifts. In the first example below 'anyone' has now become the subject instead of *ça* [that]. 'Anyone can get' is obviously much shorter than 'that can happen to anyone'. As it happens, the shorter version in the translation is also the most idiomatic one. The reformulations that are so typical of subtitling need not be for the worst.

Example 6.19

L'eczéma, ça. Ça peut arriver à n'importe qui. [Eczema, well. That can happen to anyone.]	→	Eczema, anyone can get eczema.

The change in subject in the first of the two following examples is the natural result of the change in verb, whereas in the second subtitle it is the result of a change from passive to active voice.

Example 6.20

Well, I think I know what you mean Travis.	→	Je crois vous avoir compris, Travis. [I think I've understood you, Travis.]

At the end of six months, you shall be taken to Buckingham Palace, in a carriage, beautifully dressed.	→	Dans six mois, je vous emmène à Buckingham Palace. [In six months, I will take you to Buckingham Palace.] __________. En voiture et avec une belle robe. [In a carriage and with a beautiful dress.]

- ***Manipulation of theme and rheme.*** Speech tends to manipulate the order of theme (known information) and rheme (new information) much more than writing does. Speakers normally place the rheme at the beginning of their sentence when they want to draw special attention to a particular issue or emphasize something. This may be because the issue is important to them, or because they want to bring more variation into their style. The result is a change in the neutral word order of the sentence, and the occurrence in the very beginning of lexical units that would normally be used at the end of the sentence.

  In the example below, the speaker wants to stress that the grandmother took care of quite a few chores. These are therefore placed in initial position, even though the explanation of why he mentions *le linge, le repassage* [the laundry, the ironing] follows afterwards. The enumeration is meant to signify 'many things'. In the subtitle, the word order has been changed and, in addition, the enumeration has been replaced by a generalization.

Example 6.21

Le linge, le repassage, ta grand-mère s'en chargeait. [The laundry, the ironing, your grandmother did all that!]	→	Your grandmother did all the chores.

The reversal to standard word order and grammar in the subtitles does imply an impoverishment or at least a neutralization of the ST style and a reduction of its oral features, although intonation and gestures may provide some compensation. Subtitles resort to these changes in word order to facilitate reading, as the standard theme-rheme order gives priority to known over unknown information. Theme-rheme treatment in subtitling demonstrates, as Lambert (1990:233) has pointed out, that "most subtitles follow the conventional setup of the short well-formed sentence, in which subject, verb and predicate or object follow in a stereotypical order" (our translation). Other examples of theme-rheme shifts are:

Example 6.22

And conquer it, you will!	→	Et vous serez la victorieuse. [And you'll be the winner.]
Your father isn't Mr Cohen.	→	M. Cohen n'est pas ton père. [Mr Cohen isn't your father.]

- ***Turn long and/or compound sentences into simple sentences.*** Another strategy to facilitate reading is simplifying and cutting up complex sentences that may have to be distributed over several subtitles. Shorter, simple sentences require less of a reading effort on the part of the viewers, since they do not have to rely on their memories to tie up the end and the beginning of a sentence that does not appear on screen all at once.

  Note also that the second subtitle in the first example does not equal one sentence, and it has been broken off in a logical place, at the end of the clause. Besides the risk of ending up with too telegraphic a subtitle style, the other down side of reducing long sentences to a series of shorter ones is that the connexions between the ideas expressed in coordinated and subordinated clauses may become less explicit. In the example at hand, the connective *mais* [but] expresses contrast in the ST. The woman had a beautiful body, 'but the body of a woman who had been pregnant'. This indicator of contrast has disappeared from the subtitle. Sacrificing linking words is not recommended, even though it happens in two out of the three examples cited below.

Example 6.23

Elle avait un corps – un très beau corps – mais un corps de femme qui avait été enceinte, enfin aurait pu. [She had a body – a very beautiful body – but the body of a woman who had been pregnant, or at least, might have been.]	→	Her body was still very beautiful. ——— The body of a woman who had been pregnant, ——— or who could have been.
I didn't tell you just 'cause I thought you'd get pissed off.	→	Ik heb niets gezegd. Ik dacht dat je woest zou zijn. [I didn't say anything. I thought you'd be pissed off.]

Here, I've got an idea. Suppose you agree that he can't actually have babies, not having a womb, which is nobody's fault, not even the Romans', but that he can have the right to have babies.	→	J'ai une idée. Admettons qu'il ne puisse pas faire d'enfant. [I have an idea. Let's agree that he can't have a child.] ——— Il n'a pas d'utérus. Ce n'est la faute de personne, pas même des Romains... [He doesn't have a womb. It's not his fault, nobody's, not even the Romans'] ——— mais il a le droit d'en faire. [but he has the right to make them.]

- ❑ ***Active sentences into passive or vice versa.*** The choice of the active versus the passive mode is not a neutral one, since the focus of the attention is on the performer in one case and on the action in the other, and yet, a switch from one to the other can achieve reduction without producing major shifts.

  In the first example, the switch from active to passive goes hand in hand with the use of a slightly shorter synonym that may seem stronger than the ST word, but is corroborated by the images. It is also a verb that fits better in an active sentence.

Example 6.24

Wij weten dat u al jaren door uw echtgenoot mishandeld wordt. [We know that for years you have been maltreated by your husband.]	→	We know your husband has been battering you for years.

In the second example, it is understood that 'the government' is responsible for having arrested 'our heroes' and the agent is not mentioned.

Example 6.25

We knew that was where our heroes were kept.	→	We wisten dat onze helden daar zaten. [We knew that our heroes were there.]

And finally, in the last example, the protagonist is no longer blaming himself, but the translation fits the context:

Example 6.26

Ecoutez. Vous avez un casier judiciaire vierge. Vous n'avez pas grand chose à vous reprocher. [Listen. You have a virginal judicial record. You do not have much to reproach yourself.]	→	Listen, you have a clean record, you can't be blamed for much.

- ***Use of pronouns (demonstrative, personal, possessive) and other deictics to replace nouns, or noun phrases***. Deictics are words such as pronouns and adverbs, or expressions whose meaning is dependent on the context in which they are used (e.g. here, you, that one there, him, etc.). They provide short translation solutions, as they build on a situation or on visual information that has already been established. However, beware of over-using them. The subtitle in the first example below is still understandable in the context, as the pronoun 'it' refers to the profession of 'hairdresser' mentioned in line one. The word or concept to which an adverb or pronoun refers should not be too far away in the subtitle sequence.

Example 6.27

Je suis coiffeur moi. Tout ce que je sais faire, c'est coiffer. [I am a hairdresser. The only thing I know is how to do hair.]	→	I'm a hairdresser. It's all I know.

In the examples below, the pronoun or adverb refers to a person/object on screen, as the subtitle makes use of intersemiotic cohesion between word and image.

Example 6.28

The murderer must have- like- hidden in this closet, right?	→	Le meurtrier a dû se cacher ici. [The murderer had to hide here.]
It's been a long time since we've done this. (hug)	→	Dat is lang geleden. [That is a long time ago.]
I didn't kidnap my brother (points at his brother, who's in the same room).	→	Je ne l'ai pas enlevé. [I didn't kidnap him.]
There is no food in this high mountain.	→	Il n'y a rien à manger ici. [There's nothing to eat here.]

- ***Merge of two or more phrases/sentences into one.*** Whereas long compound sentences tend to be rendered in much shorter single or co-ordinated ones, a series of short sentences in the source dialogue may also be joined, as demonstrated below. Joining sentences in this way can render the connections between actions more explicit and helps the viewer see or understand them at a glance. These apparently opposing tendencies are dictated by the same concern: improving clarity by cutting up lengthy interventions in one case, and linking up bits and pieces in the other. The ellipsis in example one ('that day' has been omitted) is filled by the context of this conversation, and the translator here gives priority to the first question over the second: whatever the interviewee remembers will include what he actually 'did' on that day.

Example 6.29

What are your memories of that day? What did you do on that day?	→	Wat herinnert u zich nog? [What do you still remember?]

In the next example, clauses that are separated by a pause in the soundtrack are joined together: the subtitle is guided by the logic of the content of the utterance, rather than the delivery.

Example 6.30

Tout simplement: j'ai envoyé une lettre. Avec ma photo. Elle m'a répondu. On s'est fixé un rendez-vous. [Very simply: I sent a letter. With a photo. She replied. We arranged to meet.]	→	Very simply. I sent a letter with a photo. ——— She answered and we arranged to meet

The two following examples speak for themselves:

Example 6.31

I want to know what I may take away with me. I don't wanna be accused of stealing.	→	Je veux savoir ce que je peux emporter sans être accusée de vol. [I want to know what I may take with me without being accused of stealing.]
Where did you find this woman? She's a genius.	→	Où tu as trouvé ce génie ? [Where did you find this genius?]

6.2.2 Omissions

Omissions or deletions are unavoidable in subtitling, as many of the examples involving mostly reformulation have shown. Indeed, omission and reformulation go hand in hand, and sometimes reformulations may be more effective than downright omissions, but foolproof guidelines do not exist. Usually, the redundancy rule will come to the subtitler's rescue. On some occasions, a word, phrase, or its content may be repeated elsewhere in the same or the previous/ following subtitle, or it may do no more than expand on an idea, rendering it more explicit. In other instances, the images may fill in a gap. However, in most cases the decision amounts to opting for the lesser loss.

Before deciding to omit, subtitlers must ask themselves: will the viewers still be able to understand the message or scene without too much of an effort, and will they not misunderstand it? Subtitlers must become experts in distinguishing what is essential from what is ancillary. The omission of some of the characters' entire turns in the example from *Secrets and Lies* below is unacceptable because it affects the interaction between the characters and possibly their characterization.

Example 6.32

A: Well, I always… thought she'd 'ad a boy…	→	Ik dacht dat ze een jongen had. [I thought she had a boy.]
B: She's a slag.		Ze is een snol. [She's a slag.]
A: No, she's not.		NO SUBTITLE
B: She fucking is.		NO SUBTITLE
A: She loves yer. We all love yer.		Ze houdt van je. Wij allemaal. [She loves you. All of us.]
B: You comin' back?		Kom je terug? [You coming back?]
A: No.		NO SUBTITLE
B: You got to.		Je moet. [You have to.]
A: Why should I?		NO SUBTITLING
B: You gotta face up to it!		Je moet 't onder ogen zien. [You have to face up to it.]
A. Face up to what?		NO SUBTITLING

6.2.2.1 Omissions at word level

The decision to omit words in the examples below is always dictated by issues of redundancy or relevance. Besides, some omissions are language-bound. When translating from English, for instance, it may not always be necessary or possible to translate question-tags. The target language will probably not have them. If the tag has a function, it can be rendered through a linguistic feature of the target language in question. If the tag is superfluous, or does little more than imitate speech, it may have to be omitted. One idiomatic translation into Dutch of 'close the door, will you?' would be *wil je de deur sluiten alsjeblief*? [Will you close the door please?].

Modifiers, mostly adjectives and adverbs, are also obvious candidates for deletion precisely because they do no more than modify the information carried by the verb or noun. The question is: how important is the modification? In the first of the two following subtitles, the context will fill in the missing 'hot' in the Spanish subtitle, and in the second it is not important that the fish are 'brightly-coloured'. What is more, they actually appear on screen.

Example 6.33

Tell me if I put too much hot fudge.	→	¿He echado demasiado chocolate? [Have I added too much chocolate?]
No. No, I get nervous when brightly-coloured fish are staring at me face-to-face, you know.	→	No, me pongo nervioso cuando se me quedan mirando los peces. [No, I get nervous when the fish keep staring at me.]

Below, the ongoing conversation signals that the character wants to know if the other is going to make the phone call immediately, even if 'now' is deleted in the Spanish subtitle.

Example 6.34

You're gonna ring Mr House, now?	→	¿Vas a llamar al Sr. House? [Are you going to ring Mr House?]

In example 6.35 the subtitle still signifies that one character knows the other merely from seeing her around, even without the qualification 'sometimes'.

Example 6.35

I, uh, I see her at the gym sometimes.	→	La he visto en el gimnasio. [I have seen her at the gym.]

To conclude, in this last subtitle, all that matters is that the character is woken up, not whether he was sleeping soundly or not.

Example 6.36

You woke me out of a deep sleep.	→	Me has despertado. [You woke me up.]

Phatic words also tend to disappear from subtitles because they do not – strictly speaking – advance the action. In mainstream cinema 'action' refers to the causal events or the actions undertaken/words spoken by characters in order to reach their goal or convey an important point of view. In documentary film the action may refer to informative content, or the argument the filmmaker wishes to present. In the first example below the emphatic *mais enfin* and *comme ça* have been deleted, and in the second, a conversation about make-up, the words 'anyway' and 'you know' do not make it to the subtitle.

Example 6.37

Mais enfin, Norah, on n'abandonne pas un bébé, comme ça, pendant des heures ! [In heaven's name, Norah, one does not abandon a baby, just like that, for hours!]	→	You don't abandon a baby for hours.
Anyway, whatever the fuck it is, she uses a lot of it you know.	→	Appelle ça comme tu veux. Elle s'en met un paquet. [Call it what you like. She puts on a load.]

Interpersonal elements that may signal power relations between interlocutors and thereby establish character tend to bite the dust too. Examples are: greetings, interjections, vocatives, formulas of courtesy, etc. Even some repetitions can be seen to fall under this heading, mainly when they express hesitation. Not only do such interpersonal features contribute little to propositional content in the strict sense, formally they also occupy a somewhat isolated position, at the beginning of the sentence, for instance, or between commas. The omission of formulaic expressions of politeness, like the request below, does not matter much, nor does the omission of 'you know', in the second example.

Example 6.38

A cup of coffee, please.	→	Un café. [A coffee.]
You know, why don't you get some plates?	→	Traiga unos platos. [Get some plates.]

As for the string of hesitations and false starters in the following example, a much briefer repetition will do in the subtitle.

Example 6.39

No, no, no, no, no. I'm-I'm-I'm-I'm I'm j- I'm-I'm ju-...um... I'm a detective. They-They-They- We-We- lowered the height requirements, so I-	→	No, no. Yo... soy inspector. Han aumentado la talla mínima, [No, no. I... am a detective. They've lowered the height requirements,] ——— y yo... [and I...]

Whether omitting such interpersonal elements is always the best choice is another issue. In the passage below, the protagonist is talking on the phone to the woman he has fallen in love with, but she refuses to see him. He is trying to re-establish contact, not really knowing how to go about it. The subtitle therefore suggests his false starts, rendering his awkwardness, which is actually what the film wants to convey in this scene.

Example 6.40

I'll come by the headquarters or something and we could em…	→	Je passe vous prendre à la permanence, je sais pas, moi, je pourrais... [I'll come and fetch you from headquarters, I don't know, I, I could...]

6.2.2.2 Omissions at clause/sentence level

Even though it is certainly not advisable to omit entire turns, sentences or even clauses, it can sometimes be unavoidable. In some cases the intervention of a particular character may actually have a very low information load. In a noisy crowded scene, for instance one that is meant to create an atmosphere rather than anything else, some interventions may not have to be subtitled. In other instances, the music may be too loud for a dialogue turn to be audible, or several people may be talking at the same time. In such cases one could say that the dialogue is part of the setting. The last turn spoken by Carolyn in the scene below from *American Beauty* does not really require subtitling beyond 'I wouldn't have the heart'. She is walking away from the camera towards her house at this point. It is the end of the scene and the music gradually takes over. By the time she pronounces the word 'heart' her voice has become virtually inaudible. The sound track and the scene as a whole convey sufficiently that Carolyn is a nervous, fast talker, and self-righteous woman. Anyhow, subtitlers working without a script would simply not be able to translate the entire last sentence.

Example 6.41

Their sycamore? C'mon! A substantial portion of the root structure was on our property. You know that. How can you call it their sycamore? I wouldn't have the heart to just cut down something that wasn't partially mine, which of course it was.

Unfortunately, though, not all scenes are that straightforward. In the example below, protagonist Eliza from the musical *My Fair Lady* is seen dancing and singing in the living-room, but she is gradually taken to the bathroom by the servants who want to get her ready for bed. While Eliza keeps on singing that she 'could dance all night', the servants are undressing her, and they sing along, saying that she needs to sleep. Their interventions are so short and quick that the subtitler could not fit them in between Eliza's lines. In other words, the subtitling gives priority to the protagonist and the viewer has to rely on the *mise-en-scène* to understand what exactly is going on.

Example 6.42

Eliza:	I could have danced all night.	→	J'aurais voulu danser sans fin.
Servants:	You're tired out.		[I would have danced forever.]
Servants:	You must be dead.		
Eliza:	I could have danced all night.		Danser jusqu'à l'aurore.
Servants:	Your face is worn.		[Danced until dawn.]
Servants:	Your eyes are red.		
Eliza:	And still have begged.		Danser jusqu'au matin.
Servants:	Now say good night, please.		[Danced until morning.]
Servants:	Turn out the light, please.		
Eliza:	For more.		
Servants:	It's really time for you to be in bed.		

The following example is an extract from a group scene from *Manhattan Murder Mystery* with four interlocutors who sometimes speak simultaneously. The subtitler has omitted turns that contain information another character rephrases differently, as well as conversational, oral features that have little more than an interactional function. The subtitler has taken care not to delete the turns spoken by the same character more than once.

Example 6.43

Ted:	Uh, you really saw his face? You saw, you saw what he looked like? No question. You know exactly who it is.	→	Vous avez vu son visage ? Vous savez qui c'est ? [You saw his face?] [You know who it is?]
Carol:	Yes. Oh, yes, I'm here to tell you...		C'était bien M. House. [It was Mr House all right.]
Larry:	Oh, no question about it. It was- It was Mr House. There was no... Not a, not a question. I mean, you could see him because, uh, you know, there was-there was just no way that you could avoid it. He was right there.		On l'a forcément vu. Il était devant nous. [We had to see him.] [He was in front of us.]
Marcia: Larry: Ted:	To me, it's obvious. Wh... How do you see it? How obvious? What do you mean?		Pour moi, c'est évident. - Comment ça ? [To me, it's obvious.] - What do you mean?]
Marcia:	Obvious he's committed the perfect murder.		Il a commis un crime parfait. [He's committed a perfect murder.]
Larry: Ted:	What do you mean? What? How? What do you mean?		C'est-à-dire ? [That is to say?]
Marcia:	Okay, look. You have to start off with another woman who bears some ballpark resemblance to Mrs House.		Commençons par une femme grosso modo genre Mme House. [Let's start with a woman style Mrs House.]

Relevance is the key in such cases and the subtitler must give priority to the person who is conveying crucial information. In the following, shorter examples, repetitions and conversational features are again exploited in order to render four turns in two.

Example 6.44

A: B: A: B:	Isn't that your door? What? Isn't that your door knocking? Yes.	→	Is dat jouw deur niet? - Ja. [Isn't that your door? - Yes.]

Occasionally, the topic of a question is incorporated in the reply of the next speaker. That is why in the excerpt below, the question has been deleted to solve problems of space.

Example 6.45

A: Why aren't you coming tomorrow? B: I'm not coming to the party because I've got other plans.	→	Ik kom niet naar het feestje, omdat ik andere plannen heb. [I am not coming to the party because I have other plans.]

Luckily, most fiction films make sure that dialogue that is really important is understood by the audience; the result being that it can also be subtitled because time constraints will not be so strict. Granted that the pace of older films is slower than that of today's productions, even group scenes are often orchestrated to such an extent that some dialogue exchanges will stand out more clearly than others. These are then obvious candidates for subtitling, even if they do not contribute to the story strictly speaking, because not subtitling such conversations would leave the viewers wondering needlessly.

In some cases, sentences or clauses have to be omitted even though they do fulfil a function. Making use of the sequentiality of dialogue (§3.4) – i.e. using information from a previous or subsequent subtitle – may be a subtitling solution. In the following example the conditional clause *si elle était partie* [If she left] has been omitted in the English subtitle, but the deletion is compensated by the question in the previous line. The conditional clause that follows the question (to which the speaker herself replies) is a repetition of that question and subsumes the question in the answer.

Example 6.46

Pourquoi elle est partie ? Si elle était partie, c'est qu'elle avait des raisons ! [Why did she leave? If she left, it's because she had some reasons!]	→	Why did she leave? She must have had a reason.

From the perspective of dialogue studies one could say that the first part of the utterance, *si elle était partie* [If she left], is the part of the turn that is context confirming. It takes care of cohesion, but does not contain new information, hence its deletion.

In the next example *mais on s'en sortait* [but we did manage] has been deleted. This clause is redundant because the following sentence, *On était heureux* [We were happy], supersedes it semantically. If people are 'happy' they are obviously doing more than 'managing'. On the other hand, 'the place was small' and 'I worked a lot' do signal that the couple was far from rich and that the extent of their supposed happiness may have been a matter of opinion.

Example 6.47

Ok, on n'habitait pas dans un palace, ok, je bossais beaucoup, mais on s'en sortait ! On était heureux ! [Ok, we did not live in a palace, ok I worked a lot, but we did manage! We were happy!]	→	OK, the place was small. OK, I worked a lot, but we were happy.

Clauses or phrases that carry less propositional content are often those that express a point of view or introduce an argument, i.e. have a presentational function. They introduce the clause that is the main focus semantically speaking. If deletion is required, these introductions are the clauses that tend to go first.

Example 6.48

I was struck during the apartheid years that you always managed to keep your sense of humour.	→	Tijdens de apartheidsjaren bewaarde u uw gevoel voor humour. [Throughout the apartheid years you kept your sense of humour.]

In some cases, even such deletions do have an effect. In the next instances, the character's uncertainty has disappeared from the subtitle. In the first example, the speaker is not sure he has done the right thing by moving in a day ahead of time, in the second, he (a child) knows he has literally 'killed a duck', if unintentionally, and his 'Mmmm, I think' only brings across the fact that he is a bit afraid to break the news.

Example 6.49

I thought I'd move in a day early.	→	Ik ben wat vroeger gekomen. [I moved in a bit earlier.]
Mmmm, I think I killed a duck.	→	J'ai tué un canard. [I killed a duck.]

Finally, in the following two subtitles it is the interaction between the characters that suffers. In the first example, the speaker is not only telling the others 'we don't know this is all true', he is also warning them not to get carried away. In the second, the interlocutor of the ST is being admonished and asked to pay attention, whereas the subtitle merely insists on the value of the 'theory' under discussion.

Example 6.50

Hold, hold on, for a second. We don't know this is all true. This is just a theory.	→	No sabemos si todo es cierto, sólo es una teoría. [We don't know if all this is true, it is just a theory.]
Yeah, but it's a great theory. Have you been paying attention? This is a great theory.	→	Sí, pero es una teoría genial. [Yeah, but it's a great theory.]

6.3 Linguistic cohesion and coherence in subtitling

Coherence is a property of texts that are well written, and helps the message come across, whereas the term cohesion refers to the techniques writers have at their disposal to promote such coherence. Intersemiotic cohesion in subtitling refers to the way it connects language directly to the soundtrack and to images on screen, making use of the information they supply to create a coherent linguistic-visual whole (§3.2 and §3.3).

In the above-mentioned scene from *American Beauty*, Carolyn Burnham refers to the movers carrying furniture into the neighbouring house. Both film dialogue and subtitle rely on visually conveyed information to make sense of her first sentence. What is more, the 'it' in the third subtitle refers to 'that house' in the character's second sentence. The subtitler makes use of the visuals once again and thanks to this intersemiotic cohesion between words and image the viewers will have no problems connecting the pronoun 'it' with the neighbouring house.

Example 6.51

So, we've finally got new neighbours. You know, if the Lomans had let me represent them, instead of 'The Real Estate King', that house would never have sat on the market for six months.	→	Eindelijk, nieuwe buren. [Finally, new neighbours.] ——— Als de Lomans mij als makelaar hadden genomen [If the Lomans had hired me as estate agent] ——— was het veel eerder verkocht. [it would have been sold much earlier.]

All the same, the condensation and reduction that is so typical of subtitling, as well as the disruption created by the layout or distribution of a sentence over more than one subtitle, can lead to coherence breakdowns. So even if the visual and aural channels contribute their bit, it does no harm to avoid low cohesion, and thereby possible coherence problems in the subtitles themselves. Such lack of coherence can be due to fuzzy references or jumpy transitions, a kind of 'telegram-style', ill-structured sentences, clauses without verbs, or illogical segmentation.

Earlier on in this chapter we pointed out how omission often goes hand in hand with reformulation; as subtitlers delete they must also make sure that the logic of the ST is maintained within and across the subtitles. They must continually look back at what they have already translated and anticipate what is still to come. It may very well be that it is difficult to keep track of this while translating, but having finished a scene, it is good to do some editing, taking extra care to check transitions and cross-references, or typical examples of anaphoric and cataphoric references. Short circuits in the information flow must be avoided. This is why many subtitling software programs, including WinCAPS, have a function that allows subtitlers to check the list of subtitles they have created.

6.4 Segmentation and line breaks

A careful segmentation of the information can help reinforce coherence and cohesion in subtitling. Translators are responsible for creating subtitles that can be easily understood in the little time they appear on screen, and considering their relative isolation – physical, though not logical – from previous and following subtitles. To attain this objective, one of the golden rules in the profession is to structure subtitles in such a way that they are semantically and syntactically self-contained. Ideally, any subtitle ought to have a clear structure, avoid any undue ambiguities, and be a complete sentence. However, this is not always possible, and it is then that segmentation becomes crucial (§4.7.1).

To segment means to divide something into separate parts or sections. In subtitling, segmentation is the division of the ST dialogue, narration etc. into sections or segments – subtitles – that the viewers can understand at a glance. Segmenting is done on two levels. A sentence may have to be distributed over the two available lines of a subtitle – line breaks – or it may run on, into two or more subtitles. The segmentation rules are basically the same within and across subtitles, but when dividing text over more than one subtitle, one should keep in mind that the memory span of viewers of any age group is limited. Complex sentences are difficult to keep track of and should be split into smaller ones.

When making use of the two lines of a subtitle, the segmentation of the text should follow syntactic and grammatical considerations rather than aesthetic rules, e.g. having lines with a symmetrical layout. Neither should the translator wait to fill the top line before venturing to the bottom one. The second line can be shorter than the first one or vice-versa.

Karamitroglou (1998) sees subtitling segmentation as follows:

> Subtitled text should appear segmented at the highest syntactic nodes possible. This means that each subtitle flash should ideally contain one complete sentence. In cases where the sentence cannot fit in a single-line subtitle and has to continue over a second line or even over a new subtitle flash, the segmentation on each of the lines should be arranged to coincide with the highest syntactic node possible.

His tree diagram (ibid.) of the sentence 'The destruction of the city was inevitable' is developed as displayed in figure 6.1.

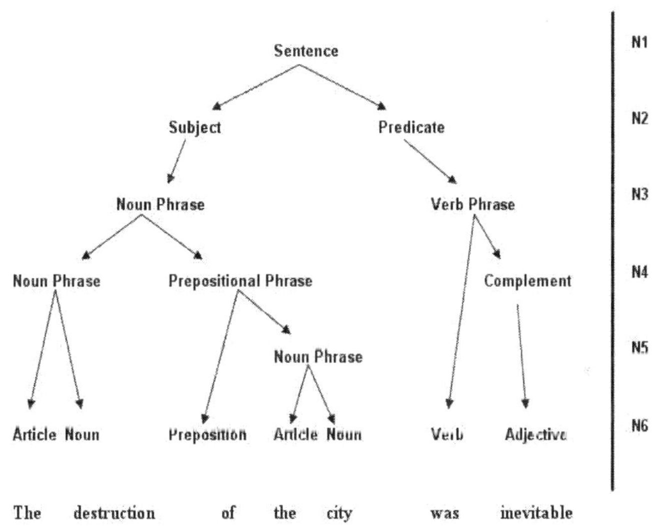

Figure 6.1

Out of the two line breaks, it is the second that flows as more readable. This occurs because the higher the node, the greater the grouping of the semantic load and the more complete the piece of information presented to the brain. When we segment a sentence, we force the brain to pause its linguistic processing for a while, until the eyes trace the next piece of linguistic information. In cases where line breaks are inevitable, therefore, we should try to force this pause on the brain at a point where the semantic load has already managed to convey a satisfactorily complete piece of information.

A segmentation on the fifth node (N5) would create the two-line subtitle:

The destruction of the
city was inevitable.

A segmentation on the second node (N2) would create the two-line subtitle:

The destruction of the city
was inevitable.

In our next example, one subtitle equals one sentence, and the distribution of text over the two available lines follows the above logic.

Example 6.52

How do you go about answering an ad?

Very simply,
I sent a letter with a photo.

She answered
and we arranged to meet.

In practice, however, it is not always feasible to match a sentence with a subtitle, so it is important to keep in mind that each subtitle should make sense in itself, while somehow indicating or suggesting that the sentence continues in the next subtitle. Segmentation always benefits from a division into parts that can function independently, and this is achieved more easily with coordinated than with subordinated clauses. Consider the example below.

Example 6.53

Either God exists, and there are things
he alone understands,

---

or he doesn't exist
and there's nothing to understand.

The ST sentence in the next example just rambles on, so some form of intervention is inevitable: it must be subdivided into short sentences.

Example 6.54

...and he was standing on the other side from me...we were shouting at one another and there were other people, other prisoners and their families, and it was such a lot of noise...sometimes I couldn't even hear what he was saying.	→	Hij stond daar, ik hier, en we schreeuwden naar mekaar. [He was there, I here, and we shouted at each other.] __________ Er stonden nog andere gevangenen en hun verwanten. [There were other prisoners and their relatives.] __________ Er was zoveel lawaai dat we mekaar soms niet verstonden. [There was so much noise that we didn't always understand each other.]

Long sentences occur in different genres, both in fiction and non-fiction films, especially when someone is reporting, telling a story, explaining a problem, or giving instructions. The example above is from a woman describing to a journalist what happened when she went to see her husband in prison for the first time. Part of the message is no doubt the confusion at the prison, but the subtitler should not render the confusion in the woman's description and must segment the ST logically. Not only has her sentence been segmented into three subtitles, in the third one the connection between the two clauses that compose it has become more explicit.

Besides syntactic-semantic segmentation, rhetorical and visual segmentation may also have a role to play. According to Reid (1996:100):

> The translator will determine the segments which later become one subtitle grammatically (on the basis of semantic units), rhetorically (on the basis of speech rhythms), or visually (on the basis of what happens on the screen in the way of cuts, camera angle changes etc.).

In our view, 'visual segmentation' as defined by Reid, belongs to the domain of spatial considerations, rather than linguistic ones. It refers to the technique of cueing or spotting and its relation to the visual narration of film (§4.7). In what follows we therefore offer more concrete examples of syntactic-semantic and rhetorical segmentation only.

6.4.1 Line breaks within subtitles: syntactic-semantic considerations

In the following examples the version preceded with the symbol ✓ is the preferred one by the authors.

① Do not hyphenate words under any circumstances.

Example 6.55

✗	It's really hard when you have sacri- ficed everything.	✓	It's really hard when you've sacrificed everything.

② If a subtitle consists of two, or more, sentences, put one sentence on each line.

Example 6.56

✗	That's his second wife. She killed herself.	✓	That's his second wife. She killed herself.

③ If a subtitle consists of a sentence with two subordinated or coordinated clauses, and inserting one after the other is impossible because the maximum number of characters per line would be exceeded or would result in an extremely long subtitle, use one line for each clause.

Example 6.57

✗	I don't need him here because I can manage perfectly.	✓	I don't need him here because I can manage perfectly.
✗	We can't take him along and we can't leave him here.	✓	We can't take him along and we can't leave him here.

Sometimes it will be impossible to make such clean-cut divisions. Bear in mind that it is not necessary to fill the first line completely before going to the second. Some subtitlers feel a degree of equilibrium in line length is more pleasing aesthetically, sometimes the customer will dictate the layout rules, in other cases a close-up may call for a shorter top line, but generally speaking which line is the longest is first determined by word groups that must be kept together (§4.6.3). More examples are given below.

④ Any disruption of a sense-unit will slow down reading. It is therefore ill advised to separate adjective from noun or adverb, adverb form verb, article from noun, preposition from prepositional clause and the like.

Example 6.58

✗	You're right, you're absolutely right.	✓	You're right, you're absolutely right.

✗	My mum will drive the car when we go to the beach.	✓	My mum will drive the car when we go to the beach.
✗	Could you lock up this place before leaving?	✓	Could you lock up this place before leaving?

⑤ If the sentence contains a to-infinitive, a phrasal verb, or collocation, try not to split them up.

Example 6.59

✗	Is someone who refuses to help a victim guilty of a crime?	✓	Is someone who refuses to help a victim guilty of a crime?
✗	I have no idea what got into him this morning.	✓	I have no idea what got into him this morning.
✗	The suspect hasn't really committed murder.	✓	The suspect hasn't really committed murder.

⑥ If the sentence contains a compound verbal form, do not separate auxiliary from lexical verb (past participle or infinitive).

Example 6.60

✗	Now listen, I'm going to give him a last chance.	✓	Now listen, I'm going to give him a last chance.
✗	I have never seen the girl in my life.	✓	I have never seen the girl in my life.

⑦ Avoid separating a verb from its direct or indirect object. If a simple sentence has to be distributed over two lines, the subject should ideally go on line one and the verb plus predicate on the second.

Example 6.61

✗	And I just can't give you the address either.	✓	And I just can't give you the address either.
✗	The nurse can get the doctor for you now.	✓	The nurse can get the doctor for you now.

⑧ If a particular sentence is the reply to a question, or a reaction to a statement, the reply/reaction is best placed on the second line, rather than in the next subtitle, unless this would give away information too soon.

Example 6.62

×	Give me those damn keys. __________ Enough! Stop!	✓	Give me those damn keys. - Enough! Stop!
×	Am I a dog who deserves to die? __________ Take the keys and let me go.	✓	Am I a dog who deserves to die? - Take the keys and let me go.

6.4.2 Line breaks across subtitles: syntactic-semantic considerations

Sometimes it is impossible to make sure sentence and subtitle coincide, because the information load is too great, or because the sentence structure does not lend itself to a division into closed off units. In that case a sentence will have to run over two or more subtitles, and the same rules regarding syntactic-semantic segmentation have to be applied when deciding where to break off. The clause or word group that constitutes it must make sense and anticipate the ending that is still to come.

Example 6.63

×	You said you didn't know her, that you had never met her, but that __________ was obviously a lie.	✓	You said you didn't know her, that you had never met her, __________ but that was obviously a lie.

Still, it is not advisable to continue a sentence over too many subtitles. In that case, dividing it up will avoid stretching the viewer's memory, as in the following example taken from Ivarsson and Carroll (1998:91):

Example 6.64

×	Welcome to the first of four programmes __________ in this series that every four weeks will show how big money __________ governs England, and how your money can be used __________ to change society. We'll see a commercial, soon to be shown __________ in our cinemas.	✓	Welcome to the first of four programmes in this series. __________ Every four weeks we will show how big money governs England __________ and how your money can be used to change society. __________ We'll see a commercial, soon to be shown in our cinemas.

6.4.3 Rhetorical segmentation

Subtitling renders speech in writing. Rhetorical segmentation tries to take some of the meaningful features of spoken language into account: hesitations and pauses, or the playfulness of quick repartees, for instance. Indeed, the way subtitles are segmented and distributed must reflect some of the dialogue's dynamics. Good rhetorical segmentation helps convey surprise, suspense, irony, hesitation, etc. These prosodic features of spoken language serve a purpose in supporting and qualifying the speaker's message. Actually, syntactic-semantic and rhetorical segmentation overlap to some extent since the linguistic and paralinguistic features of speech usually collaborate. Chances are that respecting syntactic and semantic units as well as punctuation will automatically take care of rhetorical segmentation. In some cases, however, the subtitler has to make a decision. Should the reply to a question or an ironic comment be rendered in the same subtitle? What is the best break-off point? Consider the following examples:

Example 6.65

Remind me to go to the bak- er's in the morning… and to kill him.	→	Herinner me eraan naar de bakker te gaan… [Remind me to go to the baker's…] ______ en hem te vermoorden. [and kill him.]
You are looking really good for… a twenty-one-year- old.	→	You are looking really good for… ______ a twenty-one-year-old.

Another question is whether or not a short pause or a hesitant oral delivery should be reflected somehow in the subtitle. Breaking off a sentence and continuing with it in the next subtitle may render a character's hesitation, but it may also disrupt the syntactic unity of the subtitle. Is the rhetorical impact of the disruption more relevant than the semantics of the utterance? Sometimes this is a matter of personal preference. Compare the following versions of the same subtitle. The one on the left renders the simple sentence in one subtitle; the one on the right respects the pause after 'to':

Example 6.66

I'm scared. I would like to get out of here.	←→	I'm scared. I would like to… ______ get out of here.

A related issue is the preference for more short one-line subtitles rather than fewer two-line ones. The latter group information and facilitate reading, but do not follow the rhythm of the speaker that closely.

In the following example, the character has just witnessed a car accident. He is addressing the girl who has been hit as she is lying in the road. His voice sounds worried and urgent, his sentences are short and repetitive: he appears to be prodding her with his words, trying to make her respond. In the version on the left, his sentences have been joined, which is quite all right technically speaking, in terms of space-time constraints, but not from a dramatic-prosodic perspective. In the version on the right, the subtitler has opted for almost as many short subtitles as there are sentences, following the rhythm of the speaker and retaining most of his hesitations, brief pauses and repetitions.

Example 6.67

×	✓
Miss, you have to stay awake. Answer me.	Miss, you have to stay awake. Answer me.
Count with me. Miss, answer me. Count out loud.	Count with me.
Stay with me. Stay with me.	Miss, answer me.
	Count out loud.
	Stay with me. Stay with me.

To conclude, in the last example, the subtitles on the right are not very efficient in terms of the space they use, versus the information load they carry. In another type of film (but possibly also another type of scene), it might have been better not to render any of the speaker's hesitations or false starts at all and concentrate on the message. The golden rule is: if the speaker's hesitations do not contribute to the message, do not convey them.

6.5 Discussion points

6.5.1 Reconsider each of the examples under the suggestions for condensation and reformulation at clause or sentence level (§6.2.1.2).

- ❶ What kind of translation shifts do they involve if one does not consider the context that might be provided by visual information?
- ❷ Is there a system in the shifts that you have detected?

6.5.2 The example from *Secrets and Lies* in §6.2.2 (example 6.32) shows that Dutch subtitlers tend to omit a great deal when the SL is English.

❶ Is this trend discernible in your country too?
❷ What do you think of this increasingly 'ancillary' form of subtitling, i.e. subtitles that tend to relay only the gist of the original?
❸ Are you in favour of applying this approach in the subtitling of all programmes? Or only in particular cases? Which ones?

6.5.3 Accepting that most people know some English and that they will be able to understand words from the original soundtrack, to which one of the two following opinions do you subscribe? Why?

> ❶ Given the need for reduction in subtitling, I prefer not to translate the English words that I know most people will hear and understand directly from the soundtrack. That way, I can use the space available to relay other details from the dialogue.
>
> ❷ My strategy, on the contrary, is to relay in my subtitles those English words that I know my audience is going to hear and understand. It is true that I have less space left for other information, but by translating those words in my subtitles I know my audience is not going to feel cheated.

6.5.4 Basing yourself on what you have read so far, and on your own opinion about subtitling, propose three strategies that would help to reinforce intersemiotic coherence between subtitles and the rest of audio and visual systems that operate in any audiovisual production.
[Pathway to suggestions: *DVD > Chapter 6 > Discussion points > Discussion point 6.5.4*]

6.6 Exercises

Translation as rewriting

6.6.1 Read the following excerpt (with back translation) and the English subtitles from *J'ai toujours voulu être une sainte*. Identify exactly what has been rewritten and what has been deleted. Explain the subtitler's choices.

> C'était la voisine qui avait prévenu les flics. Elle avait entendu le bébé hurler pendant des heures. Elle était venue frapper, mais personne n'avait répondu...
> [It was the neighbour who had informed the police. She had heard the baby cry for hours on end. She had knocked on the door, but no one had come...]
>
> The neighbour had rung the police.
> The baby was crying but nobody was in.

6.6.2 Go to DVD > Chapter 6 > Exercises > Exercise 6.6.2
Identify what has been rewritten and what has been deleted in this excerpt from a group scene in *Manhattan Murder Mystery*, where the characters are discussing a suspicious death. Explain the subtitler's choices.

Reduction

6.6.3 Go to DVD > Chapter 6 > Exercises > Exercise 6.6.3
Reduce in English the bits of conversation you find in the document by about 50%, making good use of redundancy and expendable repetitions.

❶ Omit and rephrase as required.
❷ Distribute your rewritten version over one or two hypothetical subtitle lines as indicated.
❸ Translate the resulting dialogue into your working language.
[Pathway to suggestions: *DVD > Chapter 6 > Exercises > Exercise 6.6.3 > Key to exercise 6.6.3]*

6.6.4 Go to DVD > Chapter 6 > Exercises > Exercise 6.6.4
Edit the text you find in the document to the required number of words, retaining as much as possible of the original meaning.
[Pathway to suggestions: *DVD > Chapter 6 > Exercises > Exercise 6.6.4 > Key to exercise 6.6.4*]

6.6.5 Go to DVD > Chapter 6 > Exercises > Exercise 6.6.5
Translate the proposed master titles from an interview with Desmond Tutu, rewriting the long sentences and using a reading speed of 160 words per minute to determine subtitle length.

Line breaks

6.6.6 Go to DVD > Chapter 6 > Exercises > Exercise 6.6.6
You will find in this document a compilation of subtitles in which line breaks could be done in a more appropriate way. Propose some alternative solutions.
[Pathway to the key: *DVD > Chapter 6 > Exercises > Exercise 6.6.6 > Key to exercise 6.6.6*]

WinCAPS

6.6.7 Go to DVD > Chapter 6 > Exercises > Exercise 6.6.7 > *Cemetery*
It is the opening scene from the film *Night of the Living Dead*, in which a brother (Johnny) and a sister (Barbara) are having a conversation inside their car. They have just arrived at a graveyard to pay their annual visit

to their father's grave, in accordance with their mother's wishes. [Pathway to dialogue list: *DVD > Chapter 6 > Exercises > Exercise 6.6.7 > Transcription of Dialogue]*

❶ Watch the clip and indicate on the script what you think is essential information.

❷ Mark on the script what you think might be the ideal segmentation. Think about the following issues:

- ❑ Should Johnny's brief 'what?' at the beginning of the scene be translated?
- ❑ If you decide to translate it, will you spot it together with Barbara's first intervention?
- ❑ What would you do with the information coming from the radio?

❸ Using WinCAPS, spot the clip and type in a shorter English version or a translation, and evaluate the result. Use a reading speed of 160 words per minute.

7. Translation Issues

7.0 Preliminary discussion

7.1 Translation challenges that are due to the different grammatical and lexical make up of languages are translators' daily fare; however, they are also confronted with various types of culture-bound translation issues that are not of a linguistic nature in the strict sense, but rooted in language all the same.

❶ Give a few examples of such culture-bound problems and discuss the difficulties.
❷ What kind of additional challenges might such culture-bound items hold for subtitlers? Why?

7.2 One of the advantages generally attributed to subtitling is that it respects the original soundtrack, encouraging the learning of foreign languages, particularly English. Given that most audiovisual programmes are shot in English and that people are increasingly familiar with this language, what do you think of the following quote from Gottlieb (2001:258):

For future subtitling, the consequences [...] could be that in several minor speech communities, we would not have to waste time subtitling from English. Most viewers would simply argue: "All the people who can read subtitles know English anyway, and besides, our language is not that different from English anymore, so why bother?"

7.1 Linguistic variation

Language, and spoken language especially, is as changeable as human beings and their surroundings, whereas writing is traditionally connected with the preservation of knowledge and with prestigious verbal art forms that appear to have more permanent and worthy functions than speech.

However, the changeability of speech is also one of its riches and, volatile as it may be, it is anchored in the community that it produces it. This makes it all the more interesting for films, especially those aiming to offer a realistic view of society. As a result, film language in its narrowly linguistic sense, often reflects this changeability. In other words, even though both fictional and non-fictional film dialogue are also shaped by film's other semiotic systems, they remain a reflection of society – if only a fictional one – since fiction is based on representations or interpretations of reality. And each society has not just one, but many 'languages'.

As a result, linguistic choices are never random in film. The way characters speak tells us something about their personality and background, through idiosyncrasies and through the socio-cultural and geographic markers in their speech, which affect grammar, syntax, lexicon, pronunciation, and intonation. Since linguistic variants are rooted in the communities that produce them, they are often used as a kind of typology in film, carrying a connotative meaning over and above their denotative functions. Sometimes, regional linguistic features are merely hinted at, but the current trend is for film language to exhibit more rather than less variation. In fact, such linguistic variants and the way they are introduced can also be indicators of the linguistic attitudes of the filmmakers. Consider, for instance, the works of British filmmakers such as Mike Leigh and Ken Loach, or recent blockbusters like *Brokeback Mountain.*

Subtitling, being a hybrid language form with its own limitations, is therefore faced with a formidable challenge: how does one translate the sophistication of spoken language variants into a regimented written form? The following discussion offers a survey of the difficulties and pitfalls, the partially resolvable or seemingly irresolvable challenges, and the aptitudes and creativity required to tackle them.

7.2 Denotative versus connotative meaning

Most subtitles display a preference for conventional, neutral word order, and simple well-formed stereotypical sentences (§6). Such sentences are the result of the various kinds of linguistic processing and rewriting discussed in previous pages, as well as subtitling's concern with clarity, readability, and transparent references. Indeed, the best subtitle is the one the viewer reads unknowingly.

This is one of the reasons why many of the interpersonal functions of dialogue get lost in the subtitles: they are perceived to relate to form rather than content. The same concern with denotative meaning underlies the rule, contained in most instructions and guidelines, that subtitling must use standard language. Besides, many people consciously or unconsciously improve their linguistic skills thanks to intralingual and interlingual subtitling, which also plays a part here.

And yet any translation student or scholar, any translator, any linguist, indeed any writer knows that the distinction between content and form is actually untenable. This is also why subtitling instructions are bound to contain contradictions. Ivarsson and Carroll (1998:157) state in their Code of Good Subtitling Practice:

8. The language register must be appropriate and correspond with the spoken word.
9. The language should be (grammatically) "correct" since subtitles serve as a model for literacy.

True, a linguistic register that corresponds with 'the spoken word' is not necessarily incorrect, but rule 9 above implies that subtitlers should correct grammar as well as other mistakes, if they do occur. In the following example, from a documentary about Robben Island, an ANC member is being interviewed. He mixes present and past tenses, whereas the Dutch subtitle does not: the turn has been rewritten in the simple past.

Example 7.1

We knew that that is where our leaders were kept.	→	We wisten dat daar onze helden zaten [We knew that our leaders were there.]

Here, the minor correction does no harm and helps improve the readability of the sentence. However, major rewriting, including the correction of mistakes, is quite common in the subtitles of interviews with non-native speakers, as well as in any other film featuring linguistic variation. In the example below regionally coloured vocabulary and grammar have been neutralized. The subtitle only indicates this is spoken language by using the single negative *j'étais pas* rather than the standard *je n'étais pas*.

Example 7.2

I'd'av walked if my dogs wasn't pooped out.	→	J'aurais marché si j'étais pas crevé. [I'd have walked if I wasn't exhausted.]

The question is: how important are such variants? Are they typical of the population group this person represents? And where does the borderline lie between correcting grammatical mistakes and interfering in the way a person speaks? The far-reaching effect such forms of rewriting can have on a film belonging to the documentary genre is discussed by Kaufmann (2004) in her study into the colourful and meaningful variation in the Hebrew spoken by immigrant interviewees in Israel. ARTE, the TV channel broadcasting the film, insisted that they should be subtitled in standard French. The scholar clearly demonstrates that part of the denotative meaning of the film was lost in the translation because of its homogenizing effect. Simply dismissing such features as either unwanted or untranslatable will not do. If all characters speak the same linguistic variant, not that much may be lost, but if one or a few stand out because of the type of language they speak, this should somehow be reflected in the dialogue exchanges. In such cases connotative meaning contributes to denotative meaning.

7.3 The translation of marked speech

Marked speech is broadly defined here as speech that is characterized by non-standard language features or features that are not 'neutral', even though they do belong to the standard language, and may therefore have more or less specific connotations. Speech can be marked by style or register, and it can also be either idiosyncratic or bound to socially and/or geographically defined population groups. Besides, marked speech includes taboo words, swearwords, and emotionally charged utterances such as interjections and exclamations.

In the best of worlds, the production company or customer commissioning the subtitles will supply a dialogue list that also contains a glossary, explaining all such instances of marked language, and a host of other linguistic and cultural particularities (§4.3). All the same, it remains up to the subtitler to determine how to translate a given term or expression. If no professional dialogue list is at hand, some Internet slang dictionaries and other websites, such as screenplay sites, can come in handy.

7.3.1 Style

Speaking is a social activity, i.e. when people speak, they address someone and they do so in a particular context. Speakers usually make their conversational contributions as adequate to the purpose and the situation as possible (Grice 1975), even if that purpose is no more than 'being sociable' or trying to avoid uneasy silences (Weigand 1992). Conversation analysis devotes much attention to locally generated phenomena in speech, and the impact of the immediate institutional setting or context on language use (Psathas 1995). In other words, people's background will have an influence on how they speak, but also the situation in which they find themselves. Film makes good use of this, carefully manipulating linguistic styles and register to narrative ends.

Following Wales's definition (1989:435-6), we understand style as "the manner of EXPRESSION in speaking or writing [...] We might talk of someone writing in an 'ornate style', or speaking in a 'comic style' [...] So style can be seen as variation in language use, whether LITERARY or non-literary". It depends on the choice of words, grammatical structures, use of literary devices, etc.

Ideally subtitlers should respect characters' manner of speaking, not only the content of their interventions. Still, the relevance of such stylistic features varies. Some films are so replete with them that they become an integral part of the story. Heritage films or literary films such as *Shakespeare in Love* are a case in point. In this particular film different literary and non-literary would-be Elizabethan styles are mixed.

Non-fictional literary programmes (e.g. a documentary about a poet), or filmed period plays can present similar challenges. In the BBC's *Bookmark* series, for instance, actors read lengthy passages from authors' novels and plays in order to acquaint the public with their writing style. The episode about Samuel Beckett, for instance, features long excerpts from his play *Krapp's Last Tape*. How does one subtitle such difficult literary styles?

The issue of what to do when subtitling Shakespeare plays, for instance, is taken up by Reid (1996:106-107). When Dutch television decided to broadcast a BBC Shakespeare series in the late 1980s, the subtitled series covered the complete range of possible subtitling strategies: from simple ancillary subtitles that did not try to imitate the playwright's poetic style to fully rhythmic and rhyming translations. What is the best solution? Leaving instructions issued by the customer or channel to one side, the target public, if it is known, may be an important factor. A full literary rendition will not be possible, but then again, it may not be required either. As Reid (ibid.) also mentions, viewers who are interested in drama, literature or poetry may well want to listen to the original, using the subtitles only for support. Besides, rendering a touch of the literary style of any ST is possible through lexical flourishes in the translation. It may be preferable not to adapt the grammar of the subtitles to that of an older or literary language variant since that might slow down comprehension rather than allow the viewer to enjoy the programme. The audience of a period piece will know people spoke a different variant of the source language at the time, and will get sufficient additional clues about the period from the setting, props, and costumes. So most of the time subtitles will occasionally hint at the period style, without rendering it in full, as in the example below from *Romeo and Juliet*.

Example 7.3

A: What sadness lengthens Romeo's hours? B: Not having that, which, having, makes them short.	→	Welk verdriet maakt de tijd zo lang? [What sadness makes time so long?] ——— Dat ik niet heb wat hem korten zou. [That I not have what would make it shorter.]

Subtitlers regularly apply the strategy of compensation when translating marked language. This means that a particular intervention becomes more 'marked' or 'colourful' in some subtitles, to compensate for the loss of such speech elsewhere in the translated film. In the next example, the neutral English word 'company' of the ST is translated as *boîte* in the French subtitles, which is much more informal in style, and suggests the way this character habitually speaks.

Example 7.4

You know in fact, I was gonna put one of your stickers on my taxi, but the company said it was against their policy.	→	Je voulais mettre un autocollant dans mon taxi... [I wanted to put up a sticker in my taxi...] ——— mais la boîte a dit que c'était contre sa politique. [but the joint said it was against their policy]

7.3.2 Register

The term register is "commonly used for those systematic variations in linguistic features common to particular non-literary situations, e.g. advertising, legal language, sports commentary" (Wales 1989:398-399). Register, in Trudgill's words (1999:online), is:

> a variety of language determined by topic, subject matter or activity, such as the register of mathematics, the register of medicine, or the register of pigeon fancying. In English, this is almost exclusively a matter of lexis, although some registers, notably the register of law, are known to have special syntactic characteristics.

By extension, the concept of register is used to denote the language produced by a particular social situation and characterized by the different degrees of formality linked to that situation. Halliday (quoted in Johnson and Johnson 1998:272) describes register as variation, not according to the 'user' but according to the 'use'.

Whereas technical registers may indicate a profession, others may reveal a character's prestige or social position. Subtitlers usually try to respect registers in as far as they fulfil a function in the narrative. A good example is provided by hospital series such as *ER*: the doctors use the register or jargon of their profession and this is somehow retained in the subtitles or replaced by target language equivalents (§7.4). As for registers determined by social relations and hierarchies, a certain degree of informality that implies closeness, or formality that suggests social difference, can simply be rendered through lexical choice.

A particularly thorny issue for translators generally, is the translation of formal versus informal second person forms of address, such as *vous* versus *tu* in French, *Sie* versus *du* in German, *usted* versus *tú* in Spanish, *u* versus *je/ge* in Dutch, etc. Some of the factors that make interlocutors opt for one rather than the other alternative are age, sex, group membership, and position of authority (Anderman 1993), but the use of the formal versus the informal personal pronoun can also have emotional connotations. In his analysis of the French film *Gazon maudit*, Mailhac (2000) points out how a character reverts back from *tu* to *vous* after a violent fight once he has calmed down, and wants to re-establish some kind of distance. He first shouts *Tu crois que ça va m'empêcher de te foutre mon poing dans la gueule!* [You think that will stop me from fucking hitting you in the face!], to then continue with a formal *vous*, in *Si je vous revois dans le coin, je vous démolis la tête. Et en prime, la batte de cricket, je vous l'enfonce dans le cul!* [If I see you again in the neighbourhood, I'll bash your head in. And as a bonus, I'll push this cricket bat up your arse].

Each case must be evaluated carefully, since the (unwritten) rules for choosing the formal versus the informal variant also differ from language to language. This means that problems can even occur when translating from, say French into German, languages that both have the morphological contrast. When translating from English, subtitlers have to resort to other visual, linguistic and narrative clues in the source film to determine relationships between characters. They might have to ask themselves questions such as: is this couple's relationship a professional one or a personal one? For how long have these two people known each other? Then they have to determine what this would mean in the target culture and decide whether the characters should address each other as *tu* or *vous* at that particular point. When translating into English, the use of first names or nicknames in one case, and 'Mr + family name' or a person's function, in the other, are obvious solutions for signalling informality versus formality. An example is given below, but usually quite a fair amount of creativity will be required.

Example 7.5

A: Gina… ¿Usted siguió dando clase? [Gina … Did you (formal) carry on teaching?]	→	Gina! Do you still teach, Professor?
B: Ay, no me trates más de usted. [Oh, do not address me with 'usted']		Gina will do.
A: ¿Seguiste dando clase? [Did you (informal) carry on teaching?]		Still teaching?

7.3.3 Dialects, sociolects, and idiolects

Whereas register affects the lexicon mostly, dialects and slang are characterized by non-standard grammar, specific lexical features, and a distinctive accent.

Dialect usually refers to a variety of language that is associated with subsets of users in a geographical area (e.g. regional and urban dialects), but also with a social group, i.e. a class dialect associated with socio-economic status (Wales 1989:119-120). The latter is also referred to as a sociolect, a term used in sociolinguistics to refer to a language variety distinctive of a particular social group or class. The word slang is used to denote a kind of jargon, but it is often close to anti-language, because standard lexical items are replaced by re-lexicalizations that are very informal, and purposefully designed, like a secret language. Tramps might use the word 'scrump' for 'steal', for instance (ibid.:423). Finally, an idiolect refers to "the speech habits of an individual in a speech community, as distinct from those of a group of people" (ibid.:230), and can be considered as the linguistic equivalent of a fingerprint. It is a system of individual stylistic features, and therefore much like a personal style, but it also includes more or less permanent features such as lisping, monotone delivery, favourite exclamations, etc.

To begin with, dialects – a generic term that covers all the above variants – pose a challenge because of the way they are embedded in a region or social group. Ideally, any dialectic occurrence should therefore first be pinpointed within the social and geographical layout of the target culture. Then its role in the audiovisual production should be evaluated: is this linguistic variant used throughout, or do only some characters make use of it? What function does this use of different speech types fulfil? An example that will be familiar to most is the use, in *Trainspotting*, of Scottish mixed with drugs-related insider jargon. In some scenes the language used by the protagonist friends is pitted against the very proper standard English of 'straight' others. From this perspective, it is important that the contrast is conveyed.

However, it is highly unlikely that any target language should have an identical equivalent, and this is a problem most dialects pose. The connotations of different target culture dialects will never be the same as those of the source culture dialects they replace. Moreover, dialects change, and the variant spoken in a film taking place in, say, 1930s Chicago, will not even exist in the source culture today. Besides, translating one dialect into another may pose comprehension problems at the target end, since even the native speakers of a particular language will not know all its dialects. Finally, dialects do not only deviate from standard languages in terms of lexical choice, but also in terms of grammar and pronunciation.

How can these problems be tackled in subtitles? Talented subtitlers again manage to 'suggest' this kind of language variation. They rely on interaction with the film's other signs to do the job and on an estimate of what viewers from the target culture might be expected to fill in themselves. Trying to put too much of the linguistic variation into the subtitles can have a reverse effect. One striking example is that of *La Haine*, a French low budget film that was hailed as:

> an inflammatory political pamphlet [that] raised several burning issues: youth unemployment, youth culture, integration of ethnic minorities, urban violence [...] *La Haine*'s youth speak a language that some critics call 'prose-combat'. It combines the particularities of the spontaneous languages spoken today in several French *cités*. (Jäckel 2001:223-224)

As a result, it also contains a form of slang that plays with almost any imaginable deviation from standard French. Since the language is part and parcel of the film story, the English subtitlers working on the cinema version tried to somehow render it. They opted for a mixture of styles, but with a strong American slant. Indeed, some kind of choice had to be made. However, the subtitles came in for strong criticism in the UK. Jäckel (2001:227) quotes one reviewer from Vertigo, as saying:

> The subtitles, which are a sloppy pastiche of black American slang in which Vinz and Hubert [two characters] speak as if they were *homeboys* in the *hood*, hinder rather than help an understanding of this dimension of the film.

Dialects are tricky, and subtitlers should never be drawing too much attention to their invaluable but preferably 'invisible' work. Below we look at a few concrete examples of what happens in subtitles tackling dialect.

7.3.3.1 Grammar

Subtitling almost always corrects grammar mistakes or dialectal grammar. Since dialects are signalled to the viewers through different channels, it is not necessary to retain all the deviations. Double negations are very common in different English non-standard variants, for instance, and viewers with some knowledge of English will recognize them. How they are dealt with in subtitling varies:

Example 7.6

Don't do nothing you wouldn't want me to hear about!	→	Niets ondeugends uithalen, hoor. [Don't do anything naughty, you hear.]
I ain't got no parents.	→	J'en ai pas de parents. [I have none of parents.]

In the example below, both the grammar ('I done' and 'ain't you') and the lexicon ('bust a gut') have been neutralized, leaving it up to the directness of the language and semi-aggressive tone of the speaker to inform the viewer that he feels little more than contempt for his interlocutor. The subtitler also relies on the images for context and local colour.

Example 7.7

You're about to bust a gut to know what I done, ain't you? Well, I ain't a guy to let you down.	→	Je wilt dolgraag weten wat ik gedaan heb, hè? Ik zal het je vertellen. [You'd love to know what I've done, wouldn't you. I will tell you.]

In those cases where variants simply must be suggested somehow, because they are part of the narrative, this is usually done through lexical choice.

7.3.3.2 Lexicon

Lexical variants are easier to suggest in subtitling than substandard grammar, as the following literal translation shows:

Example 7.8

But he's a mate, you know.	→	Mais c'est un pote. [But he's a mate.]

In the passages below, the colourful language spoken by a character from rural Oklahoma in the 1930s has partly disappeared from the subtitles, but the translation still conveys the rather aggressive tone of the man's turn. Besides, the whole poverty-stricken rural context, the poor and rebellious character's confident behaviour, his gestures, and physical interaction with peers and superiors alike, support the reduced translation in the subtitles throughout the film. Indeed, no scene is isolated; all scenes build on each other. As for the subtitles in this particular case, the much ruder *pif* for *nez* [hooter/nose] in the first example helps to convey the speaker's mood, whereas the choice of *renifler* [to sniff at] is rather offensive, suggesting animal behaviour. In the second subtitle, the character's protest is central, not his use of language.

Example 7.9

That big nose of yours been goin' over me like a sheep in a vegetable patch.	→	Ton gros pif n'a pas arrêté de renifler de mon côté. [Your big hooter has not stopped sniffing my way.]

I don't like nobody to draw a bead on me.	→	Richt dat geweer niet op me. [Don't point that gun at me.]

In the next set of excerpts, the Yiddish slang words 'schmuck', which stands for 'contemptible or foolish person' but also means 'penis', and 'schlep' meaning 'to drag oneself', are instances of strong language that also designate the Jewish origin of the speaker. This reference to the speaker's social group is lost in the Spanish subtitles.

Example 7.10

Ted is a schmuck.	→	Ted está chiflado [Ted is crazy.]
You mean...you want to schlep...all the way out to New jersey...	→	¿Quieres ir hasta allí? [You want to go down there?]

In the previous subsection on style, we saw that compensation can sometimes lend a hand. This happens here as well. In the following subtitle from the same film, the translation underscores the Jewish origins of the speaker, using 'synagogue' for 'temple'.

Example 7.11

You know I gotta be up early, tomorrow. I gotta be in temple.	→	Mañana tengo que madrugar e ir a la sinagoga. [Tomorrow I have to get up early and go to the synagogue.]

7.3.3.3 Accents and pronunciation

Accents and pronunciation are tricky to render in subtitles, and yet they may be important. Luckily, marked accents often go hand in hand with marked vocabulary. In the BBC series *Cold Feet*, the nanny Ramona speaks with a heavy Spanish accent and her pronunciation leaves much to be desired. This is an object of concern for David, the father of the child. In the Dutch subtitles Ramona's pronunciation is rendered in an improvised phonetic transcription. Using a proper phonetic transcription system is impossible since most viewers would not be able to read it, so the subtitler adapts the spelling of the target language to suggest a foreign accent. Besides, the Spanish *excusita* [excuse me] is retained.

Example 7.12

Excusita. I think I take my chicken into the lounge, ok?	→	*Excusita.* Ik eet m'n kiep in de zietkamer. [*Excusita.* I eate my tcheaken in ze lounche.]

In the musical *My Fair Lady*, accents and pronunciation are a crucial feature of protagonist Eliza Doolittle's Cockney English. She is a working class flower-girl, who is literally plucked off the street by Professor Higgins, a phonologist who undertakes to turn her into a lady. This, of course, includes teaching her how to speak the Queen's English. Some of the original dialectal features of the girl's speech must therefore be rendered. The (rather nonsensical) French subtitles make use of an improvised phonetic transcription. Such solutions must obviously be applied only to very short stretches of text. What the girl says is of little importance, only her pronunciation matters.

Example 7.13

Eliza: The rine in Spine stais minely in the pline.	→	In imbrin inopportin à chaquin est commin dans les plaines d'Espagne. ——— Un embrun inopportun à chacun est commun dans les plaines d'Espagne.
Higgins: The rain in Spain stays mainly in the plain. Eliza: Didn't I saiy that?" Higgins: No, Eliza, you didn't "saiy" that. You didn' even "say" that.		——— C'est ce que j'ai dit. [That's what I said.] ——— Non, pas une seule fois encore. [No, not one single time.]

Finally, speech impediments can also play a crucial role in characterization and these too must then be suggested in the subtitles. The subtitling of a narratively functional speech impediment in *The Life of Brian* is discussed in §7.6.2, example 7.50.

7.3.4 Emotionally charged language: taboo words, swearwords, interjections

Taboo words, swearwords and interjections are often toned down in subtitles or even deleted if space is limited, as in the examples below.

Example 7.14

What the fuck are you talking about?	→	¿De qué me hablas? [What are you talking about?]
Oh Christ, not that again.	→	¡Otra vez no! [Not again!]

However, such words fulfil specific functions in the dialogic interaction and, by extension, in the film story, so deleting them is certainly not the only or the best option available. Emotionally charged language has a phatic or exclamatory rather than denotative function and it can be quite idiosyncratic, but usually it is also linked to situations and/or population groups. Taboo words are tied in with local traditions and are used differently by different linguistic communities, depending on those communities' religious background, for instance (Díaz Cintas 2001b).

Subtitlers must therefore first identify and evaluate the impact and emotional value of a given word or expression in the source culture, and then translate it into a target culture equivalent that is deemed appropriate in the context.

A taboo is "a social or religious custom prohibiting or restricting a particular practice, or forbidding association with a particular person, place or thing" (NOED). Taboo words are words whose use is restricted or prohibited by social custom. Since swearwords are offensive words, used as an expression of anger, despair, contentment, emotion, etc. some swearwords are also taboo words, and require careful handling. Even if the connotative meaning and the strength of an expression have been rightly assessed in the source context, it always remains to be seen whether an expression with the same or similar strength and connotative meaning can be allowed in the TT. Besides, different cultures have different sensibilities and, consequently, different swearwords and taboo words. On the other hand, sensibilities change and some words gradually become more, or less, acceptable. The classic example of a word that appears to have made an inroad into the English language is 'fuck', one of the most used four letter words. Not so long ago it was absolutely not said in many circles, even if this did not always apply to cinema conversations. In the opening scene of *Four Weddings and a Funeral* for instance, the word is fired at the unsuspecting viewer five times in a row. However, saying such words is one thing, writing them is another matter, especially if they appear in enormous letters on the cinema screen. Indeed, Díaz Cintas (2001b:51) points out that expletives do not necessarily cause problems in novels, whereas they do in subtitles, in other words:

> The context where reading takes place must also be taken into consideration then. Although reading is ultimately an individual act, it is not

the same to read a book on your own, in private, as to read (and watch) a film as part of a gregarious group.

And yet, many curses and swearwords, including 'fuck' and its compounds and derivatives, are increasingly common in subtitles, at least in Europe. In the following examples, the strength of the expletives or taboo words in the source and target texts is well matched.

Example 7.15

Oh, Christ! (moans)	→	¡Joder!
Même ça, elle a merdé !	→	She even fucked that up!
They're a bunch of jerks.	→	C'est une bande d'abrutis.
Now, did you ever see what it can do to a woman's pussy?	→	Et vous avez vu ce que ça peut faire à un con?

The translation of taboo words and swearwords is crucial when they contribute to characterization or when they fulfil a thematic function in a film. This happens, for instance, in many Almodóvar films where women use macho language normally associated with men (Arnáiz 1998). In *La flor de mi secreto*, the protagonist's use of sexually explicit taboo language is not only part of her characterization but also an emancipatory tactic. Rendering her idiosyncratic use of expletives and taboo words is therefore crucial both from a narrative and a thematic viewpoint. When Leo confides to her maid that the phosphorous pills she is taking are increasing her sexual appetite rather than helping her with her memory loss, the TV solution sticks to the coarse original expression without omitting a single element of the comparison, whilst the video version tones down the whole expression by eliminating the reference to bitch. It seems here that such a deletion is not necessary and cannot be justified in terms of space and/or time constraints, since the TV version can easily accommodate exactly the same amount of information as the video does plus the controversial second part of the comparison.

Example 7.16

A : Blanca, tenía que decirte algo, pero no me acuerdo… [Blanca, I had to tell you something, but I don't remember...] B : Tome usted la pastilla del fósforo… [Take your pill of phosphorus...] A: Ah, sí… Memoria no recuperaré, pero esto me pone cachonda como una perra… [Ah, yes... I don't recuperate memory, but this makes me horny like a bitch...]	→	VIDEO Blanca, I had to tell you something, but I forgot what. ——— Take your phosphorus pill. ——— It doesn't help my memory, but God, it makes me horny. TV I forgot what I wanted to tell you, Blanca. ——— Why don't you take your tablets? ——— Ah, yes. They don't help my memory but they make me randy like a bitch.

Obviously, not only the target culture, but also the medium can have an influence on how some expletives or taboo words are translated. In the above examples, the subtitlers could also be exerting a form of self-censorship, but the translation is ultimately determined by what is deemed acceptable in the target culture, so self-censorship is a relative concept. What exactly the deciding factor is definitely merits more research. In the following examples some subtitles are more daring than others depending on the medium in which they have been commercialized.

Example 7.17

Es igual que su padre, la 'joía' por culo. [She is the same as her father, the fucking bugger.]	→	VHS She's just like her father. DVD She's like her father, the fucking bitch.
Mira Crystal, a veces pienso que sólo tienes sensibilidad en el chocho. [Look, Cristal, sometimes I think you only have feeling in your pussy.]	→	VHS I swear you've feeling in one place only. DVD Look, I think you only feel with your cunt!

A: Ah, pues ven pasado mañana... Es que quiero estar un día entero a solas con mi marido... [Ah, then come the day after tomorrow... It's that I want to be a whole day alone with my husband...] B: No faltaría más... ¡Y hártese de follá! [Of course... And gorge yourself fucking!]	→	VHS Then the next day. I want to be alone with my husband. ——— Of course! Enjoy yourself! TV The day after, then, I want to be alone with my husband. ——— Of course, and make sure you screw.

Judging the strength of the utterance to be used in the target film is a delicate issue, not only because of the strong social and ethical implications, but also because one is translating unstable connotative rather than denotative meanings. Swearwords, taboo words and interjections will therefore often have to be translated differently in different contexts, and their meanings can be a matter of interpretation. Subtitlers could even run into problems with the interpretation of a seemingly simple interjection such as 'wow'. Does it signify relief, surprise, or indignation?

In his investigation on the use of 'fuck' as well as its dubbed Catalan TV translation, Pujol (2006) finds that the word is used to express extreme anger, emphasis, disgust, contempt, surprise, and happiness. He also finds that its translation differs even within each category, and when used to relay extreme anger it is translated as *fill de puta* [son of a whore] and *malparit* [badly born]. The same happens in subtitling, of course, since such emotionally charged words must always be interpreted in context:

Example 7.18

Choose a fucking big television.	→	Choisir une putain de télé. [To choose a whore of a television]
Choose a three-piece suite on hire purchase in a range of fucking fabrics.	→	Choisir un salon à crédit dans un choix de tissus de merde. [To buy a living-room suite on hire purchase in a range of shitty fabrics.]
All the fucking chemicals.	→	Ces saloperies chimiques. [These filthy chemicals]

Ultimately, whether a particular translation decision is justified or not, can only be judged for each case and context individually. Still, the suppression or simplification of a character or interviewee's speech can come across as a case of suppressing the 'other', i.e. the person from a 'different' population group, the man or woman who does not fit into the 'standard' or 'standard language' of the (power) centre or establishment. Changes in register and style may render films more homogeneous, and changes that affect character representation ultimately affect the message of the film, i.e. the content that is subtitling's priority. On the other hand, not each and every swearword needs to be translated in order to convey characters' registers and/or personalities: peppering their speech with the occasional well-placed expletive will often do the trick. Moreover, using synonyms is also a way out, as example 7.18 shows. Even when words like the French *foutre* and the Spanish *follar* are used in their more literal meanings, English offers many options besides the obvious 'fuck', and the subtitler can resort to synonyms like 'screw', 'bonk', or 'shag'.

Still, what often compounds the problems posed by marked language for translators of audiovisual texts as opposed to other kinds of texts, such as drama or literature, is that oral language variation tends to be greater in audiovisual material. Film is more subject to change, it reflects real-life linguistic evolutions more closely, and, last but not least, it must be rendered in a hybrid form of written language within a well-defined spatial set-up. Consequently, what also underlies all the issues related to marked language is the consideration of what is generally acceptable for written as opposed to spoken language in the target culture.

7.4 The translation of culture-bound terms

Culture-bound terms are extralinguistic references to items that are tied up with a country's culture, history, or geography, and tend therefore to pose serious translation challenges. They are also referred to as cultural references, realia, and, more recently, ECRs or extralinguistic cultural-bound references (Pedersen, forthcoming).

For a start, films are distributed worldwide and through so many different media that some of them reach an enormous and extremely diverse audience within the very first months after their release. Film's propensity to travel means that the cultural references used to give shape to the story also travel extensively. Indeed, films continue to circulate long after their first launch and are often re-translated. Subsequent translations have greater time gaps to span. Furthermore, film semiotics is an important factor since both the visual and sound systems of a film contribute to the way it gives shape to its source culture or cultures, and foregrounds subtitling's vulnerability. In short, cinema's cultural diversity presents translators with a world of challenges.

In her article on cultural references and subtitling, Nedergaard-Larsen (1993:211) proposes the following main classification: references to geography, history, society, and culture. The taxonomy given by Vandeweghe (2005:40-41) focuses on three main types: geographic, ethnographic, and social-political references. In a recent article Ramière (2004) distinguishes among extra-linguistic geographical, historical and socio-cultural references. Many alternative groupings are possible and some may be more useful than others for specific analyses. The rather detailed version below is largely based on Grit (1997) as discussed in Vandeweghe (2005:40-41). Historically bound references could, in fact, fall under any one of these three headings.

- Geographical references
  - Objects from physical geography: savannah, mistral, tornado.
  - Geographical objects: downs, plaza mayor.
  - Endemic animal and plant species: sequoia, zebra.

- Ethnographic references
  - Objects from daily life: tapas, trattoria, igloo.
  - References to work: farmer, gaucho, machete, ranch.
  - References to art and culture: blues, Thanksgiving, Romeo and Juliet.
  - References to descent: gringo, Cockney, Parisienne.
  - Measures: inch, ounce, euro, pound.

- Socio-political references
  - References to administrative or territorial units: county, bidonville, state.
  - References to institutions and functions: Reichstag, sheriff, congress.
  - References to socio-cultural life: Ku Klux Klan, Prohibition, landed gentry.
  - References to military institutions and objects: Feldwebel, marines, Smith & Wesson.

The most challenging situation arises when no similar item exists in the target culture and/or if it is unknown to the majority of the target audience. Rabadán (1991:164) has termed such occurrences 'referential vacuums'. Translators must then find an alternative that will allow the viewers to fill in the target culture gap as adequately as possible. Overall, the solutions on offer range from very literal transfers to complete recreations.

Within translation studies, numerous scholars have devised different classifications of the strategies on offer, labelling and re-labelling them in an attempt to achieve a comprehensive taxonomy. Still, all existing classifications have minor deficiencies, since categories are always bound to overlap to some extent. We propose a classification based on Díaz Cintas (2003) and Santamaria Guinot (2001). Some of the strategies discussed below are more commonly used in subtitling than others.

1). Loan
2). Calque or literal translation
3). Explicitation
4). Substitution
5). Transposition
6). Lexical recreation
7). Compensation
8). Omission
9). Addition

In the case of a **1) loan**, the source text word or phrase is incorporated into the target language and text, because no translation is possible and both languages use the exact same word. Such words often have the same foreign language source. Examples are references to drinks or culinary specialities such as 'cognac' or 'muffin', but also place names that remain unchanged such as 'San Francisco', or references to historical events such as 'perestroika'.

A **2) calque** is a literal translation, e.g. *Secretario de Estado* in Spanish for Secretary of State, when *Ministro de Asuntos Exteriores* [Minister of Foreign Affairs] would be a more common and transparent title. Sometimes such terms do require an explanation. An English or American public with no prior knowledge of Dutch history will find the English calque 'States-General' for the Dutch *Staten-Generaal*, quite mysterious. This may be problematic in subtitling, where one rarely has room for explanations, unless the context or visuals come to the rescue. The degree of transparency of calques will therefore vary. The first example below is rather straightforward; in the second one, however, the literal translation has a foreignizing effect. The question is whether this effect is desirable in the particular context.

Example 7.19

I am thinking of running the Boston Marathon.	→	Quizá me apunte al maratón de Boston. [Maybe I'll enrol for the Boston Marathon.]
A: Yeah? What's that there? B: You want? They're jelly doughnuts. You want a jelly doughnut?	→	¿Qué es eso? - Buñuelos de jalea. [What is that?] [Doughnuts of jelly.] ——— ¿Quieres uno? [Do you want one?]

In the next and last example of a calque the speaker is referring to the Anglo-Saxon practice of car boot sales. At such sales people sell second-hand items they no longer need more or less literally from the boot of their car, which serves as a shop window or market stand. Since the practice is unknown in a country like Spain, the following subtitle would no doubt puzzle a Spanish audience.

Example 7.20

You know sell blankets. We'll work off the hood of the car or something.	→	Montar una tienda en el capó del coche o algo así. [Set up shop on the hood of the car or something similar.]

In the case of **3) explicitation**, the subtitler tries to make the source text more accessible by meeting the target audience half way, either through specification, using a hyponym, or by generalization, using a hypernym or superordinate. In the first case 'tulip' or 'daisy' might be used for 'flower'. In the second case *Le Soir*, might be translated as 'a Belgian (quality) paper', or 'a pick-up truck' as *un camión* [a lorry] depending on the space available and the need to explain. Hypernyms are by far the most frequent in subtitling since generalizations usually have an explanatory function, whereas hyponyms narrow down the meaning of a word. It would be unlikely for the word 'dog' to be replaced by 'Schnauzer', for instance.

The use of hypernyms includes the translation of brand names or abbreviations by the institution or concept they stand for: the Flemish *ASO* thus becomes 'secondary school' and *VRT* 'public TV'. From a denotative point of view this works perfectly, but local colour is obviously lost. The use of hypernyms, often dictated by the need for transparency, contributes to the loss of specificity that is typical of subtitling and shows that subtitlers cannot always opt for the shortest word available, since clarity may have to come first. In the following example 'Mau-Mau', a reference to a violent African secret society of the 1950s, has been replaced in French by *cannibales*. The speaker is referring to the black Manhattan neighbourhood Harlem.

Example 7.21

Fucking Mau-Mau land.	→	Un quartier de cannibales. [A neighbourhood of cannibals.]
Whole stole all your jewellery and sold it on E-Bay?	→	Wie stal je juwelen en verkocht ze op internet? [Who stole your jewellery and sold it on Internet?]

Explicitation can also take the form of translation, as in the following English example, where the South-African source text audience was expected to know the Afrikaans *Umkhonto We Sizwe* and the target audience was not. Note also that the present tense has been turned into a simple past, the tense that is more usual for storytelling. The switch does take away some of the directness of the witness account.

Example 7.22

If you hear the name ANC or PAC or Umkhonto We Sizwe you know it is communist and that it is your enemy.	→	Als je 't woord ANC hoorde of PAC of De Speer van de natie, [If you heard the word ANC or PAC or The Spear of the Nation,] ——— wist je dat 't om communisten ging, je vijand. Zo was 't je bijgebracht. [you knew it was about communists, your enemy, so you'd been taught.]

4) Substitution, as we understand it here, is a variant on explicitation, and a phenomenon that is typical of subtitling. It is resorted to when spatial constraints do not allow for the insertion of a rather long term, even if it exists in the target culture and a hypernym or hyponym would therefore not really be required. Typical examples are the names of culinary dishes that have become popular in different countries. The French *sauce hollandaise* is literally known as *hollandaisesaus* in Dutch but it might be translated as *botersaus* [butter sauce] if the space and time limitations are very strict. A Hungarian *goulash* will be 'goulash' in almost any European language but will sometimes become a 'stew' for the same reason.

In the case of **5) transposition**, a cultural concept from one culture is replaced by a cultural concept from another. This strategy is resorted to when the target viewers might not understand the ST reference should a loan or calque be used, and there is no room for explicitation. Transposition also implies some form of explanation or clarification. The British 'Marks & Spencer's' might be replaced by the Dutch *HEMA*, although this can result in a conflict with the foreign culture presented on screen, endangering the credibility of the translation. The transposition of *een vieruurtje* to '(afternoon) tea' rather than the literal 'a four o'clock' would no doubt be more successful. Transposition works best when the concepts referred to are not too different. References to 'the Bush administration' are standardly translated in Dutch as *de regering Bush* [the Bush government] because *Bush administratie* would have a different meaning.

Measurements and currencies are often adapted to the system in use in the target culture, but not always (§5.3.4.4). In the following example 'dollars' are considered known, but the subdivisions are not.

Example 7.23

A dollar eighty-five	→	Un dollar quatre-vingt cinq.
Hey Travis, have you got change for a nickle?	→	Hé, Travis. T'as la monnaie de cinq cents? [Hey, Travis. You have change for five cents.]

When the ST contains clearly audible names, however, transposition may be problematic. The viewer will hear the character say one name and read another, which can be confusing. In the case of brand names that are not commercialized globally, the use of a hypernym might be a better solution.

Example 7.24

I've brought you some Matey bubble bath.	→	Ik heb badschuim voor je. [I've got bubble bath for you.]
Howie, no. You know, I can't be your Rice-A-Roni.	→	Howie, no. No quiero ser tu regalo de consolación. [Howie, no. I don't want to be your consolation prize.]

The names of (local) celebrities can obviously not be replaced by hypernyms. Still, a nationally known VIP may be completely unknown in the target country, so leaving his or her name in the subtitle may be just as mystifying. On the other hand, transposition is awkward because of the culture clash between the name on the sound track and the name in the subtitle. Besides, the original name may have significant connotations, so these must be considered when making a decision. Theoretically, the supposed familiarity of the name should be balanced against the message the speaker wants to bring across by mentioning it.

The degree to which subtitlers expect their audiences to know culture-bound items varies considerably from country to country. Whereas Spanish subtitlers will usually look for translations and explanations, Flemish and Dutch subtitlers increasingly tend to just retain the cultural reference in the case of English or American films, even if this might be quite mystifying for a large part of the audience.

Example 7.25

Ooh, is that root beer?	→	Is dat root beer?

However, the trend to keep cultural references unchanged in the subtitles is also becoming more pronounced in languages like Italian and Spanish, raising issues regarding comprehensibility of the translation as well as prominence of the English language and cultures. The fact that the soundtrack is heard and the audience might spot the discrepancy between subtitle and dialogue is one of the common reasons put forward to justify this type approach.

Example 7.26

You've been a hot topic of conversation ever since you've joined the Structure Family. N.B. Structure is the name of a retailer.	→	Sei spesso argomento di conversazione da quando sei alla Structure. [You're often a topic of conversation since you've been in Structure.]
A: You seem in a strange mood. B: No, no, no. I'm just probably a little drunk. A: On Perrier?	→	Te noto un poco raro. - Estaré algo borracho. [I notice you a bit strange. - I may be a little drunk.] ——— ¿Con Perrier? [With Perrier?]

6) Lexical recreation or the invention of a neologism in the target language is warranted, may indeed be inevitable, when the source text speaker makes up words as well. The neologism is placed between quotation marks in the subtitle.

Example 7.27

This definitely rates about a 9.0 on my weird shit-o-meter.	→	Esto merece un 9 en mi "rarezametro". [This merits a 9 on my oddity-meter.]
Incandiferous!	→	¡"Esplendescente"!

7) Compensation means making up for a translational loss in one exchange by overtranslating or adding something in another. It is a popular strategy in subtitling, even though it may not always be practicable due to the oral-visual cohabitation of the source and target languages: the subtitles should not deviate too much from the soundtrack if the readers/viewers can be expected to understand at least part of what they hear. All the same, compensation can be a blessing for the translation of humorous films (§7.6).

8) Omission has been discussed extensively in §6.2.2. It does not seem like much of a strategy, but is sometimes unavoidable either because of space-time limitations or because the target language does not have the corresponding term. References to ranks or professional positions, e.g. with the police force or in a medical environment, can be very difficult to translate. In the following first passage from the detective series *A Touch of Frost*, both spatial constraints and terminology play a part in the decision to omit the word 'superintendent'. In the second subtitle, the name of the restaurant, which the target viewers would probably not be familiar with, has been omitted:

Example 7.28

A: Does he know you're a policeman? B: My name is Frost, Superintendent.	→	Weet hij dat je van de politie bent? - Mijn naam is Frost. [Does he know you're a policeman? - My name is Frost.]
I thought we'd have a light dinner, you know, because we had a rich lunch at Twenty-One, I thought.	→	Cenaremos algo ligero, después de esa comilona. [We'll eat for dinner something light, after that blowout.]

Finally, and contrary to what might be expected, **9) additions** also occur in subtitling, especially in passages containing cultural references that are expected to cause comprehension problems but are essential for a good understanding of the programme. In such cases, information is added. Additions are always a form of explicitation, as in the following examples:

Example 7.29

I first saw him at Palantine Campaign Headquarters at 63rd and Broadway.	→	Je l'ai vu à la permanence du candidat Palantine sur la 63ième et Broadway. [I saw him at the headquarters of the candidate Palantine at 63rd and Broadway.]
Now, you can send him to the chair.	→	Podéis mandarle a la silla eléctrica. [You can send him to the electric chair.]
After all, this was boom-town.	→	Londres était la ville du boum. [London was the boomtown.]

7.5 The translation of songs

In this section we will limit ourselves to songs with audible lyrics, that is, lyrics that the film's first target audience has no trouble understanding and that can therefore have a bearing on the interpretation of the film. However, even within this category further distinctions must be made (§5.3.1.1).

7.5.1 Deciding what to translate

Some songs do not have to be subtitled. Firstly, the customer may have given instructions. Secondly, the dialogue list may not include the lyrics and the studio, channel, or translator may therefore decide that the songs are not important. Furthermore, the language in which a song is sung must be considered. If the lyrics are not in the same language as the rest of the film (e.g. a French song in a British film), they ought to be subtitled into a third language (say, Japanese) only if they were also subtitled in English in the original version. However, a film in Catalan, for instance, may not subtitle an Italian song, because the audience can be expected to understand it, but that same song would have to be subtitled in a German subtitled version. The linguistic gap between Italian and German is bigger than that between Italian and Catalan. If a translation is required but no dialogue list has been provided, Internet is an invaluable source for finding lyrics (see Appendix 3), although it must be used with caution. The version found on Internet may differ from that in the film, in which case the lyrics heard on the soundtrack get priority.

In the event that a song and the source film dialogue are in the same language, a number of things still need to be considered. To begin with, there may be a technical limitation. At the beginning or at the end of a film, a song may overlap with the credits. Theoretically, the song could then be subtitled, but guidelines from distribution companies may require that priority be given to the text on screen. In the middle of a film, there may be a degree of overlap with the dialogue. If this occurs, the subtitles always give priority to speech over lyrics. Indeed, should the opposite strategy be required, the film will provide cues and the song will be louder than the voices, or the voices will become gradually inaudible. In scenes with some overlap, decisions as to whether or not to subtitle a song only have to be made when lyrics and dialogue stop overlapping at some point, and the lyrics remain audible.

Then again, some songs may be internationally known, like songs by The Beatles, whereas others may be merely used to suggest a certain period, which means the melody is just as important as the words. Moreover, some songs may have very simple lyrics, and we regularly hear songs on the radio that are not translated for us. If the audience can be expected to either know the song or understand it, subtitles are not required, especially if the lyrics do not contribute much to the story. But if a song is rather long, viewers who do not understand the words will start wondering about their meaning at best, and become seriously frustrated in the worst case. It is safe to say that if directors decide to include a song, this is usually done for a purpose, and viewers who do not understand the words cannot estimate their relevance. So, when in doubt: subtitle.

Indeed, some songs actually constitute the essence of a film, as it happens in musicals. Others support the narrative more or less explicitly, whether or not they have been written for the film, and whether or not they are extraneous to the story, or part of the fictional scene (as when a character switches on the radio or walks into a bar). Others still contribute to the story in a more indirect sense, by suggesting a mood or creating an atmosphere. These cases must be given special attention, even if only half the song is truly audible.

Songs in musicals should be translated, as should songs that contribute explicitly to the film story, even in documentary films. The example on the left below is a parody on the song *Island in the Sun*, rewritten for *Boom Boom Bang*, a documentary on the country of Malaysia, which questions progress if all it means is killing local customs and ethnicity as well as nature. The lyrics of the original 1950s song by Harry Belafonte and Lord Burgess are on the right. The camera focuses on the two female singers on a stage, and the first and second stanza of their song run as follows, the words are clearly audible.

Example 7.30

Our islands in the sun Taken over for development Never mind the environment No more coral now and no more *ikan*.	This is my island in the sun Where my people have toiled since time begun I may sail on many a sea Her shores will always be home to me
This is my island Lankawie Where all the goods are duty-free They're building hotels so quickly Is this the new curse of Mahsuri?	Oh island in the sun Willed to me by my father's hand All my days I will sing in praise Of your forest, waters, your shining sand.

The lyrics obviously contribute to the message of the film, a message that is further enhanced through intertextuality for those viewers who know the song upon which the new version is based.

Unfortunately not all instances in which a song is used are as clear-cut. Even if a song does not actually provide any insight into a character's thoughts or story, but merely suggests somebody's mood, this may be relevant. In the film *About a Boy*, we hear the following song when the protagonist Marcus returns home after his mother's failed suicide and finds her suicide note. The song reflects his mood, is narratively functional, and calls therefore for its translation. The subtitler renders the content reasonably faithfully and shifts a few words around to respect, and even emphasise, the rhythm and rhyme. This may upset the standard French word order slightly, but does not come across as unusual precisely because this is a song. A few concepts are rendered more explicitly. Note that none of the other songs in this film are subtitled.

Example 7.31

There's nothing I could say To make you try to feel OK	→	*Je ne peux rien dire, rien,* *Pour te faire sentir bien.* *[I can say nothing, nothing,* *To make you feel good.]*
And nothing you could do To stop me feeling the way I do		*Et rien dans ton comportement* *Ne changera mes sentiments.* *[And nothing in your behaviour* *Will change my feelings.]*
And if the chance should happen That I never see you again		*Si le mauvais sort voulait* *Qu'on ne se revoie jamais* *[If bad luck would want* *Us never to see each other again]*
Just remember that I'll Always love you.		*Rappelle-toi* *Que je t'aimerai toujours.* *[Remember That I'll always love you.]*

The indirect but still significant way in which lyrics can have a bearing on a film are demonstrated by the following example from *The Grapes of Wrath*. During a musical evening in one of the poor immigrant camps at which the itinerant Joad family is staying, Tom sings while he is dancing with his mother, the following song about Red River Valley:

Example 7.32

> Come and sit by my side if you love me
> do not hasten to bid me adieu.
> But remember the Red River Valley
> and the boy who had loved you so true.

The scene is full of suspense. Tom's mother is afraid her son will be arrested, whereas Tom tries to reassure her. What is more, the song has a thematic value. Millichap (1983:36) points out that the melody of the song returns in a number of important scenes as background music, and he attributes a nostalgic function to it. The 'Red River Valley' symbolizes the little farm from which the family have been evicted and to which they will never return. Ideally, the song ought to be translated when subtitling the film into a foreign language.

7.5.2 Deciding how to translate

Once the decision to translate has been taken, three issues must basically be weighed up against each other: content, rhythm, and rhyme. In the song about Malaysia, above, content obviously gets priority. The song, like the entire documentary, criticizes thoughtless progress and development. The song from *About a Boy* reflects Marcus's mood and offers a comment on his relationship with his mother, which must somehow be retained. The third song refers to a 'Red River Valley' from the past that has been lost. The feelings of love, tenderness, departure, and loss must be somehow conveyed, but this can be done through a rather 'free' translation. In some cases, rendering the atmospheric quality of the lyrics will do and an accurate translation may not be required.

In a musical on the other hand, songs often take on the function of dialogue and in those cases the content must really be respected. In the following example from *My Fair Lady*, Higgins, the phonologist, is commenting on the way the working class's pronunciations betrays their lack of schooling. The French translation has undergone a shift, the reference to the man's pronunciation is gone, but the subtitle still renders the gist of the conversation.

Example 7.33

Hey, you, sir, did you go to school? 'What do ya tike me for, a fool?' Well, no one taught him 'take' instead of 'tike'.	→	Vous avez été à l'école ? " Oui... parole ! " [Did you go to school? "Why... of course!"] ――― Cela ne fait pas honneur a votre école. [That is no credit to your school.]

On the other hand, not only content matters; the melodies of film songs are important too. Subtitles that respect the rhythm of a song are easier to read because of the parallelism or synchrony between words and soundtrack. Balancing content against rhythm is therefore important. After all, subtitles are a supporting translation and should not detract too much attention from the images and soundtrack. Whereas smooth parallel rhythms may facilitate reading, rhyme schemes, and especially rhyme schemes that differ from the original ones, may attract too much attention.

7.6 The translation of humour

7.6.1 Pinning down humour

Although we all have an intuitive understanding of what humour is, defining it is such a tricky undertaking that definitions of humour and approaches to its study have accumulated over time, and continue to do so. We shall therefore not attempt to offer yet another definition at this point, but rather look at some of the recurrent features of humour and the translation challenges it poses for subtitling (see also Zabalbeascoa 2005).

In the literature on the translation of humour much attention is devoted to questions relating to its (un)translatability, or at least to the difficulties involved in its translation. However, in practice, comedies have proved to travel well, be it in book form, on the stage, or on the screen. In other words: humour is certainly translated somehow.

One feature that most respondents asked to define humour will include in their definitions is that it involves laughter or at least smiling. Indeed, the following definition from the *MacMillan English Dictionary for Advanced Learners* (2002:702) states that humour is "the quality that makes a situation or entertainment funny: *a novel full of humour*". Humour is therefore defined as a quality that has 'fun' as its consequence. However, by stating that humour is a quality that produces 'fun', the definition avoids defining what the 'quality' itself is. What is more, the dictionary also offers some epithets frequently used with humour such as black, dry, gentle, grim, morbid, sardonic, tongue-in-cheek, and wry, which suggest that humour comes in 'types' and also that not all humour, e.g. morbid humour, is necessarily funny, or funny for all concerned.

Making abstraction of different types of humour, Vandaele (1999) characterizes the phenomenon on the basis of two concepts, allegedly present in all forms, albeit in different quantities or qualities: incongruity and superiority. The author defines 'incongruity' as a contradiction of cognitive schemes, which, according to Asimakoulas (2001), can also be interpreted as a deviation from a generally accepted norm. That is, a particular phrase creates an expectation in a given context and then fails to fulfil it: it deviates from the norm that would usually regulate the utterance and the expectations attached to it. Consider the following example from *Shrek*:

Example 7.34

Donkey:	So, where's this fire-breathing pain-in-the-neck anyway?
Shrek:	Inside, waiting for us to rescue her.
Donkey:	I was talking about the dragon, Shrek.

The words 'fire-breathing' in Donkey's first turn lead the viewer to believe that he is referring to the dragon that the two heroes are about to take on. Shrek's reply is therefore unexpected and is meant to provoke laughter because 'her' refers to the princess they are supposed to rescue. Beautiful princesses do not 'breathe fire' in traditional fairy-tales, but *Shrek* is not a traditional fairy-tale, it is a parody of one, and therefore continually undermines our 'traditional' expectations or the generally accepted fairy-tale norms.

Superiority amounts to a form of increased happiness related to a heightened self-esteem (Vandaele 1999:241), that is, besides causing laughter, humour can also make all or some of the parties involved feel they are better than others. This feature highlights humour's "very visible social functioning: being superior is always being superior-to-someone" (ibid.). One can, of course, have different reasons for feeling superior; one might feel superior because one has understood an incongruity, but, as Vandaele points out, a feeling of superiority can also be related to a feeling of aggression, humour in the sense of 'laughing at'. This then takes us back to 'morbid humour', in which the person telling a morbid joke may be laughing at or trying to provoke laughter at the expense of the dead, for instance. On the other hand, superiority is a necessary but not a sufficient condition for creating humour, and the same applies to incongruity, since feelings of superiority and incongruities, or deviations from a norm, do not automatically provoke laughter. The concepts of superiority and incongruity therefore cannot fully explain what humour is nor how it works, still, they are what Vandaele (2002:167) calls essential "factors of humour" or some of its "building blocks". This means that they can go a long way in helping to identify specific instances and explaining how they work.

Incongruity is also considered to be an essential feature of irony, which Pelsmaekers and Van Besien (2002:243) adequately describe in terms of Austin (1962) and Searle's (1969, 1976) speech act theory. This theory can equally well be applied to humour more generally.

> In Austin's view, when a speaker utters a sentence, without necessarily being ironic, this constitutes a locutionary act, as well as an illocutionary act and a perlocutionary act. The locutionary act consists of saying something with a propositional content. At the same time the speaker performs an illocutionary act, i.e. in saying something he or she makes an assertion, a promise, a request and so on. By the same token, the speaker performs a perlocutionary act in that he or she causes a certain effect in the hearer.

According to these scholars, irony arises when "there is some kind of contrast or incongruity between what is said (the propositional content) and what can be inferred from the situation" (2002:243). One of irony's perlocutionary effects can then be laughter, as in the case of humour. In fact, we shall consider laughter, the effect most commonly associated with humour, as its primary perlocutionary effect. This effect, i.e. the 'fun' element in humour, will therefore guide us in our selection and analysis of examples. But we are not out of the woods yet. Indeed, some utterances provoke laughter unintentionally, whereas others fail to provoke the laughter they intended, or catch on only with a limited group. The 'fun' element in humour is very unstable, and this brings us to another one of its features.

Humour does not function in isolation. It is not only rooted in its co-text (the dialogue sequence or scene/sequence in which it occurs, for instance), but also in socio-cultural, linguistic and even personal contexts. The universality of humour is relative. Chiaro (1992) has stressed the difficulty with which some types of humour cross linguistic, geographic, temporal socio-cultural, and even personal boundaries. Indeed, not only different cultures, but also different directors conceptualize humour in different ways, and see the comic in very divergent situations. In some cases ethics may play a part, as it does in the translation of taboo words, but distance must also be reckoned with: linguistic distance (between the language pairs and cultures concerned), as well as temporal distance (some jokes rely on topical events). As Vandaele writes (2002:165):

> It is clear [...] that: we may not always be able to grasp the sender's intentions; we may have our own (conscious or unconscious) agenda while grasping intentions; many other contextual elements play a role in the interpretation process; original contexts may be absent; new contexts may emerge continuously; the humorous function of a text may be combined with other textual functions. This means that a translator of humour has to make decisions.

For translators the first challenge obviously consists in understanding what is humoristic in the source text, recognizing the clues, the incongruities, but also the comic repertoires linked to particular humoristic genres, or commonly used tricks such as exaggeration, or understatement. Then they have to find a way of transferring the perceived humour into the target text and reformulating it into a new utterance that will hopefully provoke an equivalent effect, *in casu* laughter, a smile, or maybe a smirk. Interpreting the source text humour is the first step; evaluating how the target viewer will see and interpret a particular instance is the next; rephrasing the humour is the final outcome.

7.6.2 Subtitling humour

Subtitling humour requires insight and creativity, but it is also a matter of establishing priorities. Humour can occur on different levels: it can arise from the interaction between word and image, or a play on words, but it can just as well be an integral part of the story plot, reside in experiments with genre features and intertextuality, etc. Some instances will therefore be much easier to translate than others, and their importance for the programme at hand will also vary. Identifying to what extent humour is part of the texture of the film is crucial. According to Zabalbeascoa (1997:332)

> [I]t would seem that there is often a need to strike a balance between a search for comic effect by making the translated jokes as funny as possible, on the one hand, and, on the other, finding solutions that will not put the viewer off because [...] the plot, structure and the coherence of the text are weakened for the sake of certain witty one-liners.

Sometimes laughter is more important than rendering the exact semantics of a passage, sometimes the reverse will be the case. Zabalbeascoa (1996) bases his approach to humour in audiovisual texts on the appraisal of priorities and restrictions that apply to each instance, which is itself seen to be embedded in a larger whole. He distinguishes three planes on which translation priorities should be set. First, there is a vertical scale of importance: a particular instance can have top priority, very low priority or anything in between. Second, there is a horizontal scale that indicates whether humour is a priority on a global level (for the whole text) or a rhetorical device used locally (in a particular exchange). Third, there is a scale of equivalence-non-equivalence, which dictates whether there is a priority for the translation to be equivalent to the source text in certain respects and to a certain extent, or not. Is a faithful translation required or should the joke be replaced by a different one?

As Asimakoulas (2001:54) summarizes, by way of example, "when translating comedy, rendering the ST as a humorous text is of high priority in terms of importance (vertically), a global priority (relevant for the entire text) and an equivalence priority". Still, whether or not a joke is translated or simply replaced by another is not only determined by genre. Translation is not always feasible, whereas adaptation can result in clashes with the images or the logic of the fictional world, and is also determined by external factors. When subtitling classics, subtitlers will tend to be more careful with far-reaching interventions than when subtitling soaps or sitcoms. The target context as well as co-text must be considered. What is more, subtitlers may have received instructions. Still, whatever the approach, evaluating the importance of humorous passages in the film one is subtitling both locally and on a higher level will help produce adequate translations and will limit frustration about unsolvable problems, since some jokes are not as important as others. On the other hand, an attitude of resignation should not be one's starting point, and creative subtitlers regularly come up with splendid solutions, even if humour should not be preserved at all costs, and certainly not at the expense of textual coherence, or loss of fluency and idiomatic language. The subtitles must continue to support the bigger picture and be understandable at a glance.

Detecting humour is facilitated in some soaps and television comedies by their use of so-called 'canned laughter', which indicates the very place where humour occurs. On the other hand, in films and other types of TV programmes the device is never used, and it certainly does not offer any help in understanding what is going on, in evaluating the target context, or producing an equivalent in the target text. It does call for a synchronous humoristic translation. This also happens when characters or interviewees laugh at their interlocutors' jokes. If the subtitles fail to produce a humorous translation at the right time, they enter into conflict with the image and soundtrack, and the viewers will be under the impression that they are missing something. However, a lack of synchrony is not always due to a poor translation, it can also be the result of inaccurate spotting, or simply of differences in word order in the source and target languages. Even though such shifts in synchrony may be confusing for viewers who understand the film dialogue to some extent, provoking laughter slightly earlier or later is not such a big deal, given the myriad of restrictions subtitlers face. The most important thing is that more or less similar emotions are provoked.

And sometimes humour fares better in AVT than in, say, literary translation. Subtitling may be constrained by sound and image, but both visually conveyed information and oral information in the form of sounds can at times be of great help. Even if the universality of images is limited, a lot of film humour relies on the semiotics of the image. It can work through the incongruous juxtaposition of images, for instance, or through the gestures and facial expressions of the speakers. What is more, some of us may regret the dominance of Anglo-Saxon films on our screens, but North American cinema has created an internationally known culture that limits the problems of comprehension at the target end. As Chiaro (2005:139) writes, some North American productions (e.g. *My Big Fat Greek Wedding*) are consciously poured into an international rather than a national mould in order to travel better, which, together with good marketing, certainly helps. Nevertheless, subtitlers must be aware that, like in the case of culture-bound issues, national traditions will vary in their degree of tolerance for non-translation. Subtitlers in Greece may have a different view on what their presumed target audience will understand to subtitlers in Denmark.

In the next pages, we consider different types of humour that occur regularly in audiovisual productions and the tactics that subtitlers employ in order to tackle them, tactics which are similar to those used for the translation of other cultural references such as explicitation, substitution, compensation, and addition.

In his classification of audiovisual humour, Zabalbeascoa (1996) distinguishes between six types of jokes in dubbed television situation comedies. His classification is an expansion of a more basic one designed by Raphaelson-West (1989) that distinguishes between linguistic, cultural and universal jokes. Since Zabalbeascoa's expanded classification is a useful one for distinguishing between different translation challenges, their varying degrees of complexity, and the translation strategies they require, we use it as a starting point for our discussion.

1) International or bi-national jokes: In such jokes the humorous effect "does not depend on either language-specific word play or familiarity with unknown specific aspects of the source culture" (Zabalbeascoa 1996:251). The author favours the concept of bi-national jokes, because it is difficult to ascertain when a joke can be deemed truly international. It is therefore safer to refer to specific pairs of languages in this context. The referent of such jokes is part of the source culture, but the humorous effect is retained if the joke is transferred to the target text by way of a calque. In other words, its referent is sufficiently known in the target culture for the audience to recognize and interpret it in context. Examples of such bi-national or international referents that can be the object of humour are: internationally known film stars, multinationals, well-known tourist attractions, famous artists or politicians, political events that have made the world news, well-known facts about a country's history, etc. In our view, some such referents will, indeed, be fairly international, but some might travel only shorter distances and be merely known to the viewers of neighbouring countries, or countries that share part of their history. In any of these cases, the joke should not cause major subtitling problems. In fact, space constraints permitting, a literal translation of the content and verbatim rendering of the referent is the most obvious solution.

Example 7.35

I can't listen to that much Wagner, you know? I start to get the urge to conquer Poland.	→	No puedo escuchar tanto Wagner. Me entran ganas de conquistar Polonia. [I can't listen to so much Wagner. I get the urge to conquer Poland.]

Respecting the culture-bound references does not mean that faithfulness to the ST must be complete. In the following example the original question has become an affirmative sentence in the subtitles. It is quite feasible for the subtitler to use one of the common tricks of the trade when reformulating an exchange, without losing its humour.

Example 7.36

A: I think you gotta see- I gotta- You gotta, You gotta go back to your shrink. B: What do you m- A: I want you to see Doctor Ballard again. B: Huh? Larry, I went for two years. A: I'm s- yeah, I know. But you- You know how General Motors will recall defective cars?	→	Creo que tienes que volver al psiquiatra, al Dr Ballard. [I think you should return to the shrink, to Dr Ballard.] ——— Ya fui durante dos años. - Lo sé, pero… [I already went for two years. - I know, but…] ——— La General Motors revisa su coches defectuosos. [General Motors checks its defective cars.]

Some filmmakers, Woody Allen for instance, are extremely creative with language and invent new phrases that their own linguistic community does not necessarily share. This type of idiolect can therefore also be subsumed under this heading. It is not community-specific, but characterized by a show of pyrotechnics, hyperboles, and unexpected imagery with transparent referents. As the examples below show, their translation into other languages does not usually pose major problems either.

Example 7.37

Adrenaline is leaking out of my ears!	→	¡La adrenalina me sale por las orejas! [The adrenaline comes out of my ears]
Oh, Jesus! Claustrophobia, and a dead body. This is a neurotic's jackpot	→	¡Claustrofobia y un cadáver, el colmo de un neurótico! [Claustrophobia and a dead body, a neurotic's climax.]

Yet another type of jokes that can be included in this category are those breaking internationally recognizable behavioural norms, such as references to bodily functions, a frequent topic of jokes, even though one should be careful with cultural variation and acceptability in this domain.

Example 7.38

Man, you gotta warn somebody before you just crack one off. My mouth was open and everything.	→	Je moet even waarschuwen voordat je er één laat. [You must give a warning before you release one.] ______ Mijn mond stond open. [My mouth was open.]

Sometimes subtitling's technical limitations do force subtitlers to adopt a solution that is more than a literal transposition of the semantics. The impossibility of rendering the entire information flow and the need to reformulate can then lead to a loss of strength in the hyperbole or exaggeration. This happens in the example below that relies not only on semantics but also on details in the formulation that cannot be rendered in the subtitle. Consider, for instance, how 'buy up', 'tomorrow', and 'in town' contribute to the tone of the exaggeration in the utterance below.

Example 7.39

Meanwhile, I can't get the-the Flying Dutchman theme out of my mind, you know? Remind me tomorrow to buy up all the Wagner records in town and rent a chain saw.	→	No puedo sacarme de la cabeza el tema del "Holandés Errante". [I can't get out of my head the theme of the "Flying Dutchman"] ______ Recuérdame que me compre todos los discos de Wagner, [Remind me to buy all Wagner records,] ______ y alquile una sierra mecánica. [and rent a chain saw.]

On other occasions, the subtitle will have to be more explicit and therefore becomes less subtle. In the following example, the English version suggests the character's intentions whereas the Spanish translation leaves nothing to the imagination. The ring, which is the topic of this conversation, is a wedding ring.

Example 7.40

Let's get out of here, come on. And take the ring with you. Maybe there's a pawnshop open.	→	Vámonos y llévate el anillo. Podemos empeñarlo. [Let's go, and take the ring. We can pawn it.]

2) Jokes referring to a national culture or institution: If a joke focuses on an institution or other culture-bound reference that is unknown to the target culture, adaptation is required or the humoristic effect risks being lost (Zabalbeascoa 1996:252). In the following example, the subtitler has replaced the reference, Prozac, the name of a tranquilizer, by a hypernym in order to retain the sarcasm of the ST without retaining its reference to the brand name. Such translations are based on what translators expect their audiences to know (§7.4).

Example 7.41

There's nothing wrong with you that can't be cured with a little Prozac and a polo mallet.	→	No tienes nada que no pueda curarse con una pastilla y un mazo. [You have nothing that cannot be cured with a tablet and a mallet.]

If one supposes that the audience may be familiar with the reference, even if it is a foreign one, the item is simply retained in the subtitle. However, the borderline between 'international', 'bi-national' or 'national' can be a tenuous and a subjective one. Halloween, an Irish-American export and the topic of the example below, has become popular enough worldwide thanks to North American horror films, and is now an 'international' cultural reference up to a point. Some viewers will no doubt know that Halloween is 'the night of the living dead'; others might just have heard it is a night of 'trick-or-treat' games for children. It is up to the subtitler to evaluate the scope of culture-based jokes in each instance, and determine which category they fall under.

Example 7.42

How could you see her? She's dead. Not only is she dead, she's even been cremated. It's not even Halloween.	→	¿Cómo ibas a verla? Está muerta e incinerada. [How could you see her? She is dead and cremated.] ――――― Y no estamos en Halloween. [And we're not in Halloween.]

Similarly, in the next example, unfamiliarity with the referent can result in a loss of meaning as well as humour. A character is giving a hotel porter a tip. The porter eyes the dollar bill he has just been given sceptically, upon which the tipper, commenting on the face of George Washington depicted on the dollar bill, remarks:

Example 7.43

What are you making a face for? He was the father of our country.	→	No ponga esa cara. Fue el padre de la patria. [Don't pull such a face. He was the father of the country.]

3) Jokes reflecting a community's sense of humour: Comparable, but of a somewhat different nature all the same, is the sense of humour that is typical of a particular country or nationality (Zabalbeascoa 1996:252). Many communities make jokes at the expense of sub-communities inside their borders, or poke fun at other nationalities (e.g. Dutch jokes about silly Belgians and Belgian jokes about stingy Dutch). Such jokes in a way rely on a form of intertextuality, as one must know the insider national tradition to understand them. The humour can have religious overtones, or be based on historical events, but more often than not, it is inspired by prejudice, sometimes even racism, and it can therefore target ethnic communities, not just nationalities.

That is why we define this type of humour as 'community based', rather than 'national', the term Zabalbeascoa uses. Indeed, the next example, from *The Commitments,* makes use of such more or less international prejudices, known to many with a minimal sense of recent (European) history or current affairs. The whole passage was retained almost literally in the subtitles. It may be worth remembering, however, that the expected target audience of a particular production can be a determining factor when it comes to translation strategies.

Example 7.44

The Irish are the blacks of Europe, and Dubliners are the blacks of Ireland. And the north side Dubliners are the blacks of Dublin.	→	Les Irlandais sont les Noirs de l'Europe. Et les Dublinois, les Noirs d'Irlande. [The Irish are the blacks of Europe. And the Dubliners, the blacks of Ireland.] ——— Et ceux des quartiers nord sont les Noirs de Dublin. [And those from the north boroughs are the blacks of Dublin.]

In the next example of community-based humour, at the expense of North Americans, one could say that globalization has also played its part. The first line of this joke from *Chicken Run*, a British film, could be considered a European joke, but its continuation with the unexpected wordplay on 'over here' in line two, will no doubt work well in many countries worldwide. Note that the Dutch subtitler has opted for retaining the alliteration and formal repetition, coming up with a semantic variant that is different from the ST's, but that works equally well, playing on public opinion about the USA in a slightly different manner.

Example 7.45

Pushy Americans! Always showing up late for every war! Overpaid, oversexed and over here!	→	Die arrogante Amerikanen! Komen altijd te laat in elke oorlog [Those arrogant Americans! Arriving late in every war] ——— overbetaald, oversekst en overbodig. [overpaid, oversexed and superfluous.]

Another variant on nationality or community-bound sense of humour is discussed by Chiaro (2005:137-138). She points out that the translation of humour can even be problematic between countries sharing the same language, such as the UK and the USA, which, incidentally, goes to show that the translation of humour is a cultural as much as a linguistic issue. She writes (ibid.:138):

> There is no denying that British humour on screen is based on the nation's fixation with class and is conventionally not averse to punning, unlike USA comedy which prefers to play on the characterization of the individual and the gag to the punch.

The issue is a bit problematic, which the author acknowledges. Whether or not culture-specific 'senses of humour' really exist has never been proven empirically, they may be a "figment of the imagination of pop psychologists" (ibid.:140). But on the other hand, comedy shows such as *Seinfeld* and *Friends,* imported to Britain from the USA, have been much less successful in the target country.

4) Language-dependent jokes: rely upon "features of natural language for their effect" (Zabalbeascoa 1996:253). This type of jokes also falls under Chiaro's (2005) concept of 'verbally expressed humour', and includes puns and wordplays, studied extensively by Delabastita (1996:128), whose definition of the latter reads:

> Wordplay is the general name for various textual phenomena in which structural features of the language(s) are exploited in order to bring about a communicatively significant confrontation of two (or more) linguistic structures with more or less similar forms and more or less different meanings.

Although from a referential or cultural perspective such humour might be fairly international, it can rarely be translated literally. As Delabastita (1994:223) points out, the difficulties are caused by the fact that:

> the semantic and pragmatic effects of the source text wordplay find their origin in particular structural characteristics of the source language for which more often than not the translator fails to produce a counterpart, such as the existence of certain homophones, near-homophones, polysemic clusters, idioms or grammatical rules.

Substitution and compensation are often cited as the best way out (Chiaro 2005:136), but as the examples below show they are not applicable in all cases, and, as a result, half-translations and semi-substitutions also occur, unfortunately not always with good results.

Delabastita (1996) identifies the following most common types of lexical wordplay relying on the confrontation of similar forms: homophones (different writing, identical pronunciation), homographs (same spelling, different pronunciation), homonyms (same spelling and pronunciation, different meaning), and paronyms (approximate sound and spelling). However, morphological and lexical structures can be exploited too, as in 'I can't find the oranges, said Tom Fruitlessly', and 'Britain going metric: give them an inch and they will take out a mile' (ibid.:130).

All of these forms, and probably quite a few others, occur in audiovisual programmes and do so in many different guises and combinations. In order to tackle them, subtitlers must first identify the purpose or intended effect(s) of the wordplay. This is not always humour, moreover many instances of verbally expressed humour also have propositional content, which means that humour and semantics must always be balanced against each other. Finally, occurrences of language-dependent humour must be considered in their co-text since this may supply solutions that elude word-by-word approaches. The register of the speakers may be important, for instance. A similar effect may therefore be achievable through different means, even if this leads to semantic shifts in the translation. If such shifts remain limited, they are quite acceptable. They are simply the price one must sometimes pay. In the following example a form of rewriting has taken place.

Example 7.46

A: Helen Dubin's wrong for Ted. B: Yeah? A: She's too mousey. B: Well, he's a little mousey too. They can have their little rodent time. They can eat cheese together.	→	Helen no pega con Ted. Es demasiado sosa. [Helen does not go with Ted. She is too bland.] ______________ El también. Pueden salarse mutuamente y echarse pimienta. [He too. They can sprinkle salt and pepper on each other.]

In both versions the joke comes from the semantic register of cooking. 'Mousey', which means 'timid' or 'introverted' is transformed into the Spanish *sosa*, which means 'lacking salt, bland'. This meaning is what the Spanish joke uses when it says that the two characters can add salt and pepper to each other, whereas the English suggests the two mousey people can have cheese together.

In the next example, there is still some humour in the translation, although the fun element has become more of an ironic remark. The target viewers might still smile in the same place as the ST viewers, and the jocular style of the speaker is retained. In this case, the English joke itself uses a homonym: the word 'frank', which means 'honest', but is also a man's name. In the Dutch subtitles 'frank' is translated literally as *eerlijk* [honest] and the joke therefore has to be altered completely. In order to achieve this, the subtitler has used the filmic co-text: the two characters are playing a game.

Example 7.47

A: I'll be Frank. B: Oh, so who shall I be?	→	Ik zal eerlijk zijn. - Goed, dan win ik. [I'll be honest. - Good, then I win.]

Another play on the double meaning of names, this time invented paronyms, occurs in this excerpt from *The Life of Brian*. The characters of the Roman governor, as well as the friend he mentions, are actually the victims of the joke. In the French translation similar paronyms are produced.

Example 7.48

A: Have you checked? B: Well, no, sir. I think it's a joke, sir. Like 'Sillius Soddus' or 'Biggus Dickus', sir. A: What's so funny about Biggus Dickus? B: Well, it's a joke name, sir. A: I have a very great friend in Rome called Biggus Dickus.	→	Vous avez vérifié ? [Have you checked?] ——— Non, mais je crois que c'est une blague. [No, but I think that it's a joke.] ——— Comme "Débilus Crétinus" ou "Enormus Vergus". [Like "Retarded Cretin" or "Enormous Dickus".] ——— Qu'y-a-t-il de drôle dans le nom "Enormus Vergus" ? [What's so funny about the name "Enormus Dickus"?] ——— C'est un nom inventé, gouverneur. [It's an invented name, governor.] ——— J'ai un ami à Rome qui s'appelle Enormus Vergus. [I have a friend in Rome who's called Enormus Dickus.]

In our last two examples, however, the failed attempts at recreating humour, or the rather literal translations, which do not actually take the word play into account, endanger the logic and comprehensibility of the target sentence. These are therefore examples one should not follow. In the first case, the Spanish final line loses all reference to the previous subtitle; in the second, the play on the English expression 'to wear one's heart on one's sleeve' has been translated more or less literally into Dutch, which, however, does not have a similar expression. The exchange becomes nonsensical at best.

Example 7.49

I was left for another man. A trainer named Dash. I was left for a punctuation mark.	→	Me ha dejado por otro hombre. Un entrenador llamado Dash. [He has left me for another man. A trainer called Dash.] ________ Me ha dejado de repente. [He has left me suddenly.]
Donkey: We wear our fear out there on our sleeves. Shrek: Wait a second. Donkeys don't have sleeves. Donkey: You know what I mean.	→	Wij dragen onze angst op onze mouw. [We wear our fear on our sleeve.] ________ Wacht! Ezels hebben geen mouwen. - Je weet wel wat ik bedoel. [Wait! Donkeys have no sleeves. - You know what I mean.]

Some linguistic jokes rely on metalinguistic features such as accents, but also on speech impediments. Most of these are impossible to render in subtitles (§7.3), even though occasionally attempts ought to be made because the joke is crucial and/or recurs in different places in the film. In *The Life of Brian*, the Roman governor, Pilate, has a speech impediment and cannot pronounce the phoneme 'r', which is abused by various characters in conversation with him and even by the crowds listening to his addresses. In other words, it is a meaningful linguistic-oral joke, which occurs in a comedy, and therefore ought to get priority. In practice, this does not happen, at least not on the French DVD, although the character's mispronunciation of the 'r' could easily be rendered. The excerpt is already fairly nonsensical in the English version, as it tries to render the communication lapses resulting from Pilate's speech impediment. In the French, the confusion remains, however, it is no longer clear what causes it, unless the audience relies completely on the spoken text.

Example 7.50

Pilate: Now, what's youw name, Jew? Brian: Brian, sir. Pilate: Bwian, eh? Brian: No, no, Brian Pilate: The little wascal has spiwit. Soldier: Has what, sir? Pilate: Spiwit. Soldier: Yes, he did sir. Pilate: No, no, spiwit. Bwa-vado. A touch of dewing-do. Soldier: Oh, about 11, sir.	→	Alors, comment t'appelles-tu, Juif ? [So, what's your name, Jew?] ——— Brian, gouverneur. - Brian, hein. [Brian, governor. - Brian, eh?] ——— Non, Brian. - Ce rebelle a de l'esprit. [No, Brian. - This rebel has spirit.] ——— Oui, c'est ça, oui. [Yes, that's it, yes.] ——— Non, de l'esprit. Du courage, comment dire, du cran. [No, spirit. Courage, let's say, guts.] ——— Ils étaient onze, gouverneur. [There were eleven of them, Sir.]

5) Visual jokes: get their punch from visually conveyed information, whether through editing, the gestures and facial expressions of the actors, or the typical suspense set-up in which the viewer can see more and knows more than the character(s) concerned. Zabalbeascoa (1996:253-254) distinguishes between purely visual jokes and jokes that are the visually coded version of a linguistic joke but, in our view, these would be a variant of language-bound jokes or complex jokes, making use of all or various of the film's sign systems. In spite of cultural differences, there is certain universality in gestures and mime as successful series such as *Mr Bean* demonstrate, and some forms of visual communication may have become increasingly universal due to cultural globalization and the popularity of certain film genres. Since in visual humour, the image obviously does the job, translators can rest on their laurels.

6) Aural jokes: This category was added to the original classification by Díaz Cintas (2003:264) in an attempt to include noises as well as the meta-linguistic characteristics of speech, e.g. accents and intonation. Some of these metalinguistic features do occasionally require translation, however, and have been therefore included under linguistic jokes. Aural jokes are here considered to be similar to visual jokes in that they do not require translation because they do not rely on sounds that are linguistically meaningful, but rather on noises that 'speak for themselves'.

7) Complex jokes: This ultimate category is a kind of holdall for jokes that combine two or more of the above features, that is, instances of humour in which culture-bound references, image, sound and/or linguistics are combined. Especially the combination of visual information and metaphor, or culture-bound references and wordplay can be mind-boggling.

The following excerpt from *Chicken Run* combines visually rendered information (a chicken wearing thick glasses) with a linguistic metaphor that relies on it ('four-eyes!'). The translation in Dutch is quite satisfactory. *Blinde kip* [blind chicken] is an offensive Dutch expression used to refer to people with poor sight, that also implies that the person is clumsy precisely because they cannot see very well. In other words, not only do the subtitles retain the insulting reference to the chicken's thick glasses, they add a twist by using a target language expression with 'chicken'. Disrespectful references to chickens abound in this film, but there happens to be none in this exchange. The translation therefore uses compensation for those instances in which the film did use an expression involving chickens and the subtitles did not.

Example 7.51

Don't push me, four-eyes!	→	Niet duwen! Blinde kip! [No pushing! Blind chicken!]

In our last example, from *Manhattan Murder Mystery*, the Spanish and Italian solutions are quite different, but neither works very well. Two couples are discussing the university one of the characters' sons is attending. The university is 'Brown', a rather well known one in the USA, but 'brown' is also a colour, and the word is therefore a homonym. In the Spanish version 'Brown' is replaced by 'Columbia', both a university in New York City and a Hollywood production company, which is what the subtitler exploits. The result of the operation is that the character would certainly come across as silly to an American audience (a New Yorker who does not know Columbia University), and that the joke is rather bland in Spanish. In the Italian version, however, the humour becomes quite convoluted. 'Brown' is retained, and the Italian viewer can no doubt deduce that 'Brown' is the name of a college, but the question is adapted to allow for the different answer that follows. In this case, the joke is at the expense of the son, who suddenly becomes a *risparmiatore* [thrifty]. Why this should be so is not at all clear.

Example 7.52

Lillian: Um, uh, what college, uh, does your son attend? Carol: Brown. Paul: Nice color.	Spanish	→	¿En qué universidad está su hijo? - Columbia. [At what university is your son? - Columbia] ——— Eso está en Hollywood, ¿no? [That's in Hollywood, right?]
	Italian	→	Che studi compie vostro figlio? - Economia alla Brown. [What is your son studying? - Economics at Brown.] ——— Un risparmiatore! [A thrifty fellow!]

7.7 Ideological issues: whose voice and whose message

We have pointed out that subtitling's present-day preference for propositional content over formal linguistic issues, or its tendency to emphasize the importance of the message can lead to translational choices that are not altogether neutral. The same can be said of subtitling's preference for simplified standard language: the so-called neutral language it uses is often the voice of authority, i.e. the voice imposed by the TV channel (Remael 2004, Kaufmann 2004). However, we wish to emphasize again that no translation is neutral and that translating always involves making choices and taking decisions. It is important not only for translator/subtitlers but also for the readers of translations to be aware of this. The public should be educated and learn not to simply dismiss such choices or translation shifts as shortcomings or mistakes. Any text only comes into existence in interaction with its readers, who bring their own experience to it. Subtitles are no different. Today, literary translations are regularly given a voice in newspapers' literary supplements, even though this is a fairly recent and by no means widespread phenomenon. Such inclusions make readers aware of the presence, role, possibilities, and characteristics of translations and help them be aware of their impact on what they are reading.

We may still be far removed from the time when film reviews, the reviews of new DVDs, or indeed TV programmes allocate as much as a paragraph to the programme's or film's translation. Still, the boom in university courses, occasional interviews with audiovisual translators, a growing awareness among film directors, and the incorporation of some AVT courses in film studies programmes, is encouraging. Having said this, it is important for (future) subtitlers to be aware of a number of issues. Some are related to the complexity of the film text and the many voices it is composed of, some are related to the ever-changing world of audiovisual productions. The next paragraphs touch on some of the hot research issues of today.

Due to globalization, languages travel increasingly. This means that more languages are spoken in any one place today than was traditionally the case, and that through language contact languages themselves develop new variants, new mixtures, or hybrids (Mehrez 1992). This evolution is no longer limited to the former colonies of any one European state, but has become a worldwide phenomenon, most obviously noticeable in the proliferation of different varieties of international English, and what Snell-Hornby (2003:175) has called "the hybrid text of globalization". The presence of immigrants and their continuous movement has an influence on all the languages of the one-time European centre. Brunner (2003), for instance, discusses the influence of the language spoken by Germans of Turkish origin on German language and literature. Besides, the linguistic variants of European languages spoken in Latin America, Africa, Asia, are gaining prominence as these continents' influence on the world scene grows. Since film is a 'hybrid text of globalization' *par excellence*, films increasingly reflect the world's linguistic evolutions and mixes, and, as we have pointed out in §3.3.2, co-productions actively promote multilingualism in film, thereby beginning to undermine Anglo-Saxon dominance.

The flip side of the globalization coin, however, is glocalization (personalization of a product for a small local market) and also regionalization (defined here as an ideological reaction of the population to globalizing tendencies). Indeed, not only are multinationals aware of the need to localize their products for marketing, which means a lot of work for technical writers and translators, but regionalization is rearing its head as well. In order to protect their identities, and after the disintegration of some post World War II states, smaller languages are beginning to demand recognition. This too is reflected in the production of films and TV programmes, for instance in Catalonia and Flanders, to name but two examples. A proliferation of languages and voices also means a proliferation of human relations, hierarchies and interactions. To what extent is subtitling, as it is practised today, equipped to deal with these? Is subtitling, of necessity, the voice of authority? And what happens in less linear narratives when it is no longer clear who the voice of authority is? Let us consider the following example.

In *La Bataille d'Algers* a classic docu-drama about the beginning of the Algerian independence struggle, the French colonialists speak French, and any Algerians addressing the French do so as well. However, when the Algerians speak among themselves they use the Algerian Arabic variant, a dialect with strong French influence, especially in the lexicon, but Arabic all the same. Whenever Algerian Arabic is spoken, the DVD of the film provides French subtitles. Traditional subtitling rules state that film dialogue should get priority over songs and written text, but also over other types of secondary speech, like announcements over loudspeakers, background comments, and the like. However, what happens when the loudspeaker represents the voice of authority? In *La Bataille d'Algers*, the French army uses loudspeakers to admonish and instruct the population. In a couple of scenes, these announcements coincide with comments made by bystanders in Algerian. The subtitles give preference to the loudspeakers because they are more important for the narrative development of the film: in that sense they represent authority in two different ways. As a result, the voice of the protesting population is lost. In the following scene the message of the loudspeaker (in French) and the dialogue of a few Algerian women (in Algerian) alternate (Benini 2005:101). On the English DVD, only the official government message is subtitled. The turns spoken by the women, who pay absolutely no attention to the loudspeakers but are worrying about their sons, are left untranslated.

Example 7.53

A : Ayez confiance en la France et son armée. Le FLN veut vous affamer et vous condamner à la misère.	A: Show your trust in France and its army. The resistance movement wants to starve you and condemn you to misery.
B : El-hadu-llah ela es-slâma	B: Thank God you are unharmed.
A : La France est votre patrie.	A: France is your homeland.
B : Rabbi meakum yâ_ûladi.	B: God be with you my sons.
A . Ayez confiance en la France et son armée.	A. Trust in France and its army.
B : Saeid hoya ma-sefûs? Saeid hoya ma-sefûs?	B: Have you not seen Said? Have you not seen Said?

Given the context in which these lines occur, the implication of the women's words is obviously that it is the French who might have harmed their sons and brothers, not the resistance movement. Moreover, as pointed out by Benini (2005:101), the women are in full view of the camera, whereas the loudspeaker merely repeats a message it has already broadcast before. In a word, this is actually a form of censorship. On the other hand, scenes in which voices more or less coincide can be tricky, and as voices proliferate in films, the task of decision-making may become increasingly difficult, affecting not only what ought to be subtitled (or not), but also how it is done.

Indeed, the very tendency of subtitling to develop a 'subtitling tone' or 'subtitling style' (Díaz Cintas 2003:280) characterized by simple vocabulary and short sentences, a preference for standard language, and disregard for interactional signals from dialogue exchanges, may have to be challenged. What if linguistic variation becomes more and more of an integral part of the message of films and documentaries? The examples of *Trainspotting*, *The Full Monty*, *The Color Purple*, *Cidade de Deus*, and *Mar adentro* are well known, but multilingualism and linguistic variation are now also making themselves felt on a smaller scale as various accents, and different levels of informal language, geographical, or context-bound slang become common practice even on TV screens. In Flanders, Flemish intralingual subtitles of Dutch TV series broadcast by one of the private channels, VTM, sometimes include Flemish dialectal forms to render Dutch informal or dialectal variants (Remael 2004). In such instances the question to be asked is: who are the subtitles for? What kind of language support do they really require? Subtitling is a vulnerable translation, should it really be drawing attention to itself?

Apart from matters of ideology and feasibility, the budget and time available are a crucial determining factor. The practice of pivot subtitling, especially common in subtitling for film festivals, means that languages that are less known in Europe, say Chinese or Farsi, are translated from one set of usually English subtitles into other European languages. Any of the first translator's mistakes or biases are then carried over into the subsequent versions. This Anglocentric habit can, again, lead to censorship. In the above-mentioned DVD of *La Bataille d'Algers*, the following subtitling occurs (Benini 2005:103). If the French subtitles were used for subsequent translations, these would censor the source text in a similar way.

Example 7.54

A: Waš-bik ya-yemma? B: Hakmuh. [What is the matter? They've got him.]	→	Qu'est-ce que tu as ? - Rien. [What is the matter? - Nothing.]

7.8 Discussion points

7.8.1 Linguistic variation in film often reflects social class. In TV series, it is therefore often the household staff, members of the working class, or immigrants who speak substandard or non-standard linguistic variants.

❶ Can you think of an example?
❷ Who, in your example, speaks a substandard or non-standard variant and who does not?
❸ What are the most striking features of those variants, and what

exactly is their narrative function?

❹ Do they serve a well-defined purpose?

❺ If the series/film has subtitles: do they in any way try to do justice to this linguistic variation?

❻ How would you transcribe the way the characters speak?

7.8.2 What is your view on the use of marked styles and registers in subtitles:

❶ Would you want the subtitles of a classic Shakespeare drama to respect the style of the source text?

❷ Are you in favour of an increased use of dialect and slang in subtitles?

❸ Explain your answer.

7.8.3 How do think people feel about the translation of swearwords and taboo words in your country? Is tolerance for such interjections increasing? Does tolerance vary according to the medium, i.e. television, cinema, DVD? Are taboo words usually censored?

7.8.4 Watch a TV comedy with canned laughter, paying special attention to the subtitles.

❶ Has the subtitling managed to reproduce synchronous jokes?

❷ What strategies are used and with what degree of success?

❸ Can you find instances of compensation?

7.8.5 What do you think about the following quote from Nowell Smith (1968:146) about the role of audiovisual translation:

> [N]ational differences, the specificities of social and cultural situations, are all ironed out. The final effect is of a culture both cosmopolitan and provincial. The concrete becomes abstract; and then, in an attempt to make the abstract concrete again, it is reduced to the homely and easily understood.

❶ Argue for or against this opinion by drawing on the analysis of such differences and specificities in three sequences of a film or documentary of your choice.

❷ Restrict your analysis to the impact that the linguistic manipulation of such differences may have on their reception by the target community and propose your own translations for the issues at stake.

7.8.6 Go to DVD > Chapter 7 > Discussion points > Discussion point 7.8.6 > subtitles for VHS
Go to DVD > Chapter 7 > Discussion points > Discussion point 7.8.6 > subtitles for DVD
The same two scenes from Almodóvar's *¿Qué he hecho yo para merecer esto?* have been translated differently into English.

❶ Compare the two sets of English subtitles done for VHS and for DVD and underline the main differences, paying particular attention to the way the mother is portrayed in the subtitles.
❷ Take a look at the original dialogue in Spanish with a literal back-translation in English.
[Pathway: *DVD > Chapter 7 > Discussion points > Discussion point 7.8.6 > dialogue list*]
❸ Which of the two sets of subtitles do you prefer? Why?

7.9 Exercises

Style and register

7.9.1 Test your understanding of the different translation strategies for culture-bound items discussed in this chapter. Try to think of an example for each one that you might have been confronted with in translations.

❶ Loan
❷ Calque or literal translation
❸ Explicitation
❹ Substitution
❺ Transposition
❻ Lexical recreation
❼ Compensation
❽ Omission
❾ Addition

7.9.2 Go to DVD > Chapter 7 > Exercises > Exercise 7.9.2 > Poem > Clip
Watch the excerpt *Poem* from a documentary film on the Spanish Civil War entitled *Art in the Struggle for Freedom*. Spot and subtitle it with WinCAPS, applying a reading speed of 180 words per minute.
[Pathway to dialogue list: *DVD > Chapter 7 > Exercises > Exercise 7.9.2 > Poem > Transcription of dialogue*]

7.9.3 Go to DVD > Chapter 7 > Exercises > Exercise 7.9.3 > Prayer > Clip
Spot and subtitle the excerpt *Prayer* from *Night of the Living Dead* you find on the DVD. This is a slow passage in which a reverend is saying prayers over a coffin. Try to respect the clergyman's rather formal register.

[Pathway to dialogue list: *DVD > Chapter 7 > Exercises > Exercise 7.9.3 > Prayer > Transcription of dialogue*]

7.9.4 Go to DVD > Chapter 7 > Exercises > Exercise 7.9.4 > *Will* > Clip
Spot and subtitle the excerpt *Will* from *The Snows of Kilimanjaro*, in which the protagonist Harry is having a conversation with his uncle Bill, who is very ill. The passage contains some explicit interaction between image and dialogue, as well as a visual metaphor and wordplay.
[Pathway to dialogue list: *DVD > Chapter 7 > Exercises > Exercise 7.9.4 > Will > Transcription of dialogue*]

7.9.5 Go to DVD > Chapter 7 > Exercises > Exercise 7.9.5 > Sports jargon
Metaphors relating to the field of sports can be difficult to translate. Take a look at the dialogue on the DVD and propose a translation in your language.
[Pathway to suggestions: *DVD > Chapter 7 > Exercises > Exercise 7.9.5 > Sports > Key to exercise*]

Emotionally charged language

7.9.6 Go to DVD > Chapter 7 > Exercises > Exercise 7.9.6 > Swearing
Imagine these curses occur in a film you are translating and the lines are spoken by students at a social gathering. The four-letter word should get a different translation in each instance. How would you translate them into your mother tongue, taking into account what is acceptable in your country?

7.9.7 Go to DVD > Chapter 7 > Exercises > Exercise 7.9.7 > *Confrontation*
This is a short dialogue from the film *Memento*. Translate it into your working language following the times indicated for each subtitle. Apply a reading speed of 180 words per minute.

Songs

7.9.8 Translate the lyrics of the song from *About a Boy* into your working language, trying to find a balance between rhyme, rhythm and content. You find the song in example 7.31 above.

7.9.9 Go to DVD > Chapter 7 > Exercises > Exercise 7.9.9 > *Malaysia* > Clip
Spot and translate this short clip from the documentary film *Boom Boom Bang*, discussed in example 7.30.
[Pathway to dialogue list: *DVD > Chapter 7 > Exercises > Exercise 7.9.9 > Malaysia > Transcription of dialogue*]

❶ Search the Internet to find an explanation: who is or was *Mahsuri*? Who or what is *ikan*?

❷ As you translate the song into the language of your choice, make sure you achieve a balance between respect for content, rhythm, and rhyme.

❸ Consider what might be the best solution for dealing with the cultural references: leaving the words as they are and insert them in italics or translate them?

❹ The DVD includes translated versions of the above clip into many languages. Compare and discuss the differences between these translations and your own.
[Pathway to translations: *DVD > Chapter 7 > Exercises > Exercise 7.9.9 > Malaysia*]

Humour and wordplay

7.9.10 Go to DVD > Chapter 7 > Exercises > Exercise 7.9.10 > One-liners
Try your hand at the translation of a few instances of complex humour from the film *Chicken Run.*

7.9.11 Go to DVD > Chapter 7 > Exercises > Exercise 7.9.11 > *Ketchup*
Translate the joke you find in this section into your working language. Compare it with some of the translations that have been commercialized.
[Pathway to translations: *DVD > Chapter 7 > Exercises > Exercise 7.9.11 > Ketchup > Translations*]

7.9.12 Go to DVD > Chapter 7 > Exercises > Exercise 7.9.12 > *Publishing* > Clip
Spot and subtitle the excerpt *Publishing* from *The Last Time I Saw Paris*. This is a conversation between the protagonist and his father in law. It contains a wordplay that makes use of alliteration. What would you do with the song?
[Pathway to dialogue list: *DVD > Chapter 7 > Exercises > Exercise 7.9.12 > Publishing > Transcription of dialogue*]

AVT Test

7.9.13 Go to DVD > Chapter 7 > Exercises > Exercise 7.9.13
In this exercise, you have a set of questions aimed at testing your knowledge about general issues relating to audiovisual translation.
[Pathway to key: *DVD > Chapter 7 > Exercises > Exercise 7.9.13 > Key to exercise*]

8. Further Activities

The exercises in this chapter will help you familiarize yourself with the WinCAPS subtitling software and offer extra subtitling practice, combining some of the major subtitling challenges. They have been subsumed under two headings: “WinCAPS activities” and “Extra scenes”.

8.1 WinCAPS activities

The exercises in this section ask you to revise subtitles. They focus on such matters as subtitling rhythm, reading speed, spotting and timecodes, line breaks, segmentation, punctuation and other formal conventions. All the activities are based on WinCAPS files that you need to manipulate, helping you to familiarize yourself with most typical subtitling issues, while giving you hands-on practice with the state-of-the-art WinCAPS program which is also widely used in the industry today.

Since the main purpose of the exercises in this subsection is to have you exploit some of the quite practical functions the software offers to subtitlers, some of them may appear rather simple from a linguistic or translational point of view. All the same, even the simpler exercises will make you aware of subtitling details that may be quite important when it comes to promoting easy legibility and readability, for instance. What is more, trying out the possibilities of the software is an important aspect of teaching yourself subtitling in the sense that the software should no longer hold any secrets for you once you get down to more difficult assignments, whether those from the section with extra exercises, or exercises you make up yourselves, basing yourselves on those in the book.

Indeed, all the exercises in this section are in English and you should work in English when completing and amending them; however, it goes without saying that they can be adapted, expanded, and exploited differently. For instance, you can follow the main instructions for a particular activity and decide to go one step further, translating the scene into your working language, using the English version as a kind of template.

Important: Remember that all the .w30 files and clips are automatically loaded on your computer hard drive during the installation on WinCAPS. To be able to work with one of these read-only .w30 files you have to create a working copy first. Using the .w30 file for Exercise 8.1.1 as an example, you have to do the following:

Open WinCAPS > File > Open > 811_Reef_Declaration_EXERCISE > File > Copy To

and then save it onto your hard drive or your USB memory stick. This will be your working copy. Close the read-only file you have on your screen. Go to File > Open > and browse for the location on your hard drive or USB memory stick where you saved your working copy. You will then be able to work with this new copy and make the amendments you consider appropriate. Before opening a new Exercise (or Key) file, make sure that you first 'disassociate' any clips that are open. For more details go to DVD > WinCAPS > Set-up > WinCAPS Installation Instructions.

8.1.1 WinCAPS FILE

Open WinCAPS > File > Open > 811_Reef_Declaration_EXERCISE > File > Copy to

CLIP
Open WinCAPS > Video > Open Video > 811_Reef_Declaration

TASK
The way the dialogue has been spotted in this exercise is far from ideal: there are too many one-liners and some of the subtitles are too short in duration. In some cases merging two or more short subtitles into a two-liner might be more appropriate for the reading rhythm.

PROPOSAL
Open WinCAPS > File > Open > 811_Reef_Declaration_KEY

8.1.2 WinCAPS FILE

Open WinCAPS > File > Open > 812_Reef_Loan_EXERCISE > File > Copy to

CLIP
Open WinCAPS > Video > Open Video > 812_Reef_Loan

TASK
Reconsider the line breaks and the number of lines per subtitle in this exercise.

PROPOSAL
Open WinCAPS > File > Open > 812_Reef_Loan_KEY

8.1.3 WinCAPS FILE

Open WinCAPS > File > Open > 813_BlueStar_End_EXERCISE > File > Copy to

CLIP
Open WinCAPS > Video > Open Video > 813_BlueStar_End

TASK
All the in and out times are assumed to be correct in this exercise and you do not need to adjust them. However, you will see that many subtitles are in different colours and appear all over the screen. Your task is to make sure that all the subtitles appear in the same colour (i.e. they should be all yellow), and to reposition them at the bottom of the screen, centred.

PROPOSAL
Open WinCAPS > File > Open > 813_BlueStar_End_KEY

8.1.4 WinCAPS FILE

Open WinCAPS > File > Open > 814_BlueStar_Presentation_EXERCISE > File > Copy to

CLIP
Open WinCAPS > Video > Open Video > 814_BlueStar_Presentation

TASK
As in the previous exercise, all the in and out times are again assumed to be correct and you do not need to adjust them. The problem here is that the reading speed of the subtitles is very slow because more information has been condensed and deleted from the original than necessary. Rewrite the subtitles in English adding what you consider to be the most important information but taking into consideration a maximum reading speed of 160 words per minute.

PROPOSAL
Open WinCAPS > File > Open > 814_BlueStar_Presentation_KEY

8.1.5 WinCAPS FILE

Open WinCAPS > File > Open > 815_Charade_Ambassador_EXERCISE > File > Copy to

CLIP
Open WinCAPS > Video > Open Video > 815_Charade_Ambassador

TASK
This is another clip in which the in and out times are correct, as is the reading speed. Your task here is to read the subtitles carefully and amend any transcription errors or punctuation conventions that depart from the ones set out in Chapter 5 of this book.

PROPOSAL
Open WinCAPS > File > Open > 815_Charade_Ambassador_KEY

8.1.6 WinCAPS FILE

Open WinCAPS > File > Open > 816_Charade_Puppets_EXERCISE > File > Copy to

CLIP
Open WinCAPS > Video > Open Video > 816_Charade_Puppets

TASK
The in and out times of this very short scene have not been carefully spotted. The subtitles either appear too early or disappear too late, or vice versa. In other words, the titles are not well synchronized with the soundtrack and do not remain on screen for the required period of time. As a result the reading speed is often far too high. What you need to do is produce a new subtitle file with more accurate timing, without changing the segmentation of the dialogue or the number of subtitles (6 in total). Reading speed: 180 words per minute.

PROPOSAL
Open WinCAPS > File > Open > 816_Charade_Puppets_KEY

8.1.7 WinCAPS FILE

Open WinCAPS > File > Open > 817_Charade_Snow_EXERCISE > File > Copy to

CLIP
Open WinCAPS > Video > Open Video > 817_Charade_Snow

TASK
The timing of the subtitles in this scene is correct, but the reading speed is too high, i.e. there is too much text in most subtitles. Your task is to condense/delete information where appropriate to make sure that all subtitles adhere to a maximum reading speed of 160 words per minute. Decide what to do with the few instances where

a different language than English is spoken. Keep in mind that 39 is the maximum number of characters allowed per line.

PROPOSAL
Open WinCAPS > File > Open > 817_Charade_Snow_KEY

8.1.8 WinCAPS FILE

Open WinCAPS > File > Open > 818_EPBCResources_EXERCISE > File > Copy to

CLIP
Open WinCAPS > Video > Open Video > 818_EPBC_Resources

TASK
In this exercise the spotting and segmentation of the original text could be much improved. Most of the subtitles are not self-contained sentences, but carry on over several subtitles, making it difficult and taxing to read. Look for better ways of segmenting the original in subtitles that take syntax more seriously and can therefore be read more easily. You will have to modify the in and out times, but remember to stick to a reading speed of 180 words maximum, with lines of no more than 39 characters.

PROPOSAL
Open WinCAPS > File > Open > 818_EPBCResources_KEY

8.1.9 WinCAPS FILE

Open WinCAPS > File > Open > 819_McLintock_Room_EXERCISE > File > Copy to

CLIP
Open WinCAPS > Video > Open Video > 819_McLintock_Room

TASK
You do not need to alter any of the times in this scene. The main purpose of this activity is for you to check formal subtitling conventions and punctuation. Modify the subtitles whenever you think these conventions have not been correctly implemented, following the guidelines put forward in Chapter 5. Listen carefully to the original dialogue, because there are also a few mistakes in interpretation that you will need to correct.

PROPOSAL
Open WinCAPS > File > Open > 819_McLintock_Room_KEY

8.1.10 WinCAPS FILE

Open WinCAPS > File > Open > 8110_LivingDead_Tombstone_EXERCISE > File > Copy to

CLIP
Open WinCAPS > Video > Open Video > 8110_LivingDead_Tombstone

TASK
First of all, the scene in this exercise has been wrongly timed, with most of the in and out cues out of sync with the original dialogue. Amend the times in a way you consider appropriate, bearing in mind that in some cases you may want to merge two subtitles into one. Pay attention to the needless changes in colour, special effects and displacement of the subtitles, to make sure that the end product adheres to the guidelines proposed in this book.

PROPOSAL
Open WinCAPS > File > Open > 8110_LivingDead_Tombstone_KEY

8.2 Extra scenes

The collection of clips brought together under this heading constitutes a kind of pool of material meant for extra practice, cut to measure, digitized and ready for use. It consists of scenes from different films and film genres: fiction, documentary and animation. Moreover, unlike the exercises in the body of the book, these offer practice in subtitling from different source languages, that is: Dutch, English, French, Italian and Spanish.

The excerpts contain more complex subtitling challenges, although the degree of difficulty varies. They may be especially interesting for independent and self-taught learners, but they can also serve as a starting point for class discussion since in some cases different solutions will probably be equally acceptable.

Although WinCAPS will work with most digitized scenes, having these scenes handy on the DVD is obviously more practical. Students who have worked their way through the material on offer here, can then also turn to clips that are available on Internet, on sites such as:

www.archive.org/details/movies
www.linktv.org

Most of the scenes on this DVD come with a transcription of the dialogue, but on some occasions you will have to translate directly from the screen, i.e. without the help of a typed-out version of the script. In fact, this is common practice in the profession, when subtitlers either do not have the dialogue list at their disposal or have no time to consult it. On the other hand, the opposite is not uncommon either: translators may also be asked to work from a dialogue list or audio tape without having access to the images. This, however, is a practice we certainly do not wish to promote.

The pathway on the DVD to find this wealth of material is:
DVD > Chapter 8 > 8.2 Extra scenes

Once there you find the following sections:

- 8.2.1 In Dutch
  - Films
  - Documentaries
- 8.2.2 In English
  - Films
  - Documentaries
  - Animation films
- 8.2.3 In French
  - Films
  - Documentaries
- 8.2.4 In Italian
  - Films
- 8.2.5 In Spanish
  - Films
  - Documentaries

Important: Besides being available on the DVD, all the clips mentioned above are automatically loaded onto your computer hard drive during the intallation of WinCAPS. To work with WinCAPS, we recommend you use the video clips that have been saved onto your hard drive rather than the clips on the DVD. For more details on how to work with any of these video clips and to create your own subtitles, please go to DVD > WinCAPS > Set-up > WinCAPS Installation Instructions and read section '4. Working with other clips from the DVD'.

9. A Glossary of Terms Used in Subtitling

Italics are used to indicate terms with their own entry.

4:3: *Aspect ratio* of a standard television screen.

16:9: *Aspect ratio* of a widescreen television.

16 mm, 35 mm: These are film formats and denote the actual size of the negative film, in millimetres. 16 mm is often used for documentary work, as the cameras are more portable. Major feature film projects are shot in 35 mm or larger.

Adaptation: Activity that consists in transforming a rough translation of the dialogue in subtitle chunks that respect the space and time limitations imposed by the medium.

Adapter: The professional who adapts the rough translation into subtitles, taking into account the various spatial and time constraints.

Analogue technology: Technology that allows the recording, and transmission of information (images and sound) by means of a continuous, unbroken signal. Old vinyl records and magnetic VHS tapes are good examples. One of the main drawbacks of the analogue system is the loss of quality when making copies from an original. See also *digital*.

Animation: Any process whereby artificial movement is created by photographing a series of drawings, objects or computer images one by one, as in cartoon programmes for children.

Annotated master dialogue/dubbing list: Document containing all the dialogue exchanges that can be heard in the film, with additional information on slang terms, colloquialisms, obscure cultural references and the like. It can also contain details about the camera movements and the way actors behave on screen. It is used for the dubbing or lip-sync of films and it aims at dispelling translation errors and misunderstandings.

Aspect ratio: The aspect ratio of video material is related to the shape of the screen used to display the video, i.e. the relation between the height of the projected image and its width. Standard television sets are 4:3, which is the ratio of the screen width to the screen height. Widescreen televisions are becoming more popular and their aspect ratio is 16:9. To convert from widescreen to 4:3 aspect ratio the audiovisual material has to be letterboxed, which means adding black bars to the top and bottom of the wide screen video so that it fits into a 4:3 screen. For analogue broadcasts, a 14:9 letterbox image provides the best compromise when viewing a widescreen production on a 4:3 display.

Authoring: For DVD-Video, authoring refers to the process of designing navigation screens and menus, creating, collecting, formatting, and encoding audiovisual material.

Avi: Stands for Audio Video Interleave and is currently one of the most common multimedia file formats for storing audio and video data. AVI files typically end in the .avi extension. See also *MPEG*.

AVT: Abbreviation for Audiovisual Translation.

Betacam-Digital: A professional system similar to *Betacam-SP* but based on *digital* technology rather than *analogue*.

Betacam-SP: A professional system used for the recording and transmission of video and audio material. Based in *analogue* technology, it has been the industry equivalent of the domestic *VHS*.

Bit: The most basic information unit used in a *digital* file.

BITC: Burnt-In Time Code.

Blanking lines: Also known as the blanking interval. Lines outside the visible image on a television screen; used to transmit conccalcd signals such as *teletext* or a *VITC time code*.

Caption: (a) Term used to refer to a *subtitle* aimed at the deaf and the hard-of-hearing audiences, usually in the USA. (b) It can also refer to written text that appears superimposed somewhere on the original picture. See also *closed caption* and *insert*.

Captioning: Term used to refer to the *subtitling* of programmes aimed at the deaf and hard-of-hearing audiences.

Celluloid: Term used to refer to the cinema or a film, originally the transparent flammable plastic made in sheets from camphor and nitrocellulose, formerly used for cinematographic film.

Character generator: A device that transforms *digital* signals into typographic characters. It can be located either in the television broadcasting system (for *open subtitles*) or inside a TV receiver (for *closed subtitles* or *teletext*).

Closed captions: Subtitles aimed primarily at the deaf and the hard-of-hearing viewers, although they can also be enjoyed by people learning an additional language, people first learning how to read, and others, in order to read a transcript of the audio portion of a video, film, or other presentation. It is closed because it is not engraved on the film. It is hidden in the video signal and to watch it an external or internal *decoder* needs to be used, such as *teletext*. In North America, closed captions are hidden in what is called line 21 of the vertical blanking interval (VBI).

Closed subtitles: The *subtitles* are encoded into the video signal but are not visible on screen until they are activated by means of a *decoder*. They are not an integral part of the audiovisual programme and can be added to the original version by the viewer. These are the typical *subtitles* found on *teletext* and many DVDs. See *open subtitles*.

Codec: A circuit or software module used to compress and/or decompress data. When an *analogue* video signal is converted to a *digital* signal, the resulting *digital* data is a massive 20MB per second. The codec is used to compress this data for recording, and then to decompress it to its original form for playback.

Combined continuity and subtitle/spotting list: Document that contains the *combined continuity* of a film together with the list of *master titles*.

Combined continuity: Working document that contains the complete list of dialogues together with additional information on the actors' performance and the camera movements. The most detailed ones also offer information on potential translation problems and annotations on issues that can help translators, such as obscure cultural referents and plays on words.

Compression: A technique for reducing the number of bits in a *digital* signal, usually by lowering the quality of the record.

Cue(ing): The process of defining the in and out times of individual *subtitles*. See also *timing* and *spotting*.

Cut: Any *editing* of the programme that involves a change from one image to another. A cut is hard or clear when the difference in images is sharp and noticeable, and it is soft when the change is less pronounced, e.g. one image fades into another. Cuts are usually referred to as *scene changes* or *shot changes*.

Decoder: (a) An electronic apparatus that transforms *digital* signals into information like letters or words. (b) An apparatus attached to a TV set that permits the viewing of encoded satellite or cable programmes or *closed subtitles*.

Dialogue list: Document that compiles the dialogues of a film or audiovisual programme. It is used as a general term that refers to all documents containing the dialogue and any other type of information.

Dialogue subtitle: A *subtitle* conveying the speech of two people. It covers two lines, one per person, and the second line is preceded by a dash.

Diegetic sound: Any voice, music or sound effect whose source is present on screen or belongs to the narrative space.

Digital technology: A technique for signal transmission and recording where, in contrast to *analogue technology*, each value of a video and audio signal is transformed into binary information with only two levels, 1 and 0. This permits transmission, recording, copying and storage without any loss of quality.

Display: Text that is an integral part of the picture, e.g. banners in demonstrations or road signs. See *insert*.

Distribution: One of the three branches of the film industry; the process of supplying the finished film to the places where it will be shown. See *exhibition*, *production*.

Distribution company: Company in charge of distributing films at national and international levels. The films can be their property or that of a different company. In many cases they also work as *production companies*.

DVD: Introduced in 1996, it was originally known as Digital Video Disc but soon became known as Digital Versatile Disc. It is the next generation of optical disc storage technology. It has the same overall dimensions of a CD, but a significantly higher storage capacity of many gigabytes, sufficient for containing films dubbed and subtitled into many different languages.

Editing: (a) In filmmaking, the task of selecting and joining camera *takes*. (b) In the finished film, the set of techniques that govern the relations among *shots*.

Electronic subtitles: These *subtitles* are produced by a character generator and beamed by a projector onto the screen, without damaging the original copy. Frequently used at film festivals.

Encoding: The use of hardware or software to convert a video or audio signal file into a specific format, often using compression algorithms to reduce the overall amount of data.

Engraving: Last phase in the *subtitling* of a cinema movie that consists in inscribing the *subtitles* on the film copy in such a way that they appear and disappear in sync with the dialogue exchanges. Nowadays, *laser* engraving is the most used technique.

ESIST: European Association for Studies in Screen Translation.

Exhibition: One of the three general areas of the film industry; the process of showing the finished film to audiences. See *distribution*, *production*.

Feature film: A movie of usually about 90-120 minutes in length on one particular topic.

Foot/feet: Together with the *frame* is the unit of measurement of a movie picture and equals 30.48 centimetres. A foot contains 16 *frames*. See also *footage*.

Footage: Total length of a movie picture in *foot/feet* and *frames*, the basic units of measurement of a film.

Forced subtitles: *Subtitles* of the burnt-in *captions* of the original film that have to appear in the translated versions of the film, including the dubbed versions. In the case of *DVDs*, where the viewers are given the option to select the audio, even if the subtitle track is not activated, forced *subtitles* will still appear.

Frame: One of a series of still transparent photographs on a strip of film used in making movies. When a series of frames is projected onto a screen in quick succession, an illusion of movement is created. In cinema, there are 24 frames per second and a *foot* of *celluloid* contains 16 frames. Television allows 25 frames per second.

Full frame: Picture touching both sides, top and bottom of the television screen.

Genesis file: A file containing the *master titles*, usually in English, from which subtitlers have to produce their *subtitles*. The in and out times have already been decided by a technician, and the original dialogue is usually shortened to comply with the media limitations.

Glass master: Process by which a film is transferred to *DVD* and compressed via *MPEG*.

Hang: To hang a *subtitle* is to let it stay on the screen for a bit longer after the speech it represents has finished. This is done to give viewers enough time to read it.

HDTV: High Definition TeleVision. A technique for improving the quality of the TV image and increasing its size. It usually works with 1125 or 1250 scanning lines instead of 625 or 525 and has around five times as many luminous points. The *aspect ratio* is usually widescreen, 15:9 or 16:9.

Insert: Any written text that appears in the original programme. It may have been recorded by the camera (e.g. letters, road signs, grafitti, banners) or added afterwards during the *editing* (e.g. text locating the scene, both in terms of time and space). See also *narrative title* and *display*.

Interlingual subtitles: *Subtitles* that imply the translation from a source language into a target language.

Intertitle: In silent motion pictures, an intertitle is a piece of filmed, printed text edited into the midst of (i.e. -inter) the photographed action, generally to convey character dialogue, or descriptive narrative material related to the material photographed. Intertitles were a mainstay of silent films, but the development of the *soundtrack* largely eliminated their usefulness, except as an occasional artistic device. They are considered the predecessors of *subtitles*.

Intralingual subtitles: *Subtitles* in the same language as the dialogue of the audiovisual programme. They are mainly used for *subtitling* programmes for the deaf and the hard-of-hearing, following conventions that are different to the ones regulating *interlingual subtitles*. Intralingual subtitles are also used for teaching purposes and for karaoke.

Kerning: Adjusting the horizontal spacing between letters.

Laser subtitles: *Subtitles* that are engraved onto the film copy by means of a laser beam, and become, therefore, an integral part of the film.

Laser subtitling: A method of *subtitling* cinema film by means of a high power, very narrow laser beam, developed in the late 1980s and frequently used nowadays.

Latency: The time that elapses between the appearance of a *subtitle* on the screen and the eye registering it.

Letterbox: Picture touching both sides of the television screen, but with a black border top and bottom.

Live subtitling: (a) *Subtitling* produced during the broadcasting of a live programme. Today live *subtitling* is often produced with *speech recognition* technology. It requires a mixture of *subtitling* and interpreting skills. See *real-time subtitling*. (b) *Subtitling* that, although prepared beforehand, is fed manually during transmission or projection of an audiovisual programme, e.g. *electronic subtitles* at a film festival.

Localization: Process by which multiple language versions of a product are created.

LTC: Longitudinal Time Code. A *timecode* recorded alongside the images on a magnetic recording, often on one of the *soundtracks*.

Master list: A script of a film or audiovisual programme containing subtitles of the actors' lines in the original or a *pivot language*, to be used by subtitlers translating into other languages. The master list gives the essence of what is said as well as suggesting a proper length of the *subtitle*. See *template*.

Master (sub)titles: *Subtitles* that have already been cued in the original or a *pivot language*, usually English. They normally come accompanied by annotations and comments aimed at helping translators.

Métrage: French term to refer to the length of a film in meters. A meter of film contains some 52 *frames*. A 90-minute film is usually some 2.5-kilometre long and contains some 130,000 *frames*.

MPEG: Stands for Motion Picture Experts Group and represents a family of *digital* audio and video coding standards. It enables data compression of sound and images without great loss of quality so that they take up less capacity. This makes them easier to store and access over the web, a PC, a data card, etc. MPEG4 is the latest variant.

Multilingual subtitling: *Subtitling* an audiovisual programme in several languages to be shown on the screen or distributed simultaneously.

Narrative title: Term used in *dialogue lists* to indicate that we are dealing with a written text on the screen that offers information about the diegesis (narrative). See also *insert*.

NTSC: National Television System Committee, responsible for setting *analogue* television and video standards mainly in the United States, Canada, Japan and some Latin American countries. In Europe and the rest of the world, the dominant television standards are *PAL* and *SECAM*. It uses 525 lines and delivers approximately 30 *frames* of video per second.

Offline subtitling: *Subtitling* that is done in advance with no further interference at the time of transmission. See *online subtitling*.

Offscreen: Happening in the space of the scene but in an area outside what is visible onscreen.

Online subtitling: *Subtitling* that is done while the event that is being broadcast and subtitled is actually happening. See *offline subtitling*.

One-liner: A *subtitle* of one line, conveying one person's speech. It can be anything from a short monosyllable to a full line of some 40 characters maximum. It usually goes at the bottom of the screen to minimize the intrusion of the written text on the picture. Not to be confused with the 'one-liner' of comedy: a short joke or witty remark. See *two-liner*.

Open subtitles: *Subtitles* that are not encoded into the video signals and are instead burned on the images. They are an integral part of the audiovisual programme since they cannot be removed and are always visible on the screen, like the *subtitles* on a cinema film. See *closed subtitles*.

Optical subtitling: A method of *subtitling* cinema film by copying photographed *subtitles* onto the film print, in use in different forms since the 1930s. It has fallen into disuse nowadays. See *laser subtitling*.

Origination: The creation of a *subtitle* file from scratch.

PAL: Phase Alternate Line. A commonly used colour TV system, the standard for all TV and video equipment used in most European countries. The PAL system uses 625 lines at 25 *frames* per second to make up a video or TV picture. See *SECAM, NTSC*.

Photochemical subtitling: A traditional method of *subtitling* cinema film by impressing the photographic type plate *subtitles* directly onto the film copy after chemically removing the emulsion. In use since the 1930s, it has now fallen into disuse. See *laser subtitling*.

Pivot language: An intermediary language, usually English, used in the *master list* for the preparation of multilingual *subtitles* of films shot originally in lesser-known languages, e.g. *subtitles* in English for a film in Farsi used for the translation of the film into French or Italian.

Pixel: Short for Picture Element. Pixels are the smallest point of light or colour that make up a *digital* image. The more pixels, the higher the image resolution will be. In *subtitling*, it is being used to work out the maximum length of a *subtitle* line, taking over the traditional number of characters per line and allowing greater rationalization of the available space.

Post-production script: Document based on the *pre-production script* or *screenplay* that has been prepared or edited after shooting in order to incorporate any changes made during the shooting of the programme.

Pre-prepared subtitles: *Subtitles* that have been prepared beforehand and are just cued in manually at the time of transmission.

Pre-production script: Text prepared for the shooting of a film or other audiovisual programme containing information about *scenes* and actors' dialogue. In most cases it is not suitable for *subtitling* as dialogue and the order of *scenes* may have been changed during the actual shooting. Sometimes also referred to as *script* or *screenplay*. See *post-production script*.

Production: One of the three branches of the film industry; the process of creating the film. See *distribution, exhibition*.

Projection: Last phase in the *subtitling* of an audiovisual programme, which consists in projecting the *subtitles* onto the programme in such a way that they appear and disappear in sync with the dialogue exchanges. These *subtitles* are not an integral part of the programme. *Electronic subtitles* are always projected onto the screen. See *engraving*.

Real-time subtitling: Also known as *simultaneous subtitling* and *live subtitling (a)*.

Reel: A (large) portion of a motion picture that contains two smaller units, called also reels, and has a length of some 2,000 feet (600 meters) in total. It lasts for some 20 minutes. Since the reel contains two smaller units of

10 minutes each, it is common to see a reference to *reel-5A* and *reel-5B*, (or *5AB*) at the top of the *dialogue lists*. In some countries, it is used as the unit to pay translators working for dubbing.

Reformatting: Converting an already existing file to a different master for another release of the same film, usually the *DVD* or video release.

Safe Area: The term refers to the portion of the television picture that will definitely be displayed on screen. The safe area on a screen is where text is less distorted and graphics do not spill into one another, away from the edges. Picture safe area is defined to be 80% of the screen area. Title safe area is the area within which *subtitles* need to be placed to make sure that they will appear on screen and will not be cut off at the ends.

Sans serif: Used to describe letters that have straight lines without short adorning strokes, *serifs*, at the ends. Considered more readable in *subtitles*. See *serif*.

Scanning lines: The lines that build up the image on the television screen, 625 lines in the *PAL* and *SECAM* systems, 525 in *NTSC* and 1250 or 1125 in *HDTV*.

Scene: Any continuous part of a programme that takes place in one time and space, e.g. a classroom or an airport lounge.

Scene change: A cut that moves the plot from one scene to the next. Typical changes are when the story moves to a different location.

Screenplay: Text prepared for the shooting of a film or other audiovisual programme containing information about *scenes* and actors' dialogue. In most cases it is not suitable for *subtitling* as dialogue as well as the order of *scenes* may have been changed during the actual shooting. Sometimes referred to as the *(pre-production) script*, but the term *screenplay* is usually reserved for the published versions of such texts. However, even in published format screenplays remain unstable text forms; they are often mixtures of pre-production and post-production versions, and therefore seldom reliable renderings of the finished film.

Script: Text prepared for the shooting of a film or other audiovisual programme containing information about *scenes* and actors' dialogue. In most cases it is not suitable for *subtitling* as dialogue as well as the order of *scenes* may have been changed during the actual shooting. Often used as a short form of *pre-production script* or as a synonym for an unpublished *screenplay*. In screenwriting manuals *script* and *screenplay* are sometimes equated with the 'blueprint' of the film.

SDH: Subtitles or Subtitling for the Deaf and the Hard-of-hearing.

SECAM: SÉquentiel Couleur À Mémoire. Colour television system used for all TV and video equipment in France and some African countries. Like *PAL*, it uses 625 lines scanned at 50Hz, 25 *frames* per second and a *4:3 aspect ratio*. See *NTSC* and *PAL*.

Serif: The short strokes that mark the ends of the straight (and some of the curved) lines of a letter. See *sans serif.*

Shot: See *take.*

Shot change: A cut between two *takes* or shots within a *scene*. A typical shot change is when the camera moves from one speaker to another within the same *scene.*

Simulation: Prior to the *engraving* of the *subtitles,* the subtitler or an editor reviews the film or programme in a simulation session: a screening with the *subtitles* on the video screen just as they will appear on the final product. Modifications of text and *timing* can be made at this stage.

Simultaneous subtitling: See *real-time subtitling, live subtitling (a).*

Soundtrack: Technically, this term refers to the audio component of a movie or audiovisual programme, including the dialogue, musical score, narration, and sound effects that accompany the visual components.

Speech recognition: computerized transfer of speech to written text. Products such as IBM's ViaVoice and DNS-Nuance (originally Dragon's Naturally Speaking) are some of the most popular. Speech recognition is used increasingly by TV broadcasters for *live subtitling.*

Spot(ting): Based on the *timecode*, it is the process of dividing the original dialogue into units to be subtitled, taking into consideration both the length of each of the exchanges and the media limitations. It indicates the in and out times of each individual *subtitle*. See *timing* and *cueing.*

Spotting list: See *master (sub)titles.*

Spotter: Technician in charge of spotting the dialogue, i.e. of noting the start and end of every utterance.

Studio: Company in charge of the *subtitling* process.

S-VHS: An enhanced version of the *VHS* video cassette system. The 'S' stands for Super and offers superior picture quality from videotapes.

Subtitle: Any of the written projections that appear on screen and represent what is being said on the screen or other information that needs to be conveyed. They are sometimes added to films when they are released in a country that speaks a different language to that used in the film to enable the viewers to understand what is being said. Subtitles can be of one, two or three lines. Depending on the conventions applied, each line of a subtitle can contain from 28 to 41 spaces.

Subtitling: Audiovisual translation practice that consists of presenting a written text, generally in the lower part of the screen, that endeavours to recount the original dialogue of the speakers, as well as the discursive elements that appear in the image (letters, inserts, graffiti, inscriptions, placards, and the like), and the information that is contained in the *soundtrack* (songs, voices off).

Supertitle: See *surtitle.*

Supratitle: See *surtitle.*

Surtitles: *Subtitles* used in the *surtitling* of operas and theatre performances, also known as *supertitles* and *supratitles*.

Surtitling: Type of audiovisual translation commonly used in opera, other musical performances and theatre plays. The translated or transcribed text is prepared beforehand and projected on a screen usually suspended above the stage.

Synchronization: Coincidence in point of time between the appearance and disappearance of a *subtitle* and the delivery of the dialogue exchanges.

Synchrony: See *synchronization*.

Take: Also known as *shot*, it is any continuous, uninterrupted film footage between *cuts*. There can be several takes within a *scene*.

Tape: video format. See *DVD*.

TCR: Time Code Reader. A clock recorded alongside each *frame* and containing 8 digits that reads hours: minutes: seconds: *frames*.

Telecine: The process by which a film, usually shot at 24 *frames* per second, is converted to television video, usually at 25 *frames* per second (*PAL*) or 30 *frames* per second (*NTSC*).

Teletext: A system by means of which written information is superimposed on a television signal and broadcast. It is used in many countries to broadcast *intralingual subtitles* for the deaf and the hard-of-hearing. The signals, concealed in the *blanking lines*, activate a *character generator* in the television set, which creates the characters and mixes them into the television picture when a specified teletext page is selected.

Template: A list of *master (sub)titles* with the in and out times already spotted. See *master list*.

Territory: Term used in the industry to refer to the country, usually non-English speaking, in which an audiovisual programme is being released.

Theatrical subtitling: cinema *subtitling*.

Timecode: 8-digit time code that locates with exact precision the hour, minute, second and *frame* in which we are in the programme (e.g. 01:35:29:11). It helps to time the exact length of a *scene*. Note that the last two digits represent 24 *frames*/second in a normal film, 25 *frames*/second for *PAL* and *SECAM* video systems and 30 *frames*/second for *NTSC* video system. When the recording is played, the signal is read and the time code information picked up and used by the *subtitling* equipment. It can be displayed in or outside the image and is indispensable in present day *subtitling*. *BITC*, *VITC* and *LTC* are all types of timecode.

Timecue: An instruction for the *subtitling* equipment as to when to insert or clear a specific *subtitle*. To timecue is to give the *subtitling* equipment these instructions. See also *spotting* and *cueing*.

Timing: The process of defining the in and out times of *subtitles*. See also *spotting*, *cueing* and *timecue*.

Trailer: A short segment of film that cinemas and television stations use to advertise a feature film.

Two-liner: a *subtitle* of two lines. See also *one-liner*.

VAM: Value Added Material. Additional material that is put on a *DVD* apart from the feature film, such as commentary tracks, featurettes, extra footage, outtakes, etc.

VCR: Video Cassette Recorder.

VHS: Video Home System. Video recording and cassette system, also used in professional contexts, where the image and sound quality does not demand broadcast standard.

VITC: Vertical Interval Time Code. A *timecode* usually found on lines 19 to 21 of the *blanking lines*; traditionally used for *subtitle* preparation on a *VCR* because it remained accurate with slow motion and stills.

***Voice-over*:** A narration that is played on top of a video segment, usually with the audio for that segment muted or lowered.

***Voice recognition**:* in its initial inception, technology used for identifying people by their voice. However, it has of late become a synonym of *speech recognition*.

Widescreen: Technically, a particularly wide *aspect ratio* used for some films, but commonly used to describe content (such as appears on many *DVDs*) that displays at wider *aspect ratios* than are normally in use, such as on standard televisions. It is a way of shooting and projecting a movie in theatres. The original *footage* does not get cut off because of the *4:3 aspect ratio*. With the advent of high definition video, widescreen *16:9* video is coming into more popular use.

Wrap: A feature in *subtitling* programs which automatically takes a word that will not fit onto one line down to the next line.

Related glossaries can be found on the following websites:

www.transedit.se/glossary.htm
www.panasonic.co.uk/glossary/index.htm#V

10. References

10.1 Bibliography

Anderman, Gunilla (1993) "Untranslatability: the case of pronouns of address in literature". *Perspectives: Studies in Translatology* 1(1): 57-67.

Arnáiz, Carmen (1998) "El humor de las chicas de Almodóvar. La liberación de la lengua femenina". *International Journal of Iberian Studies* 11(2): 90-100.

Asimakoulas, Dimitrios (2001) *Subtitling Humour and the Humour of Subtitling: A Theoretical Approach to the Translation of Verbal Humour and Subtitling with Respect to the Greek Subtitled Versions of* Airplane! *and* Naked Gun. MA Dissertation. Manchester: UMIST.

Assis Rosa, Alexandra (2001) "Features of oral and written communication in subtitling", in Yves Gambier and Henrik Gottlieb (eds.) *(Multi)Media Translation: Concepts, Practices, and Research.* Amsterdam and Philadelphia: John Benjamins, 213-221.

Austin, John L. (1962) *How to Do Things with Words*. Oxford: Oxford University Press.

Baker, Mona (1992) *In Other Words: A Coursebook on Translation.* London and New York: Routledge.

Ball, Alan (2000 [1999]) *American Beauty*. London: Film Four Books.

Baxter, Sarah (2004) "Prim America blanks out British TV's naughty bits". *The Sunday Times*, 16th May: 24.

BBC (1994) *The BBC Subtitling Guide*. London: BBC.

Becquemont, Daniel (1996) "Le sous-titrage cinématographique: contraintes, sens, servitudes", in Yves Gambier (ed.) *Les transferts linguistiques dans les médias audiovisuels*. Villeneuve d'Ascq (Nord): Presses Universitaires du Septentrion, 145-155.

Benini, Nadia (2005) *Sous-titrage vers le néerlandais du film* La Bataille d'Alger. MA Dissertation. Antwerp: Hoger Instituut voor Vertalers en Tolken, Hogeschool Antwerpen.

Bhaba, Homi (1994) *The Location of Culture*. London and New York: Routledge.

Bogucki, Lukasz (forthcoming) "Amateur subtitling on the Internet", in Gunilla Anderman and Jorge Díaz Cintas (eds.) *Audiovisual Translation: Language Transfer on the Screen.* Basingstoke: Palgrave Macmillan.

Bordwell, David, Janet Staiger and Kristin Thompson (1996 [1985]) *The Classical Hollywood Cinema.* London and New York: Routledge.

Branigan, Edward (1992) *Narrative Comprehension and Film*. London and New York: Routledge.

Brondeel, Herman (1994) "Teaching subtitling routines". *Meta* 34(1): 26-33.

Brunner, Maria E. (2003) "Literarische Mehrsprachigkeit und Transkulturalität. Der Dialog zwischen den Kulturen und das Rcho von Mimikry und sprachlicher Hybridität im Werk deutsch-türkischer Autorinnen", in Aline Remael and Ilse

Logie (eds.) *Translation as Creation: the Postcolonial Influence. Linguistica Antverpiensia New Series* 2, 115-128.
Castellano, Alberto (ed.) (2000) *Il doppiaggio: materiali*. Roma: Aidac.
Castro Roig, Xosé (2001) "El traductor de películas", in Miguel Duro (coord.) *La traducción para el doblaje y la subtitulación*. Madrid: Cátedra, 267-298.
Cerón, Clara (2001) "Punctuating subtitles: typographical conventions and their evolution", in Yves Gambier and Henrik Gottlieb (eds.) *(Multi)Media Translation: Concepts, Practices, and Research*. Amsterdam and Philadelphia: John Benjamins, 173-177.
Chaume, Frederic (2004) *Cine y traducción*. Madrid: Cátedra.
Chiaro, Delia (1992) *The Language of Jokes: Analysing Verbal Play*. London and New York: Routledge.
------ (2005) "Foreword. Verbally expressed humor and translation: An overview of a neglected field". *International Journal of Humour Research* 18(2): 135-146.
Cornu, Jean-François (1996) "Le sous-titrage, montage du texte", in Yves Gambier (ed.) *Les transferts linguistiques dans les médias audiovisuals*. Villeneuve d'Asq: Presses Universitaires du Septentrion, 157-164.
Danan, Martine (1992) "Reversed subtitling and dual coding theory: new directions for foreign language instruction". *Language Learning* 42(4): 497-527.
------ (2004) "Captioning and subtitling: undervalued language learning strategies". *Meta* 49(1): 67-77.
Dancyger, Ken and Jeff Rush (1991) *Alternative Scriptwriting. Writing Beyond the Rules*. Boston: Focal Press.
Delabastita, Dirk (1989) "Translation and mass-communication: film and TV translation as evidence of cultural dynamics". *Babel* 35(4): 193-218.
------ (1994) "Word play as a special problem in translation studies". *Target* 6(2): 223-243.
------ (1996) *Word Play and Translation*. Manchester: St Jerome.
Delabastita, Dirk and Rainier Grutman (ed.) (2005) *Fictionalising translation and Multilingualism. Linguistica Antverpiensia New Series* 4.
Den Boer, Corien (2001) "Live interlingual subtitling", in Yves Gambier and Henrik Gottlieb (eds.) *(Multi)Media Translation: Concepts, Practices, and Research*. Amsterdam and Philadelphia: John Benjamins, 167-172.
Derasse, Bernard (1987) "Dubbers and subtitlers have a prime role in the international distribution of television programmes". *EBU Review. Programmes, Administration, Law* 38(6): 8-13.
Díaz Cintas, Jorge (1999) "Modalidades traductoras en los medios de comunicación audiovisual", in Milagros Aleza *et al.* (eds.) *El contacto lingüístico en el desarrollo de las lenguas occidentales*. Colección *Quaderns de Filologia, Estudis Lingüístics IV*. Valencia: Universidad de Valencia, 85-99.
------ (2001a) *La traducción audiovisual: el subtitulado*. Salamanca: Almar.
------ (2001b) "Sex, (sub)titles and videotapes", in Lourdes Lorenzo García and Ana María Pereira Rodríguez (eds.) *Traducción subordinada II: el subtitulado (inglés – español/galego)*. Vigo: Universidade de Vigo, 47-67.
------ (2003) *Teoría y práctica de la subtitulación: inglés-español*. Barcelona: Ariel.

------ (2005a) "El subtitulado y los avances tecnológicos", in Raquel Merino, José Miguel Santamaría and Eterio Pajares (eds.) *Trasvases culturales: Literatura, cine, traducción 4*. Vitoria: Universidad del País Vasco, 155-175.

------ (2005b) "Audiovisual translation today: a question of accessibility for all". *Translating Today* 4: 3-5.

------ (Forthcoming). "Back to the future in subtitling", in Heidrun Gerzymisch-Arbogast (ed.) *Multidimensional Translation: Challenges*. Manchester: St. Jerome.

Díaz Cintas, Jorge and Pablo Muñoz-Sánchez (2006) "Fansubs: Audiovisual Translation in an amateur environment". *The Journal of Specialised Translation* 6: 37-52. www.jostrans.org/issue06/issue06_toc.php

Díaz Cintas, Jorge and Pilar Orero (2003) "Course profile: postgraduate courses in audiovisual translation". *The Translator* 9(2): 371-388.

Dollerup, Cay (1974) "On subtitles in television programmes". *Babel* 20: 197-202.

Dwyer, Tessa (2005) "Universally speaking: *Lost in Translation* and polyglot cinema", in Dirk Delabastita and Rainier Grutman (eds.) *Fictionalising Translation and Multilingualism. Linguistica Antverpiensia New Series* 4: 295-310.

D'Ydewalle, Géry and Ubowanna Pavakanum (1992) "Watching foreign television programs and language learning", in Frits L. Engel *et al.* (eds.) *Cognitive Modelling and Interactive Environments in Language Learning*. Berlin: Springer Verlag, 193-198.

D'Ydewalle, Géry *et al.* (1987) "Reading a message when the same message is available auditorily in another language: the case of subtitling", in J.K. O'Regan and A. Lévy-Schoen (eds.) *Eye Movements: From Physiology to Cognition*. Amsterdam and New York: Elsevier Science Publishers, 313-321.

Elosua Francia, Arantza (2005) *Pulp Fiction. An Audiovisual Analysis of the Lost Translation and the Bewildering dubbing into Spanish and Catalan*. MA Dissertation. Edinburgh: University of Edinburgh.

Ferrer Simó, María R. (2005) "Fansubs y scanlations: la influencia del aficionado en los criterios profesionales". *Puentes* 6: 27-43.

Franco, Eliana (2000) *Revoicing the Alien in Documentaries. Cultural Agency, Norms and the Translation of Audiovisual Reality*. PhD Thesis. Leuven: Katholieke Universiteit Leuven.

Gambier, Yves (1994) "Audio-visual communication: typological detour", in Cay Dollerup and Annette Lindegaard (eds.) *Teaching Translation and Interpreting 2*. Amsterdam and Philadelphia: John Benjamins, 275-283.

------ (2003) "Introduction. Screen transadaptation: perception and reception". *The Translator* 9(2): 171-189.

Georgakopoulou, Panayota (2003) *Reduction Levels in Subtitling. DVD Subtitling: A Compromise of Trends*. PhD Thesis. Guildford: University of Surrey.

------ (Forthcoming) "subtitling for the DVD industry", in Gunilla Anderman and Jorge Díaz Cintas (eds.) *Audiovisual Translation: Language Transfer on the Screen*. Basingstoke: Palgrave Macmillan.

Goodwin, Charles (1979) "The interactive construction of a sentence in natural conversation", in Psathas, George (ed.) *Everyday Language: Studies in Ethnomethodology*. New York: Irvington Publishers, 97-121.

Gottlieb, Henrik (1994) "Subtitling: diagonal translation". *Perspectives: Studies in Translatology* 2(1): 101-121.

------ (2001) "Anglicisms and TV subtitles in an anglified world", in Yves Gambier and Henrik Gottlieb (eds.) *(Multi)Media Translation: Concepts, Practices, and Research*. Amsterdam and Philadelphia: John Benjamins, 249-258.

Grice, H. Paul (1975) "Logic and conversation", in Peter Cole and Jerry L. Morgan (eds.) *Syntax and Semantics III*. New York: Academic Press, 41-58.

Grit, Diederik (1997) "De vertaling van realia". *Filter* 4(4): 42-48.

Gutt, Ernst-August (1991) *Translation and Relevance: Cognition and Context*. Oxford: Blackwell.

Hannay, Mike and Lachlan Mackenzie (2002) *Effective Writing in English. A Sourcebook*. Bussum: Coutinho.

House, Juliane (1981) "Translation quality assessment", in Andrew Chesterman (ed.) (1989) *Readings in Translation Theory*. Helsinki: Oy Finn Lectura Ab, 157-161.

Ivarsson, Jan (1992) *Subtitling for the Media: A Handbook of an Art*. Stockholm: TransEdit.

Ivarsson, Jan and Mary Carroll (1998) *Subtitling*. Simrishamn: TransEdit.

Izard, Natàlia (1992) *La traducció cinematogràfica*. Barcelona: Publicacions de la Generalitat de Catalunya.

Jäckel, Anne (2001) "The subtitling of *La Haine*: a case study", in Yves Gambier and Henrik Gottlieb (eds.) *(Multi)Media Translation: Concepts, Practices, and Research*. Amsterdam and Philadelphia: John Benjamins, 223-235.

Jakobson, Roman (1959) "On linguistic aspects of translation", in Lawrence Venuti (ed.) (2000) *The Translation Studies Reader*. London and New York: Routledge, 113-118.

Johnson, Keith and Helen Johnson (1998) *Encyclopedic Dictionary of Applied Linguistics. A Handbook for Language Teaching*. Oxford: Blackwell.

Karamitroglou, Fotios (1998) "A proposed set of subtitling standard in Europe". *Translation Journal 2(2)*.
http://accurapid.com/journal/04stndrd.htm

Kaufmann, Francine (2004) "Un exemple d'effet pervers de l'uniformisation linguistique dans la traduction d'un documentaire: de l'hébreu des immigrants de 'saint-Jean' au français normatif d'ARTE". *Meta* 49(1): 148-160.

Kayahara, Matthew (2005) "DVD Technology and the Possibilities for Audiovisual Translation Studies". *The Journal of Specialised Translation* 3: 64-74.
www.jostrans.org/issue04/issue04toc.htm

Koolstra, Cees M. and Johannes W.J. Beentjes (1999) "Children's vocabulary acquisition in a foreign language through watching subtitled television programs at home". *Educational Technology Research & Development* 47(1): 51-60.

Kovačič, Irena (1994) "Relevance as a factor in subtitling reductions", in Cay Dollerup and Annette Lindegaard (eds.) *Teaching Translation and Interpreting 2*. Amsterdam and Philadelphia: John Benjamins, 245-251.

Kriek, Bartho (2002) "Kijk wie er spreekt. Halve vertalingen in ondertitels". *Onze Taal*, 276-278.

Krogstad, Morten (1998) "Subtitling for cinema films and video/television", in Yves Gambier (ed.) *Translating for the Media. Papers from the International Conference Languages and the Media*. Turku: University of Turku, 57-64.

Lambert, José (1990) "Le sous-titrage et la question des traductions. Rapport sur une enquête", in Rainer Arntz and Gisela Thome (eds.) *Übersetzungswissenschaft. Ergebnisse und Perspektiven. Festschrift für Wolfram Wilss zum 65 Geburtstag*. Tübingen: Gunter Narr, 228-238.

Leboreiro Enríquez, Fernanda and Jesús Poza Yagüe (2001) "Subtitular: toda una ciencia... y todo un arte", in Miguel Duro (coord.) *La traducción para el doblaje y la subtitulación*. Madrid: Cátedra, 315-323.

Lefevere, André (1987) "'Beyond interpretation' or the business of rewriting". *Comparative Literature Studies* 24(1): 17-39.

Lomheim, Sylfest (1995) "L'écriture sur l'écran: stratégies de sous-titrage à NRK, une étude de cas". *Translatio, Nouvelles de la FIT/FIT Newsletter* XIV(3-4): 288-293.

------ (1999) "The writing on the screen. Subtitling: a case study from Norwegian Broadcasting (NRK), Oslo", in Gunilla Anderman and Margaret Rogers (eds.) *Word, Text, Translation. Liber Amicorum for Peter Newmark*. Clevedon: Multilingual Matters, 190-207.

Luckmann, Thomas (1990) "Social communication, dialogue and conversation", in Ivana Markovà and Klaus Foppa (eds.) *The Dynamics of Dialogue*. Hemel Hempstead: Harvester and Wheatsheaf, 45-61.

Luyken, Georg-Michael *et al.* (eds.) (1991) *Overcoming Language Barriers in Television: Dubbing and Subtitling for the European Audience*. Manchester: European Institute for the Media.

MacMillan English Dictionary for Advanced Learners. (2002), edited by Michael Rundell. Oxford: MacMillan Education.

Mailhac, Jean-Pierre (2000) "Subtitling and dubbing, for better or worse? The English video versions of *Gazon Maudit*", in Myriam Salama-Carr (ed.) *On Translating French Literature and Film II*. Amsterdam and Atlanta: Rodopi, 129-154.

Marleau, Lucien (1982) "Les sous-titres... un mal nécessaire". *Meta* 27(3): 271-285.

Martín, Laurentino (1994) "Estudio de las diferentes fases del proceso de doblaje", in Federico Eguíluz *et al.* (eds.) *Trasvases culturales: literatura, cine, traducción*. Vitoria: Universidad del País Vaco, 323-330.

Mayoral Asensio, Roberto (2001a) "Campos de estudio y trabajo en traducción audiovisual", in Miguel Duro (coord.) *La traducción para el doblaje y la subtitulación*. Madrid: Cátedra, 19-45.

------ (2001b) *Aspectos epistemológicos de la traducción*. Castellón: Universidad Jaume I.

Mayoral Asensio, Roberto, Dorothy Kelly and Natividad Gallardo (1988) "Concept of constrained translation. Non-linguistic perspectives of translation". *Meta* 33(3): 356-367.

Mehrez, Samia (1992) "Translation and the postcolonial experience: the Francophone North African text", in Lawrence Venuti (ed.) *Rethinking Translation. Discourse, Subjectivity, Ideology*. London and New York: Routledge, 120-138.
Millichap, Joseph R. (1983) *Steinbeck and Film*. New York: Frederick Ungar.
Moreno Latorre, Trinidad (2003) "Subtitulado para personas sordas a través del teletexto". *Faro del Silencio* 195: 44-49.
Munday, Jeremy (2001) *Introducing Translation Studies. Theories and Applications*. London and New York: Routledge.
Myers, Lora (1973) "The art of dubbing". *Filmmakers Newsletter* 6(6): 56-58.
Nedergaard-Larsen, Birgit (1993) "Culture-bound problems in subtitling". *Perspectives: Studies in Translatology* 2: 207-251.
Neves, Josélia (2005) *Audiovisual Translation: Subtitling for the Deaf and the Hard-of-Hearing*. PhD Thesis. London: Roehampton University.
NOED (1998) *The New Oxford Dictionary of English*, edited by Judy Pearsall. Oxford: Clarendon Press.
Nowell Smith, Geoffrey (1968) "Italy sotto voce". *Sight and Sound* 37(3): 145-147.
Papadakis, Iannis (1998) "Greece, a subtitling country", in Yves Gambier (ed.) *Translating for the Media. Papers from the International Conference Languages and the Media*. Turku: University of Turku, 65-70.
Pedersen, Jan (forthcoming) "How is culture rendered in subtitles?". Paper presented at the conference *Between Text and Image: Updating Research in Screen Translation*. Forlì, 27-29 October 2005.
Pelsmaekers, Katja and Fred Van Besien (2002) "Subtitling irony. *Blackadder* in Dutch". *The Translator* 8(2): 241-266.
Pommier, Christophe (1988) *Doublage et postsynchronisation*. Paris: Editions Dujarric.
Poyatos, Fernando (1997) *Nonverbal Communication and Translation*. Amsterdam and Philadelphia: John Benjamins.
Psathas, George (1995) *Conversation Analysis: The Study of Talk-in-Interaction. Qualitative Research Methods* 35. Thousand Oaks: Sage Publications.
Pujol, Dídac (2006) "The translation and dubbing of 'fuck' into Catalan: The case of *From Dusk till Dawn*". *The Journal of Specialised Translation* 6: 121-133. www.jostrans.org/issue06/issue06_toc.php
Rabadán, Rosa (1991) *Equivalencia y traducción: problemática de la equivalencia translémica inglès-español*. Zamora: Universidad de León.
Ramière, Nathalie (2004) "Comment le sous-titrage et le doublage peuvent modifier la perception d'un film. Analyse contrastive des versions sous-titrée et doublée en français de film d'Elia Kazan, *A Streetcar Named Desire* (1951)". *Meta* 49(1): 102-114.
Raphaelson-West, Debra (1989) "On the feasibility and strategies of translating humour". *Meta* 34(1): 128-141.
Ravenhill, Mark (1996) *Shopping and F***ing*. London: Methuen.
Reid, Helen (1996) "Literature on the screen: subtitle translating for public broadcasting". *SQR Studies in Literature 5*: 97-107.
Reiss, Katharina (1977) "Text types, translation types and translation assessment",

in Andrew Chesterman (ed.) (1989) *Readings in Translation*. Helsinki: Oy Finn Lectura Ab, 105-115.
------ (1981) "Type, kind and individuality of text: decision making in translation". *Poetics Today* 2(4): 121-131.
Reisz, Karl and Gavin Millar (1997) *The Technique of Film Editing*. 2nd edition. Oxford: Focal Press.
Remael, Aline (1998) "The poetics of screenwriting manuals: a reflection of some of mainstream cinema's manifest and hidden tangles with the written word", in Paul Joret and Aline Remael (eds.) *Language and Beyond. Actuality and Virtuality in the Relations Between Word, Image and Sound.* Amsterdam and Atlanta: Rodopi, 203-218.
------ (2001) "Some thoughts on the study of multimodal and multimedia translation", in Yves Gambier and Henrik Gottlieb (eds.) *(Multi)Media Translation: Concepts, Practices, and Research.* Amsterdam and Philadelphia: John Benjamins, 13-22.
------ (2003) "Mainstream narrative film dialogue and subtitling. A case study of Mike Leigh's *Secrets & Lies*". *The Translator* 9(2): 225-247.
------ (2004) "Irak in het vizier. Hedendaagse internationale politiek in ondertitels". *Filter* 11(3): 3-12.
Robson, Gary D. (2004) *The Closed Captioning Handbook*. Amsterdam: Elsevier.
Santamaria Guinot, Laura (2001) *Subtitulació i referents culturals. La traducció com a mitjà d'adquisició de representations socials*. PhD Thesis. Barcelona: Universidad Autónoma de Barcelona.
www.tdcat.cesca.es/TDCat-0726101-095437
Searle, John (1969) *Speech Acts*. Cambridge: Cambridge University Press.
------ (1976) "A classifcation of illocutionary acts". *Language in Society* 5: 1-23.
Smith, Stephen (1998) "The language of subtitling", in Yves Gambier (ed.) *Translating for the Media. Papers from the International Conference Languages and the Media*. Turku: University of Turku, 139-149
Snell-Hornby, Mary (2003) "Re-creating the hybrid text: postcolonial Indian writings and the European scene", in Aline Remael and Ilse Logie (eds.) *Translation as Creation: the Postcolonial Influence. Linguistica Antverpiensia New Series* 2: 173-190.
Sperber, Dan and Deirdre Wilson (1995 [1986]) *Relevance: Communication and Cognition*. 2nd edition. Oxford: Blackwell.
Televisió de Catalunya (1997) *Criteris lingüístics sobre traducció i doblatge*. Barcelona: Edicions 62.
Titford, Christopher (1982) "Sub-titling: constrained translation". *Lebende Sprachen* 27(3): 113-116.
Törnqvist, Egil (1995) "Fixed pictures, changing words. Subtitling and dubbing the film *Babettes Gæstebud*". *TijdSchrift voor Skandinavistick* 16(1): 47-64.
Torregrosa, Carmen (1996) "Subtítulos: traducir los márgenes de la imagen". *Sendebar* 7: 73-88.
Trudgill, Peter (1999) "Standard English: what it isn't", in Tony Bex and Richard Watts (eds.) *Standard English: The Widening Debate*.
www.phon.ucl.ac.uk/home/dick/SEtrudgill.htm

UNESCO (1976) *Recommendation on the Legal Protection of Translators and Translations and the Practical Means to improve the Status of Translators.* 22 November. http://portal.unesco.org/en/ev.php-URL_ID=13089&URL_DO=DO_TOPIC&URL_SECTION=201.html

Vandaele, Jeroen (1999) "Each time we laugh. Translated humour in screen comedy", in Jeroen Vandaele (ed.) *Translation and the (Re)Location of Meaning. Selected Papers of the CETRA Research Seminars in Translation Studies 1994-1996*. Leuven: CETRA, 237-272.

------ (2002) "(Re)Constructing humour: Meaning and means". *The Translator* 8(2): 149-172.

Vandekerckhove, Reinhild, Annick De Houwer, Aline Remael and Isabelle Van der Niepen (2006) "Intralinguale ondertiteling van Nederlandstalige televisieprogramma's in Vlaanderen: linguïstische en extra-linguïstische determinanten", in T. Koole, J. Nortier and B. Tahitu (ed.) *Artikelen van de vijfde sociolinguïstische conferentie*. Delft: Eburon, 503-513.

Vanderplank, Robert (1988) "The value of teletext sub-titling in language learning". *ELT Journal* 42: 272-281.

------ (1992) "Non-native speaker viewers' use of teletext subtitles in English: some exploratory studies", in Graham Davies and Michael Hussey (eds.) *New Technology in Language Learning*. Frankfurt: Peter Lang, 89-102.

Vandeweghe, Willy (2005) *Duoteksten. Inleiding tot vertaling en vertaalstudie*. Gent: Academia Press.

Vanoye, Francis (1985) "Conversations publiques". *Iris* 3(1): 99-118.

Wahl, Chris (2005) "Discovering a genre: the polyglot film". *Cinemascope* 1. www.madadayo.it/Cinemascope_archive/cinema-scope.net/index_n1.html

Wales, Katie (1989) *A Dictionary of Stylistics*. London and New York: Longman.

Weigand, Edda (1992) "A case for an integrating procedure of theoretical reflection and empirical analysis", in Sorin Stati and Edda Weigand (eds.) *Methodologie der Dialoganalyse*. Tübingen: Max Niemeyer Verlag.

Weinberg, Herman (1985) *Booze, Cigars, and Movies*. New York: Anthology Film Archives.

Zabalbeascoa, Patrick (1996) "Translating jokes for dubbed television situation comedies". *The Translator* 2(2): 235-267.

------ (1997) "Dubbing and the nonverbal dimension of translation", in Fernando Poyatos (ed.) *Nonverbal Communication and Translation*. Amsterdam and Philadelphia: John Benjamins, 327-342.

------ (2001) "La traducción del humor en textos audiovisuals", in Miguel Duro (coord.) *La traducción para el doblaje y la subtitulación*. Madrid: Cátedra, 251-266.

------ (2005) "Humor and translation – an interdiscipline". *International Journal of Humor Research* 18(2): 185-207.

10.2 Filmography

A Touch of Frost (1992-2004), Roger Bamford, Roy Battersby *et al.*, UK.
Abba Live in Concert (1979).
About a Boy (2002), Chris Weitz and Paul Weitz, USA.
Aislados (2005), David Marqués, Spain.
American Beauty (1999), Sam Mendez, USA.
Amores perros / Love's a Bitch (2000), Alejandro González Iñárritu, Mexico.
Art in the Struggle for Freedom (2000), Obe Osheroff, USA.
Átame / Tie Me Up! Tie Me Down! (1990), Pedro Almodóvar, Spain.
¡Ay, Carmela! (1990), Carlos Saura, Spain/Italy.
Baby Cart in the Land of Demons / Kozure Ôkami: Meifumando (1973), Kenji Misumi, Japan.
Bang! Bang! In Da Manor (2004), Sean Mendez and Negar Esfandiari, UK.
Bataille d'Algers, La (1965), Gillo Pontecorvo, Italy.
Beneath the 12 Mile Reef (1953), Robert D. Webb, USA.
Big Lebowski, The (1998), Joel Coen, USA.
Blue Star Camp (2000), Adrian Smith, UK.
Blue Velvet (1986), David Lynch, USA.
Bookmark (1993), Randall Wright, UK.
Boom Boom Bang (1998), Hanno Baethe and Zaki Omar, Germany.
Bowling for Columbine (2002), Michael Moore, USA.
Brokeback Mountain (2005), Ang Lee, USA.
Broken Hearts Club, The (2000), Greg Berlanti, USA.
Cabaret (1972), Bob Fosse, USA.
Cachorro / Bear Cub (2004), Miguel Albaladejo, Spain.
Cage aux folles, La / Birds of a Feather (1978), Edouard Molinaro, France.
Cardiac Arrest (1994-1996), David Garnett and David Hayman, UK.
Casablanca (1942), Michael Curtiz, USA.
Charade (1963), Stanley Donen, USA.
Chicken Run (2000), Peter Lord and Nick Park, UK.
Cidade de Deus / City of God (2002), Fernando Meirelles and Kátia Lund, Brazil/France/USA.
Cielo abierto, El / Ten Days Without Love (2001), Miguel Albaladejo, Spain.
Cold Feet (1998-2003), Nigel Cole, Ciaran Donnelly *et al.*, UK.
Color Purple, The (1985), Steven Spielberg, USA
Commitments, The (1991), Alan Parker, Ireland/UK/USA.
Crying Game, The (1992), Neil Jordan, UK/Japan.
Cyrano de Bergerac (1900) Jean-Paul Rappeneau, France.
Depuis qu'Otar est parti... / Since Otar Left (2003), Julie Bertucelli, Belgium/France.
Elling (2001), Petter Næss, Norway.
ER (1994-present), Michael Crichton *et al.*, USA.
Erin Brockovich (2000), Steven Soderbergh, USA.

European Picture Book Collection (2003), Penni Cotton, UK.
Father's Little Dividend (1950), Vincente Minnelli, USA.
Faulty Towers (1975-1979), John Howard Davies and Bob Spiers, UK.
Flikken (1999-present), Pierre De Clerq *et al.*, Belgium.
Flor de mi secreto, La / Flower of my Secret, The (1995), Pedro Amodóvar, Spain/France.
Fond Kiss... Ae (2004), Ken Loach, UK/Belgium/Germany/Italy/Spain.
Four Weddings and a Funeral (1994), Mike Newell, UK.
Frasier (1993-2004), David Angell *et al.*, USA.
French Lieutenant's Woman, The (1981), Karel Reisz, UK.
Friends (1994-2004), David Crane, Martha Kauffman *et al.*, USA.
From Dusk till Dawn (1996), Robert Rodriguez, USA.
Full Monty, The (1997), Peter Cattaneo, UK.
Gazon Maudit / French Twist (1995), Josiane Balasko, France.
Gone with the Wind (1939), Victor Fleming, USA.
Grapes of Wrath, The (1940), John Ford, USA.
Guantanamera (1995), Tomás Gutiérrez Alea and Juan Carlos Tabío, Cuba/Spain/Germany.
Haine, La (1995), Matthieu Kassovitz, France.
Hard Talk (1997-present), BBC-TV interview series, UK.
Have Your Cake and Eat It (1997), Paul Seed, UK.
Head on (1998), Ana Kokkinos, Australia.
Historia oficial, La / Official Story, The (1985), Luis Puenzo, Argentina.
Hola, estás sola? / Hi, Are You Alone (1995), Icíar Bollaín, Spain.
Holcroft Covenant, The (1985), John Frankenheimer, UK.
Hollow Man (2000), Paul Verhoeven, USA.
Hours, The (2002), Stephen Daldry, USA.
J'ai toujours voulu être une sainte / I Always Wanted To Be a Saint (2003), Geneviève Mersch, Belgium/Luxembourg.
Jamón, jamón / A Tale of Ham and Passion (1992), José Juan Bigas Luna, Spain.
Joseph and the Amazing Technicolor Dreamcoat (1999), David Mallet and Steven Pimlott, UK.
Last Time I Saw Paris, The (1954), Richard Brooks, USA.
Liaison Pornographique, Une (1999), Frédéric Fonteyne, France/Switzerland/Belgium/Luxembourg.
Life of Brian, The (1979), Terry Jones, UK.
Lijmen (2000), Robbe De Hert, Belgium.
Loaded (1994), Anna Campion, New Zealand/UK.
Lois & Clark: The New Adventures of Superman (1993-1997), Joe Shuster, USA.
Look Who's Talking (1989), Amy Heckerling, USA.
Lost in Translation (2003), Sofia Coppola, USA.
Mamaman (2002), Iao Lethem, Belgium.
Man with the Golden Arm, The (1955), Otto Preminger, USA.

Manhattan Murder Mystery (1993), Woody Allen, USA.
Mar adentro / Sea Inside, The (2004), Alejandro Amenábar, Spain/France/Italy.
Max et Bobo (1998), Frédéric Fonteyne, Belgium/Luxembourg/France.
McLintock! (1963), Andrew V. McLaglen, USA.
Memento (2000), Christopher Nolan, USA.
Men in Black (1997), Barry Sonnenfeld, USA.
Mobutu, Roi du Zaïre / Mobutu, King of Zaïre (1999), Thiery Michel, Belgium/France.
Moulin Rouge (2001), Baz Luhrmann, Australia.
Mr Bean (1990-1995), John Birkin, John Howard Davies *et al.*, UK.
Mrs Doubtfire (1993), Chris Columbus, USA.
Mujeres al borde de un ataque de nervios / Women on the Verge of a Nervous Breakdown (1988), Pedro Almodóvar, Spain.
My Big Fat Greek Wedding (2002), Joel Zwick, USA/Canada.
My Fair Lady (1964), George Cukor, USA.
My Name is Joe (1998), Ken Loach, Spain/Italy/France/UK/Germany.
Night of the Living Dead, The (1968), George A. Romeo, USA.
Nueve reinas / Nine Queens (2000), Fabián Bielinsky, Argentina.
Pourquoi se marier le jour de la fin du monde ? / Why Get Married the Day the World Ends? (2000), Harry Cleven, Belgium/Luxembourg.
Prime Suspect (1991-2003), Christopher Menaul *et al.*, UK.
Princess Mononoke / Mononoke-hime (1997), Hayao Miyazaki, Japan.
Pulp Fiction (1994), Quentin Tarantino, USA.
¿Qué he hecho yo para merecer esto? / What Have I Done to Deserve This? (1984), Pedro Almodóvar, Spain.
Rich and Famous (1981), George Cukor, USA.
Rocky Horror Picture Show, The (1975), Jim Sharman, UK.
Romeo and Juliet (1968), Franco Zeffirelli, UK/Italy.
Russia House, The (1990), Fred Schepisi, USA.
Secrets and Lies (1996), Mike Leigh, France/UK.
Seinfeld (1990-1998), Larry David, Jerry Seinfeld *et al.*, USA.
Shakespeare in Love (1998), John Madden, USA/UK.
Shrek (2001), Andrew Adamson and Vicky Jenson, USA.
Sicilia, La (1997), Luc Pien, Belgium.
Simpsons, The (1989-present), Matt Groening *et al.*, USA.
Snows of Kilimanjaro, The (1952), Henry King, USA.
Sound of Music, The (1965), Robert Wise, USA.
Star Wars (1977), George Lucas, USA.
Stargate (1994), Roland Emmerich, USA.
Stranger, The (1946), Orson Welles, USA.
Stuart Little (1999), Rob Minkoff, USA.
Sweet Sixteen (2002), Ken Loach, UK/Germany/Spain.
Taxi Driver (1976), Martin Scorsese, USA.
Thelma & Louise (1991), Ridley Scott, USA.
Trainspotting (1996), Danny Boyle, UK.

Voices from Robben Island (1995), Adam Low, UK.
Zatoichi's Pilgrimage / Zatôichi umi o wataru (1966), Kazuo Ikehiro, Japan.

Index